18th Edition

Legal
Research

How to Find & Understand the Law

Editors of Nolo

EIGHTEENTH EDITION	AUGUST 2018
Editor	CARA O'NEILL
Cover Design	SUSAN PUTNEY
Book Design	TERRI HEARSH
Proofreading	ROBERT WELLS
Index	RICHARD GENOVA
Printing	BANG PRINTING

ISSN: 1539-4115 (print)

ISSN: 2377-7214 (online)

ISBN: 978-1-4133-2564-5 (pbk)

ISBN: 978-1-4133-2565-2 (ebook)

This book covers only United States law, unless it specifically states otherwise.

Please note

We believe accurate, plain-English legal information should help you solve many of your own legal problems. But this text is not a substitute for personalized advice from a knowledgeable lawyer. If you want the help of a trained professional—and we'll always point out situations in which we think that's a good idea—consult an attorney licensed to practice in your state.

Acknowledgments

This book wouldn't be possible without original author, Stephen R. Elias. Until his death in late 2011, Stephen R. Elias was a practicing attorney, president of the National Bankruptcy Law Project, and the author or coauthor of many Nolo books, including *Bankruptcy for Small Business Owners, Special Needs Trusts: Protect Your Child's Financial Future, How to File for Chapter 7 Bankruptcy,* and *Chapter 13 Bankruptcy.* Steve was also one of the original authors of Nolo's bestselling *WillMaker* software. He held a law degree from Hastings College of the Law and practiced law in California, New York, and Vermont before joining Nolo in 1980.

Over the years, other wonderful people have also contributed to this book in different ways, particularly Susan Levinkind, an original coauthor, Alayna Schroeder, a subsequent author, and many of the researchers and editors of Nolo.

Table of Contents

Your Legal Research Companion

If you're new to legal research, you might be apprehensive about how to find, understand, and apply the law. Whether you're in front of a computer or in a law library, it's common to feel like you're searching for the proverbial needle in the haystack. After all, there are so many different research resources and so many places to look. If you're struggling to locate the relevant material, worry no more. With a little practice, you'll find everything you need

Legal research isn't as difficult as it might seem, and, after you research a couple of topics, it will start to make sense.

That's where this book comes in. And we'll do more than help you navigate the process of legal research. We'll also cover:

- the basics of the law, so you understand what you're looking at
- where to find legal resources, so you'll know where to go
- how to frame your legal issue, so you approach your research efficiently
- how to find and use legal resources including background resources, statutes, cases, and more
- how to validate that what you have reflects the current status of the law, and
- how to organize your research and put it to use.

In short, when it comes to finding what you need, don't fear. If it's out there, we'll help you find it.

Understanding the Basics of the Law

Trying to research the law can be a daunting task—and there used to be a time when it was virtually impossible for nonlawyers to access legal information themselves. Fortunately, the Internet has been a game changer and that's no longer the case. Today, many people find it easy to do their own legal research, whether to resolve a private dispute, understand and work with a legal professional, or assist in their own academic or professional development. Often, that research can start from the comfort of a home or office.

In this book, we'll help you find the resources you need as you conduct your own legal research. But before we get started, we think it helps to have a basic understanding of how the law works. In this chapter, we'll cover:

- what "the law" is
- understanding state versus federal law
- sources of law, and
- how U.S. courts are structured.

These basics will provide the framework for understanding how to conduct legal research, helping you frame your legal questions and find the answers you're looking for.

What Is the Law?

Most of us don't spend much time thinking about what "the law" means. The law doesn't enter our daily lives in a recognizable way, and only becomes visible to us when we get a traffic ticket, are denied a government service, buy or sell a house, or dispute a bill. In the real world, the law is an amorphous set of rules that govern individual and group behavior. We don't even know about many of these rules, or we understand them only generally. For example, you don't need to see a written law to know that it's a crime to steal or destroy someone else's property. But the rules have force because if we break them, we can be held responsible by our legal system.

That being said, even if we understand what "the law" is, it doesn't mean it always functions in a predictable way (although that's the goal).

After all, prosecutors choose whether to bring charges against defendants, so committing a crime doesn't necessarily lead to prosecution. And while we might be entitled to a government service—a Social Security payment, for example—that doesn't help much when the Social Security Administration denies a claim. The reality is, laws are applied by real people in the real world, so things don't always play out as perfectly as we might want or expect.

This explanation also applies to other parts of the the legal profession, such as the availability and interpretation of evidence used to prove a case in court. Different people have different understandings not only of factual events—for example, whether you or the other driver ran a stop sign— but different understandings about what the law means. It's because of these different interpretations that people often end up in court.

Simply put, successful litigation starts with solid preparation—and the first step is finding the law that applies to your case.

Sources of Law

The law is not found in a single set of books.. Instead, it is several separate collections, one or more of which might apply to any given situation. Law includes:

- **The U.S. Constitution.** This high-level document is comparatively short, but lays out some of the most important principles for how our legal system is structured. It gives the authority to the various branches of government and states to make new laws. Also, the amendments guarantee fundamental rights to citizens, such as the right to free speech and to bear arms.
- **Federal statutes.** As we'll explain below, Congress frequently passes new laws that become statutes. These written laws are called statutes.
- **Federal cases.** Federal courts decide cases about federal law, and explain how to interpret federal statutes (how a statute should be applied in certain situations isn't always clear—or even anticipated). They also hear cases between two parties that are from different states.

- **Federal administrative regulations.** The legislature cannot write all the statutes needed to regulate society—there simply isn't enough time. Instead, the legislature shifts specific law-making authority to government agencies through an "enabling statute." For instance, agencies like the Equal Employment Opportunity Commission, the Internal Revenue Service, and the Environmental Protection Agency, are created by the U.S. Congress and are part of and overseen by the executive branch. They issue regulations (law) in the area of authority granted by the enabling statute. Regulations are part of federal administrative law.

CAUTION
Sovereign Native American tribes have their own courts and laws. These essentially function outside the system we describe here, and are beyond the scope of this book.

- **State constitutions.** Like the federal government, state governments have constitutions that form the basis of their legal structure.
- **State statutes.** Like Congress, state legislatures pass statutes, which constitute state statutory law. While federal laws apply everywhere, these laws apply only within the state.
- **State cases.** State courts decide cases about state law.
- **State administrative regulations.** As at the federal level, agencies are created by state legislatures but overseen by state governors. They write regulations, which constitute state administrative law.
- **Local ordinances.** Local governments pass ordinances that become police codes, building codes, planning codes, health codes, and so forth.

In most cases, your legal research will probably touch on only two or three of these legal sources. For example, if you want to sue your automobile mechanic because he didn't properly fix your brakes, causing an accident, this will probably be an area of state statutory and case law, but won't require you to look at the federal Constitution or local ordinances. We'll explain more about these sources of law below.

Constitutions

Both state constitutions and the federal Constitution are the founding documents that form the basis of authority for all other forms of law—that is, they tell the various branches of government what authority they have to create new law. As we'll explain below, legislatures and judges create law, but that law cannot conflict with the constitution.

Statutes: Legislative-Made Law

What most of us tend to think of when we think of the law are the acts passed by our national and state legislatures. We might understand, for example, that Congress has decided the income tax rate, or that our state legislators have determined that it's illegal to discriminate against someone in the workplace based on sexual orientation.

When bills are passed, they are written down, given an identification number, and arranged in numerical order in a code book (or "codified"). They create what are known, collectively, as statutes. Both federal and state statutes are usually grouped together by subject matter—for example, the California Family Code includes most of the laws that affect families that are facing divorce, legal separation, or child custody disputes, while Title 12 of the Connecticut code deals with state taxation. When it comes to legal research, this makes it much easier to find relevant materials. As new bills are passed, they either amend existing statutes or add new ones and are incorporated into the existing code books.

We'll discuss how to use and understand statutes in greater detail in Chapter 5.

Common Law: Judicial Interpretation

While statutes are a very important part of our law, they actually make up a small part of it. That's primarily because we don't always agree on what the statutes, and other sources of law like the Constitution, mean. As a result, interpreting what these laws say is largely a responsibility of our court system. For example, in a child custody case, a law might say that custody should be determined with the "best interests" of the child in mind. The child's mother might think that means living with her with occasional visits to the child's father, whereas the father might feel the child should live part-time with each parent. On each side, the parties have a different interpretation of what the law means and how it protects them.

As a result, in many cases judges must look at what the law says, then try to determine what it means in light of the circumstances of the people before the court, the ones involved in the lawsuit. When they do, they might create a document explaining or summarizing their rationale, called an "opinion." Judicial opinions form what is known as "common law" or "case law." In essence, case law is a judge's view of what the statute means when applied to the particular facts of the case before the court.

Common law is developed over time as opinions build on one another (most jurisdictions require judges to follow the logic of certain earlier opinions—more below). So you won't find common law written down in one place, like a statute, with a bright-line rule. Instead, the courts publish opinions in books called "reports" or "reporters." Federal and state courts have separate sets of reporters which organize opinions, or "cases," by date.

Because common law is part of the law, judges have to consider not only what statutes say, but what judges before them have said on the same issue. In other words, court opinions serve as authority or "precedent," that other judges are sometimes required to consider when deciding similar cases. Sometimes this is referred to as "binding" authority, because the judge in a subsequent case is bound to follow it.

As we'll explain below, courts are arranged in a hierarchal system that means that not every judge has to consider the opinion of every other judge in the country each time a similar issue comes up. However, when they do have to rely on the interpretations of others, they turn to judicial opinions. When you're researching a legal issue, you will have to learn how to read judicial opinions to gather the salient facts and law that apply to your issue. We'll explain more about how to do that in Chapter 7.

What If a Judge Was Wrong?

The system of judicial precedent works great when judges correctly interpret the law. But what if they don't—for example, what if judges decide, as they did many years ago, that it's okay to segregate people based on their race? Is a judge bound to follow a law that is wrong?

Fortunately, the answer is no—but judges don't deviate very often so you should never expect a trial-level judge to deviate from existing law. Judges respect a legal principle called stare decisis—Latin for "let the decision stand." Unless there is a very good reason to depart from current law, judges generally do not. In fact, most lawyers will tell you they've never had a trial judge agree to disregard current law. Instead, trial judges expect litigants seeking legal change to appeal the case to a higher court with the authority to do so.

This does not mean that every judge's decisions stand forever. Courts do recognize mistakes, take current social values and mores into account, and in rare instances, liberally interpret the law to fit the desired result, when so inclined. But the principle of stare decisis is a strong one.

The reality is that no one—including judges—want to be found wrong (or "appealed" in a judge's case), and therefore judges are reluctant to discard well-established rules and take pains to explain and justify a significant departure from precedent. Since convincing a judge to diverge from the law would take stellar advocating on your part, it's usually best to confine your arguments to those that fit within existing law.

If Congress disagrees with a court's decision, however, it can usually pass a new law that contradicts it. (This isn't true if the case interprets the Constitution, though, because Congress's power to legislate can't conflict with the Constitution.) For example, Lily Ledbetter sued her employer, claiming that it had discriminated against her by paying her less than her male peers. But the Supreme Court held that she had filed her suit too late, and upheld the trial court, which had thrown the case out. (*Ledbetter v. Goodyear Tire & Rubber*, 510 U.S. 618 (2007).) The Court decided Ledbetter hadn't met the legal requirement to bring her claim within 180 days, because the decision to pay Ledbetter less had happened many years before. Ledbetter argued that each time she received a paycheck that was for less than her peers, it was a "continuing violation" of the law, so the 180 days started to run from the time she received her last paycheck. Even though the Supreme Court disagreed with Ledbetter, shortly thereafter Congress passed the Lily Ledbetter Fair Pay Act, taking Ledbetter's side. Now, employees in Ledbetter's shoes have the benefit of the act. Without it, courts would be required to treat those employees the same way the Supreme Court treated Ledbetter.

Administrative Regulations

Both the federal and many state governments have administrative agencies that work in specific areas of law—for example, the U.S. Department of Labor oversees the wages and working conditions of the nation's workers. These agencies are created by Congress and state lawmakers, but are under the leadership of an executive branch—either the president or a governor. The agencies are given the authority to adopt regulations that specify how certain laws will be carried out. While Congress passes laws that provide the framework for how the law is implemented (an enabling statute), regulations often provide detail, frequently based on the experience and feedback from citizens who have questions about the law. For example, while the existence of a mileage reimbursement rate is part of federal law, the amount of that rate is set each year by the IRS.

Local Ordinances

Some areas of the law aren't covered by either state or federal law, or at least they aren't covered completely. In that case, local bodies like city councils or county boards have authority to regulate. You may have come across local ordinances if you have needed a building permit or have questioned zoning laws, for example. Often, these ordinances are enforced and regulated by the bodies that create them, and there are options to resolve disputes that don't involve the court system—for example, appealing a decision by the local planning commission might involve a hearing before the commission, rather than going to court.

State Versus Federal Law

The law comes from more than one source. The primary sources are state law and federal law, though as we've explained, local bodies regulate some areas too.

Describing the difference between state and federal law could send us into a long-winded explanation of constitutional principles, but we'll try and keep it simple. The main legal text that creates federal law is the U.S. Constitution. The Constitution lays out several specific areas that the federal government regulates fully, without state intervention—for example, maritime law. Then there are areas the federal government is allowed to regulate. And finally, the Constitution also says that if an area doesn't fall within the areas regulated by the federal government, then only states have the power to regulate that area.

Of course, what falls within each realm has resulted in a lot of judicial interpretation and opinion, and there are many areas that are regulated by both state and federal law. The general principle, however, is that certain areas—federal taxes and immigration, for example—are governed solely by federal law, and lots of other areas the federal government doesn't regulate—such as landlord-tenant law—are primarily regulated by the states.

Issues Covered by State Law

Each state has its own set of statutes, as well as common law. Most states have laws regulating the following areas: child custody, conservatorships, contracts, corporations, crimes (in most cases), divorce, durable powers of attorney for health care and financial management, guardianships, landlord-tenant relationships, licensing (businesses and professions), living wills, motor vehicles, partnerships, paternity, personal injuries, probate, property taxation, real estate, trusts, wills, workers' compensation, and zoning. Except in rare cases (for example, the federal government regulates disclosure of lead-based paint hazards in residential rentals), these issues will not be covered by federal law.

Issues Covered by Federal Law

For most of our country's history, federal law was limited to court interpretations of the U.S. Constitution and the Bill of Rights, as well as the topics that Congress is specifically authorized to address under the Constitution, such as the regulation of commerce and immigration. But as courts have interpreted the Constitution to allow the federal government to regulate more areas, federal law might control a broad range of social welfare, health, and environmental issues.

Federal law generally controls areas like agriculture, bankruptcy, copyright, customs, food and drug regulation, immigration, interstate commerce, maritime activity, patent, Social Security, and trademark.

Issues Covered by Both State and Federal Law

A large number of legal areas now involve both state and federal law. Federal and state governments both are concerned about such topics as environmental law, consumer protection, and the enforcement of child support statutes; and the Constitution doesn't limit who can do what.

This is primarily true because Congress is authorized by the Constitution to spend money for the general welfare, and it creates programs under which federal funds are offered to state governments under certain conditions. (Usually, states must meet the conditions and contribute financially too.) A good general rule is that if federal funds are involved, at least one element of federal law is involved.

When states participate in one of these programs, typically, federal law gives some latitude in how the program is conducted, so states pass their own laws and regulations to govern the operation. Of course, courts interpret these statutes and regulations to create common law on the issue. So, federal cost-sharing programs result in new state law, too.

Areas covered by both state and federal law include consumer protection, criminal law, employment, environmental protection, health law, labor law, occupational safety, subsidized housing, taxes, transportation, unemployment insurance, veterans' benefits, and welfare law. If you have a problem that is affected by both federal and state law, you might have to look to both state and federal law background resources to get a firm handle on your problem. We'll explain more about how to do that in Chapter 4.

The Court System

As explained above, when drafting opinions that interpret the law, judges are bound by the opinions of other judges. But judges don't have to follow every prior opinion interpreting a statute. Courts are arranged in a certain hierarchy, which makes judges bound by the decisions of only those higher up in the hierarchy.

How Courts Are Structured

Both state and federal courts are structured in a similar way. If you wish to bring a lawsuit, you will usually file a suit in the trial court. This might go by one of several different names—for example, the superior court, the municipal court, or in New York (confusingly enough), the supreme court. But the function of this first court is the same: Everything up to and including a trial will happen here. For the most part, trial courts do not issue opinions that other courts are required to follow.

After the trial court, the next level up is called the appellate court. If you reach a final resolution in the trial court—for example, the judge rules against you—and you believe the decision is wrong, you have the right to appeal the decision. In most instances, the role of the appellate court isn't to start your trial over, hearing the evidence again. Instead, they look at what the trial court did and decide whether it made any mistakes applying the law to the facts. Appellate courts often issue opinions, and those opinions are binding on the trial courts below them within the state.

The highest court is usually called the supreme court—though not always (as explained, that's the name for the trial court in New York). Also, some states have no intermediate appellate court, so appeals go straight to the supreme court of that state.

Most Cases Don't Go to Trial

Even though our court system is set up to take cases to trial, in the vast majority of disputes, this isn't what happens. Here are some of the most common reasons why:

- **Charges are dropped.** In criminal cases, prosecutors might decide not to pursue the case for several different reasons—they find new evidence that changes their minds, they do not think they have enough evidence to convince a jury, or they do not have the time or resources to deal with the case.
- **The parties reach an agreement.** In criminal cases, this is called a "plea bargain." The prosecutor and defendant might agree that the defendant will voluntarily plead guilty to a lesser crime with lesser penalties—for example, a misdemeanor theft charge instead of a felony. In civil suits, the parties might settle the case, perhaps with the defendant agreeing to pay something to the plaintiff, but less than was asked for.
- **The court might rule on a "dispositive motion."** To avoid wasting court time and resources, parties can ask the judge to issue a ruling or an order before the case goes to trial. Some of these rulings have the effect of ending the case, and those decisions can be appealed. We'll explain more about dispositive motions in Chapter 9.

The supreme court is another appellate court and will usually only decide whether the court below it correctly interpreted the law and applied it to the facts; it won't gather new evidence or start things over. Except in certain kinds of cases—for example, death penalty cases—most supreme courts get to decide which cases they will hear. If you don't agree with the decision made by the appellate court (again, except in certain cases that can come right from the trial court to the supreme court), you can ask the supreme court to hear your case, but it might refuse, in which case, the appellate court's ruling stands.

There are all kinds of exceptions to this general structure. For example, in many states, claims under a certain amount are heard in small claims court, not the trial court. The trial court might act as the appellate court and can review the entire case, like new. (This is called *de novo* review.) Or, if you are filing for bankruptcy and your creditors challenge it, that case will be handled in federal bankruptcy court. We won't be able to point out every exception to you, so you might have to do some research to figure out the procedure in the court system you're in. We'll explain how to do that in Chapter 2.

Federal Courts

If you have a lawsuit that involves a federal issue or is otherwise within the court's jurisdiction—meaning it covers an area that federal courts are allowed to hear—you can file it in the federal trial court, called the U.S. District Court. You can't file your lawsuit in any district court, however. As we'll explain in Chapter 9, there are rules to prevent you from showing up at a Nebraska courthouse if you and the defendant both live in Oregon, and the incident that resulted in a lawsuit took place in Oregon. There is at least one district court in every state, but often more, breaking the state into regions. District courts don't usually issue "published" opinions (opinions that are considered binding on other courts), though other courts might take these decisions into account.

Above the district court is the appellate court, called the circuit court in the federal system. There are 13 circuits, divided by area of the country. Most of the circuits are numbered, except for the DC Circuit and the Federal Circuit. The First through Eleventh Circuits all cover specific parts of the United States, while the DC and Federal Circuits are based in Washington, DC. The DC Circuit hears appeals from cases in the District of Columbia, while the Federal Circuit deals with nationwide claims based on particular areas of law including international trade, government contracts, patents, trademarks, certain money claims against the United States government, federal personnel, and veterans' benefits.

The decisions of the circuit courts are binding on all the district courts that are part of that circuit, but not on other circuit courts or the district courts in those other circuits. For example, the Fifth Circuit includes Texas, Louisiana, and Mississippi. If the Fifth Circuit issues a ruling, it will bind all district courts in those three states; however, it will not be binding on the Eleventh Circuit. The Eleventh Circuit might consider it "persuasive," meaning it might find the logic compelling and might consider it to craft its own decisions. But it is not bound to do so.

 RESOURCE
Want to find the federal court where you live? Visit www.uscourts.gov/court-locator to see both the district and circuit courts.

At the very top of the hierarchy in the federal court system is the U.S. Supreme Court. Most of us have heard of the Supreme Court, and maybe even some of the major cases that have come out of it, like *Roe v. Wade*, *Brown v. Board of Education*, and *Bush v. Gore*. The Supreme Court is made up of nine members who are appointed for an unlimited term by the president of the United States. As appointees who don't have to worry about reelection, the Supreme Court is supposed to be less politically biased than the legislature or president.

Except for "appeals of right"—those situations in which parties have an automatic right to Supreme Court review—the Court chooses which cases it will hear. Very frequently, the Court will choose cases involving conflicting opinions in the circuit courts. So if the Ninth Circuit says it's okay to do something and the First Circuit says it isn't, the Supreme Court might issue a rule that will bind both. All federal courts must follow the Supreme Court's decision.

State Courts

Most state court systems follow a similar structure to the federal system. Usually, the only state court opinions that are published are those issued by appellate courts, including the state's supreme court.

It's important to recognize that state court opinions don't generally bind federal courts, and vice versa. This makes sense. For the most part, federal courts are dealing with federal law issues, and state courts are dealing with issues related to state laws. So neither judicial system tells the other how to interpret its own laws.

But this gets tricky when state or federal court systems must interpret each other's laws. This happens, for example, when both state and federal issues are part of a single lawsuit. Let's say you believe your employer discriminated against you based on your race. You might file a lawsuit alleging that the employer violated federal and state anti-discrimination laws. But it wouldn't make sense to have two different cases, in two different courts, with two different judges. So you are permitted to bring both claims in one place.

If you choose state court, the state court will have to apply federal law to decide whether your rights under federal law have been violated. If there's an issue of federal law that the judge must interpret, the judge will turn to federal law to find the answer, not state law. In that case, the judge is bound by federal law.

Finding Legal Resources

Understanding what the law is and how it's structured is just the beginning of learning how to conduct legal research. In addition, you need to know where to find it. In this chapter, we're going to discuss the resources that are available to you. In future chapters, we'll discuss how to use these resources to find answers to the specific legal question or questions you have.

Where Legal Information Is Located

In years past, legal research took place in one place: a law library. Legal research looks very different today, however, for a variety of reasons. One is that courts, recognizing that many litigants represent themselves and need access to resources, have become more user-friendly. They often provide self-help centers and other materials—for example, instructions on how to file a small claims court action without the help of a lawyer. Additionally, book publishers, lawyers, and professional organizations have all recognized the value of providing information directly to consumers, who will buy their products, hire them, or join their groups.

But the biggest explanation for the shift is the way in which research is conducted online. We can find information on all kinds of legal topics online, without the hassle of going out to a law library. If you're trying to figure out the rules for forming a corporation in your state, you can most certainly find instruction online. The same is true if you want to read the Supreme Court's latest opinion on a particular topic. There are many, many things you can find within minutes—but you have to know where to look.

It isn't always the only, or even the best, way to conduct legal research, however. Here, we'll cover several different options.

Law Libraries

Law libraries remain an excellent resource for the legal researcher. For one thing, they usually have a lot of legal books and resources that aren't available online, or at least not without paying a high fee.

Additionally, libraries come with another helpful resource you'll have trouble replicating online—librarians. When you're having trouble finding a source, are confused about where to begin, or just need help understanding something you find, a librarian can help. In a law library, you'll be able to gain access to expensive online legal resources that we'll discuss in further detail below.

To find a law library near you, do an online search or check your local phone book. A local law school will likely have a law library, but states, counties, and other government agencies might as well. Call or look online to make sure the facility is open to the public. Also, plan on spending most of your time researching in the library itself. You won't usually be able to check out the most useful resources.

Law School Libraries Have Useful Websites, Too

Many law school libraries have useful websites. Here are a few examples:

WashLaw (www.washlaw.edu). A comprehensive website created by the Washburn University School of Law, this gives state-by-state legal resources, links to online periodicals, the online catalogs of many law libraries, and more.

Emory University School of Law (www.law.emory.edu). Under "Law Library," you'll find links to legal materials (select "Databases: Free" under the "Electronic Resources" heading).

Boalt Law Library (www.law.berkeley.edu/library.htm). This website for Berkeley's law school includes several different research guides by subject, in addition to information about online legal resources and how to access them. Select "Legal Research" from the top navbar, and then "Research Guides."

D'Angelo Law Library (www.lib.uchicago.edu/e/law/index.html). The University of Chicago's law library website also includes relevant research guides on a variety of legal research topics. Click on "Law Library Research Guides" under "Course Support."

Court Offices and Self-Help Centers

Another good resource for a lot of legal material is your local court. As we mentioned, today, many courts recognize that litigants representing themselves need some help understanding legal processes. Some courts have self-help offices or offices staffed by attorneys or clerks who help litigants figure out what forms to file, what deadlines to meet, and so forth. These offices also often have basic information and documents to explain the process litigants must go through to resolve a legal issue in the court system. However, these attorneys or clerks do not represent you and cannot give you legal advice. They are just there to help you understand the legal requirements for working your way through the court system, or to explain your options to you.

Many courts also have helpful information online. It should be relatively easy to find your court's website by using a search engine like Google and typing in the name of the county and the word "court." You might be able to find necessary forms, court rules (discussed further below), and information about your legal issue and how to file a lawsuit.

Online Research

Most legal researchers will spend at least some of their time researching online (and many will spend most of their time there). This approach is useful at every stage: when you're trying to get general information about a topic, when you're zeroing in on specific legal sources, and when you're trying to figure out what to do with the information you have uncovered. We'll discuss online research in "Looking for Legal Resources Online," below.

Primary Sources and Secondary Sources

All legal resources can be broken down into two categories: primary and secondary sources. Primary sources are the law itself—for example, the statutes, cases, and regulations that explain whether and how the federal government is to distribute Social Security benefits. Secondary sources are those that interpret or explain a primary source. For example, an article, a treatise, or a summary of how Social Security benefits must be distributed is a secondary source.

Primary Sources

The law found in primary sources can take many different forms. They include cases, statutes, administrative regulations, local ordinances, state and federal constitutions, and more.

Why Use Primary Sources

Primary sources are often more difficult to read and digest than secondary sources, but it isn't wise to rely solely on secondary sources. That's because laws can quickly change as courts issue new decisions or the legislature passes new laws. You won't always see these changes reflected in secondary sources. On the other hand, looking at primary sources is the quickest way to get the most up-to-date information.

Another reason it's important to rely on primary sources is that it's possible to get a lot more detail—that is, to find information that's much more helpful, specific, and targeted than you'll find in a secondary source. For example, assume your dog broke through the fence enclosing its dog run and bit a neighbor who was stealing sports equipment from your yard. You want to know whether you are liable for the neighbor's injuries given that the dog was fenced in and it was not intentionally released; and that the neighbor was trespassing on your property. You might find a secondary source that explains your liability when your dog bites someone, or your responsibility to a trespasser injured on your property. But by looking at primary sources, you might find a case or series of cases with very similar facts to the situation you're in, helping to put these two legal issues together into one. This will allow you to see how a court might apply the law to the facts of your case.

Finally, primary sources are very important because courts give them much more weight than they do secondary sources. Secondary sources only tell courts what legal scholars say about a legal principle, and courts want to see the actual source of the law itself. If the court is required to follow the primary source—for example, because it was issued by a higher court in the same jurisdiction—the court will certainly want to see it in original form.

Where to Find Primary Sources

The most popular method for accessing relevant primary material is to use law libraries or to go online. It usually isn't too difficult to find a case, statute, or regulation just by doing some searching around online. We'll explain how in future chapters.

Once you have a primary source, however, you have to ensure that it is still "good law." Legislatures pass new laws, courts overrule previous decisions by lower courts, and administrative regulations are amended or repealed. All this means that even once you've found a relevant primary source, you have to ensure nothing has happened in the meantime that undermines its validity. We'll explain how you do this in Chapter 8.

When to Use Primary Sources

It's important to use primary sources when you're trying to put together a document or an argument that carries legal weight. As we've explained, courts grant greater deference to primary sources than secondary sources.

It's also very important to use primary sources when you want to know exactly what the law says. Secondary sources might explain the law, but they won't be able to give you the full detail of what's actually there. Though reading primary law can be difficult, it's important to do it if you really want to understand the details. In Chapters 5 through 7, we'll explain more about how to read legal documents.

Secondary Sources

While primary sources are the texts of laws themselves, secondary sources are documents that interpret or discuss the primary sources. This might include legal journals, newspaper articles, online posts, and so forth.

The depth of treatment you get from any given secondary source can vary a great deal. Some secondary sources are very detailed, very law intensive, and very helpful. Others might provide only a broad, general overview of a topic. Finding the appropriate secondary source will depend, in large part, on where you are in your research. At the beginning, you might need only enough information to get "the lay of the land." But as your research progresses, you might want to find secondary sources that provide much more specific treatment of your legal issue.

When to Use Secondary Sources

Secondary sources are a logical place to start when you do not know anything about the topic you are researching. A secondary source can often explain the basic concepts you'll encounter in primary sources, making it easier to read them. It will also often cite to primary sources, thus helping to deepen and expand your research.

Secondary sources are also useful when you want to learn how things are generally done, or how they are done in other states. Many national secondary sources give a broad overview of the law, which can vary from place to place. This can be helpful when you're trying to learn the basics of how the law works, or when you need to compare how different jurisdictions handle the same issue (for instance, while conducting legal research for an academic paper). Keep in mind, however, that the law varies between states. If your legal issue involves state law, you'll be better off using a state-specific secondary source.

Where to Find Secondary Sources

Secondary sources can be found in lots of different locations—from websites to newspapers to books to legal texts available only in law libraries. For the most part, you should be able to find more general secondary sources online. However, you might find that when you want to get more detailed information—for example, when you want to find a secondary source that will help you find specific, legal primary sources—you'll have to head to the library or use a fee-based online research service like those described later in this chapter.

Popular Secondary Sources

The usability and helpfulness of secondary sources can vary widely. One excellent source of plain English discussions and explanations of legal topics is the books and articles published by Nolo, found at www.nolo. com. Like this book, these use everyday language to discuss complicated legal topics. We recommend visiting the website when you have a legal question, to see if there is an article or book that discusses it. Often, these resources will be a good jumping off point to the text of primary sources themselves, giving you a foundation to better understand the primary texts. You will have the option of searching using keywords or following the logical topical categories and subcategories that appear on the home page. For example, if you want to find out about an immigration-related issue, you can either type "immigration" in the search box, or click on "Immigration" under "Get Informed."

There are a couple other well-known secondary sources that give you a broad overview of the law. One is an encyclopedia called *American Jurisprudence* (commonly referred to as *"Am. Jur."*). *Am. Jur.* is organized by legal topic and covers each issue broadly, discussing any general legal principles and sometimes, specific state applications. We will explain more about *Am. Jur.*, and how to find and use it, in Chapter 4. Another similar secondary source is *American Law Reports* (called *"A.L.R."*). *A.L.R.* contains a series of articles organized much like *Am. Jur.* We'll also cover using *A.L.R.* in Chapter 4.

Many states have their own secondary sources that provide detailed information about state law. For example, in California, the well-known publisher B.E. Witkin has a series of state-specific volumes, such as *Summary of California Law* and *California Procedure,* which practicing lawyers refer to frequently. These books and others like them often provide greater detail than sources like *Am. Jur.* or *A.L.R.*, with lots of references to primary sources.

Finally, the websites of local, state, and federal government agencies are great secondary resources. For example, if you have a question about federal tax law, the IRS website at www.irs.gov has many summary documents that explain the legal principles laid out in the otherwise cumbersome federal tax code.

Looking for Legal Resources Online

Conducting online research can be much more efficient, and potentially thorough, than doing the same research in a legal library. Without having to wander around, physically look through books, or speculate as to which source will be most useful, you can save yourself a lot of time and cover a lot more territory. And by creating narrow, focused searches, you can get reliable, comprehensive results.

In Chapter 4, we'll discuss using online research to get reliable background information on topics you're researching. And in Chapters 5 and 6, we'll talk about how to narrow searches to get relevant primary source materials. For now, we're just going to familiarize you with some of the major online resources, so you'll know where to look once you are ready to get started.

Court Websites

As already explained, court websites are often a great resource for finding information on a variety of legal topics. Sometimes they provide access to primary sources like court opinions and rules, too.

For example, if you go to the United States Supreme Court site (www.supremecourt.gov), you can look up opinions written by the Court, as well as briefs submitted by parties. (Briefs are the legal documents each side submits to argue its case, which judges read and evaluate before the parties have a hearing to decide the issue.) Many other courts have similar accessibility. And at www.uscourts.gov, you can find links to all the courts in the federal system using the "Court Locator" box.

⚠ **CAUTION**

Not every opinion you find is good law. Remember, the decisions of lower courts can be overruled by higher ones, and the decisions of any court can be undone by a new law created by the legislature (as long as it doesn't conflict with the state or federal constitution). In Chapter 8, we'll explain how you determine whether a source is still "good law." For now, remember that just because a source is online doesn't mean it holds legal weight.

The Public Access to Court Electronic Records system (PACER, www.pacer.gov) is another excellent resource for court documents. It allows users to obtain information from a variety of federal cases. PACER compiles the legal documents filed in federal lawsuits in various courts across the country. For a small fee, users can download and read these documents. If you are curious about a particular lawsuit or want to know if a party you're going to sue has been sued in federal court before, for example, PACER is a useful resource.

Local state court websites also often have a lot of information. Many have online filing services that allow members of the public to access legal documents like briefs and judicial opinions. Some states even compile these types of resources in one location—usually, the website for the entire state court system. To see an example, visit the New York State Unified Court System's website (www.nycourts.gov). Under the "E-Courts" heading, click on "Decisions" to access rulings and opinions from the state's trial and appellate courts (you'll select the court from the menu on the left).

Legislative Websites

Many state legislatures have online information about bills under consideration or recently passed. You can use these websites to find current statutes or potential changes to the law, too.

At the federal level, the database many legal researchers find helpful is the GPO's Federal Digital system (FDsys)(www.gpo.gov/fdsys), a service of the U.S. Government Printing Office, which compiles information from all three branches of government, including Congressional legislation, the U.S. Code, and the Code of Federal Regulations.

Administrative Agencies

Many state and federal administrative agencies also have websites that allow you to access legal information. For example, if you visit the website for the Connecticut Department of Labor at www.ctdol.state. ct.us, you can access Connecticut labor laws and regulations, as well as explanatory information (click the "Regulations of CT State Agencies" box at the bottom left of the screen). If you know the area of law you are researching (we'll discuss how you figure this out in the next chapter), you might be able to go directly to the websites of the relevant administrative agency to get more information.

If you're looking for federal regulations, regardless of subject matter, you can find them at www.gpo.gov/fdsys. Look for "Code of Federal Regulations" under "Browse."

Using Search Engines

Many researchers today turn to a search engine like Google to find relevant information on almost any topic; and legal topics are no exception. Search engines are usually based on the words in all the indexed online sites, so they work much like pulling book indexes off the shelf and reading through them, only on a much bigger scale and through a very complex process.

The good part of automatic indexes is that they are thorough. But of course, they often produce more results than you need, and sometimes, those results aren't relevant or reliable. And although most search engines try to rank their results according to how relevant they are likely to be, this ranking can be unpredictable. For example, one automatic search engine might put exactly what you are looking for at the top of a list of 200 entries, while another might put it far down the list or even at the bottom. This can be challenging when the list is thousands of documents long.

Legal Search Engines

To even further narrow your research, you can choose to work in search engines that focus just on legal websites. You'll want to make sure they have the same flexibility to do Boolean searching (described below) as more general search engines. And you might want to go back and forth between various engines, comparing and contrasting results. A few sites to try include:

- https://scholar.google.com (select "Case law")
- www.lexisweb.com
- www.law.com/search.

Boolean Searching

To make the most of a tool as powerful as online research, you want to ensure you get all relevant results when conducting a search—and without the irrelevant ones. Many times, typing a few keywords into the search box will quickly pull up resources that are useful to you. But in other cases, you'll be inundated with more than you can handle, and some of it won't be relevant.

To avoid this problem, we suggest you learn how to write targeted searches that will narrow your results. The best way to do this is in a search engine that uses Boolean logic, as many do. The point of Boolean logic is simply that it can "read" specific words and symbols (called "operators") to help narrow our searches.

Before we explain the various Boolean search terms, we want to mention that with some search engines, you can get the benefit of Boolean logic without having to master the use of the various terms. On Google, for example, you'll find advanced search options.

See "Boolean Searching Cheat Sheet," below, for the current Google search pages.

If you are using a professional legal research site such as Westlaw, you might see yet more choices, as shown in the "Boolean Searching Cheat Sheet," below.

Here are the common Boolean operators and their functions:

- **And.** If you use the word *and* in your search, it will not be indexed like other words. That is, the search engine will not go looking for documents that use the word *and*. (Several other common terms, like *the, or,* and *so forth,* also don't get indexed.) Instead, *and* acts as an operator. The search engine will only look for documents containing the words that appear on either side of the *and*. For example, the query *box and container* produces every document that has both the word box and the word container. That is, it doesn't produce any document that doesn't have both words. Some search engines use the + symbol instead of the word *and* for the same purpose. As shown on the "Boolean Searching Cheat Sheet," below, Google simply gives you a text box in which to type all of your "and" words; in Westlaw, you must enter an ampersand (&)—if you simply list the two words, separated by a space, Westlaw will look for one term *or* the other.

- **Or.** *Or* instead of *and* means the engine will search for documents containing either word. You might use *or* when you're not sure which word is likely to be used to describe something relevant to your search, for example, *box or container* will produce documents with either or both words. Remember, if you are using Westlaw, simply separating the terms by a space will result in an "or" search.

- **And not.** To exclude words you don't want, you can use the operator *and not*. For example, if you are searching a legal issue in criminal law and want to exclude results that deal with civil law, you can use the "and not" operator to eliminate the word "plaintiff," which describes a party to a civil, but not a criminal, lawsuit. Just keep in mind that when using this operator, it's possible you'll also exclude some relevant results, so use it carefully.

- **Near/[number].** This indicates words should appear in spatial proximity to each other, such as in the same sentence or paragraph. For example, near/3 or n/3 means the keywords (the words on each side of near/3) must not be separated by more than three words. Some search engines use the operator *w* (standing for within) instead of "near" (for example, *w/3*).

Advanced Search

Find pages with...

all these words:

this exact word or phrase:

any of these words:

none of these words:

numbers ranging from: to

Then narrow your results by...

language: | any language   ▼ |

Find pages in the language that you select.

region: | any region   ▼ |

Find pages published in a particular region.

last update: | anytime   ▼ |

Find pages updated within the time that you specify.

site or domain:

Search one site (like wikipedia.org) or limit your
results to a domain like .edu, .org or .gov

terms appearing: | anywhere in the page   ▼ |

Search for terms in the whole page, page title or web
address, or links to the page you're looking for.

SafeSearch:

no filtering   **moderate**   **strict**
Tell SafeSearch how much explicit sexual content to filter.

reading level: | no reading level displayed   ▼ |

Find pages at one reading level or just view the level info.

file type: | any format   ▼ |

Find pages in the format that you prefer.

usage rights: | not filtered by licence   ▼ |

Find pages that you are free to use yourself.

| Advanced Search |

Google's Advanced Search Page

Boolean Searching Cheat Sheet

Function	Google/Yahoo! Operator	Google/Yahoo! Example	Westlaw Operator	Westlaw Example	Results contain documents or websites which contain:
And	[space]	slip fall	&	slip & fall	both these words (slip and fall)
Or	OR	slip OR fall	[space]	slip fall	either of the words (slip or fall)
Phrase	" "	"slip and fall"	" "	"slip and fall"	the exact phrase (slip and fall)
But not	-	slip -fall	%	slip %fall	excludes the word that appears after the operator % (slip but not fall)
Near			/n	slip near/4 fall	both words within a specified proximity to one another. (slip within four words of fall)
Word extender	*	slip*	!	slip!	words that began with the letters before the wildcard ! (include slips, slippery, slipped, and so forth)
Same sentence			/s	slip/s fall	words appear in the same sentence (slip and fall accidents happen)

Other Common Boolean Operators

Function	Operator	Example	Results contain documents or websites which contain:
One or the other	Xor	Slip xor fall	one word but not both (slip or fall)
Placeholder	?	F?ll	words in which one letter can differ (fall, fell, full, and fill)
Sets of conditions	( )	(slip near/2 fall) (wet or rain)	met all the parenthetical conditions (slip within two words of fall, but must also contain either the word wet or the word rain)

- **Adj.** This operator means the words must be adjacent to each other and in the order entered. For instance, the search query *dangerous adj beauty* means that the documents must have the phrase "dangerous beauty" in order to end up on the search results list. Alternatively, some engines allow you to use adj/ [number] in connection with a specification of how close the keywords should be. For instance, *adj/3* means the keywords must appear in the order they are entered in the search engine query box and not be separated by more than three words.

- **Quotes.** Putting quotes around a set of words means the engine will search only for the exact phrase. These are sometimes referred to as "string searches," because they involve a specific string of alphanumeric characters (letters and numbers). Google gives you a text box to enter "this exact wording or phrase."

- **xor.** The xor logical operator allows you to pull up documents that have either of the words separated by the operator but not documents that have both terms in them. For example, *box xor container* will give you results with box or container, but not box and container.

- ***.** For most search engines, the asterisk serves as a word (or part of a word) extender. By placing an asterisk at the end of a string of letters (known as the root), you are asking the search engine to search for any word that starts with the letters preceding the asterisk. For instance, if we used the word *driver* in a search request dealing with the suspension of a driver's license, the search engine would only look for that exact word and would skip over documents that use closely related words such as drivers, driver's, drivers', or driving. And the document with one of these variations on driver might be just the one you want. Typing in *drive** instead of *driver* will catch them.

- **?.** A question mark, or sometimes an exclamation point, serves as a wildcard. When you insert it in a word in a query, it stands for any character occupying that position in the word. Suppose, for example, your search involves women's rights. You would want to include the term women in your search query, but would also want to capture cases that use the term woman. By using a place holder for the "e" and the "a" in these two terms (wom?n), you can have the computer search for any case containing either term.

- **Parenthesis.** You will use parentheses when you do a search with multiple operators. As you might recall from algebra, when you use parentheses, you tell the search engine to start the search with what's inside, then complete it with everything else. For example *(break or enter) and (house or car)* will look for these four combinations: break and house, break and car, enter and house, and enter and car. (Of course, it might also include results with all phrases.)

As we've found, not every Boolean search engine will have the same set of operators. However, the more available to you, the more you can narrow your search, because you can combine these operators into one search. For example, assume you are looking for information about the circumstances that trigger driver's license suspensions. You would want documents that contain both "license" and "suspend." But each of these documents should also have either the word "driver" or the word "operator" (since you don't know which of these two words will be used in the materials you are searching for). A query that would accomplish this search would look like this: *license and suspend and (driver or operator)*.

Boolean searching takes some practice. And even once you're good at it, you might find that as you do your research, new phrases come up that need to be included or excluded from your query. We encourage you to remain flexible and to keep modifying your queries as you go.

Using Google

Though many search engines are available, the most popular is Google. Indeed, Google has many useful tools to help legal researchers narrow their research and get relevant results. Here are a few special features worth mention (if Google redesigns their toolbar, which is very likely, the specific directions on accessing these features might change, but you'll probably be able to figure out how to get them with a little trial and error):

- **The Google Toolbar.** Downloading the Toolbar is convenient because it will add a Google search box to your browser's window, and you won't have to type www.google.com every time you want to enter a search. But it has other research assistance functions too. To get the Google Toolbar, type "Google Toolbar" in your search engine.

- **News searches.** Because Google's search priorities are often based on the popularity of a site—statistics that accrue over time— current information might be buried at the end of search results. Google compensates for this by allowing you to perform a news search in which the search engine looks for timely media reports on the searched terms. You can search for news results in two ways. First, you can run a search on Google's main page but then click the "News" link on the top of the search results page. Or, you can direct a search to find only news articles. To perform the latter, go to http://news.google.com and enter your query into the search box

> **TIP**
>
> **Stay on top of breaking legal news stories.** If you want to stay abreast of a specific news subject, try "Google Alerts." You will receive daily (or "as it happens") emails based on your choice of query or topic. Go to www.google.com/alerts and type in the search terms.

- **Google Scholar.** If you'd like to limit your Google search to scholarly papers, try Google Scholar. Go to http://scholar.google.com and enter your search term. You'll get results that are limited to materials such as peer-reviewed journal articles, theses, books, abstracts, and technical reports from the broad areas of research that are available online. If you're doing legal research online, you can limit your search to decisions that have been issued by appellate courts throughout the country, at both the state and federal levels. From the Google Scholar start page, select the "Case law" radio button, located just below the main search query field. You'll be given the option of limiting your search to certain jurisdictions and courts, using the "Select courts" feature.

A Few Tips and Tricks When Using Google

When performing searches with Google, here are some tips and tricks to keep in mind:

- **Google ignores many common words and characters.** Google disregards words such as where, the, how, why, and some single digits and letters. You can see which words are ignored on the search results page. If you want the search to include the common word, put a "+" sign in front of it—for example, Americans +with Disabilities Act. (Be sure to include a space before the "+" sign.)
- **You can make Google search for synonyms.** If you want to search not only for your search term but also for its synonyms, place the tilde sign ("~") immediately in front of the search term.
- **You can search for a range of numbers.** If you want to obtain results within a numerical range—for example, copyright law results between 1980 and 1990, just include the two numbers, separated by two periods, with no spaces, into the search box along with your search terms. For example, type, "copyright law 1980..1990."
- **Get rid of multimeaning terminology.** If your search term has more than one meaning, you can focus your search by putting a minus sign ("–") in front of words related to the meaning you want to avoid. (Be sure to include a space before the minus sign.) For example, if you're researching marijuana and want to use the word "pot," you don't want results concerning cooking pots, coffee pots, or melting pots. You would type "pot –cooking –coffee –melting" and it would eliminate many of the unnecessary common results.

- **Quick definitions.** Nolo's online dictionary (www.nolo.com/dictionary) will probably have the best plain-English definitions of legal terms, but you can also type "define" followed by a space and the word to be defined in your Google search box.
- **Blog search.** If you're interested in what others have to say about a subject, you can limit your searches to relevant blogs. On the Google home page click on the "Apps" icon, then select "More," then "Even More" in the drop-down list, and on the next screen click on "Blog Search" under "Specialized Search."
- **Searching books.** If you want to search through the complete text of millions of books to research your legal topic, you can do that using Google Books (http://books.google.com). Just enter your search term into the query field, and you'll see a list of books containing that term or phrase. You can access a free preview of many of the books in Google's database, and for some titles, the entire text is even available for free online.

Legal Research Websites

In addition to using search engines and general government sites to get legal information, you can find a lot of this information on websites specifically designed for legal research. We'll cover some of the most common ones here. Note that the skills you learn by using search engines will help you here—many of these sites have search functions that use the same or similar logic.

Lexis and Westlaw

In the world of online legal research, two players dominate. These are the services LexisNexis (called "Lexis," www.lexis.com) and Westlaw (www.westlaw.com). These sites provide access to almost any legal resource you can imagine. Both have user-friendly platforms which feature a single natural-language search that brings up results from across all databases. While other online legal research services exist, none have the power of Lexis and Westlaw.

Of course, this power comes at a price—and a very steep one. While Lexis and Westlaw are cost-effective for large law firms with many lawyers using them, they're rarely realistic for the average researcher. Luckily, you might be able to gain access to Westlaw or Lexis in a law library. We suggest you call around to nearby law libraries to find out whether they offer free public access. If not, becoming a regular subscriber is probably not a realistic option for you, so you'll want to consider some of the alternatives mentioned below.

 TIP

Have access to Lexis or Westlaw, and need help figuring out how to use the system? Both websites have online tutorials available—we suggest you take advantage of them before getting started, particularly if you're being charged for use. (Clicking around at random can quickly get very expensive.) Understanding what you're doing will make your research process much more efficient. And understanding Boolean searching will also help—both databases use similar and even more complex search tools.

Fortunately, there are lots of other online research options that are much cheaper or even free.

Nolo

As we've already explained, Nolo's website (www.nolo.com) has many articles and books on legal subjects. Additionally, it provides state-by-state information on a variety of legal topics, such as the employment discrimination laws of each state, making a will, getting a divorce, or filing a small claims court action. Nolo has other resources like a directory of lawyers and a host of legal forms.

Justia

Justia is a very comprehensive, free site that provides several different legal resources. Probably the most useful is its direct access to searchable federal and state primary and secondary sources, such as the U.S. Code and Supreme Court opinions since 1790, as well as federal appellate court cases since 1950 and lots of relevant state materials, too. To access this information, visit http://law.justia.com.

Justia also has a helpful feature if you're looking to learn what's currently happening with a specific topic. That's because it includes a search feature (http://blawgsearch.justia.com) that allows you to look at legal blogs. Because many lawyers, professors, and other legal professionals use blogs to keep clients and others updated about what's happening in the law, this can be an excellent resource and is more focused than a general blog search using a search engine like Google.

FindLaw

FindLaw is another online resource that will help you find primary law at no cost. Visit caselaw.findlaw.com to get access to many primary sources. FindLaw covers primary law territory similar to Justia, but doesn't have as many secondary sources or helpful links.

VersusLaw

VersusLaw is billed as a low-cost alternative to its larger, more expensive competitors—and its pricing system puts it in financial reach for many general consumers. The flip side, however, is that it does not have the same research capabilities or access to resources of the larger providers.

VersusLaw's search capability does allow the user to access lots of different legal resources at one time. However, it's limited to primary law resources. Another important limitation is that, while the system can list all cases that cite to the particular case you're researching, it does not distinguish how those subsequent cases deal with the original. This means it isn't possible to tell, from a quick glance, whether any subsequent cases overrule the current one, something that is easy to do in either Westlaw or

Lexis. Finally, VersusLaw does not give citations to the "official reporter." You might need those citations if you plan to cite cases in an official court document.

When you search statutes (except the U.S. Code) on VersusLaw, you will be linked to the publicly available websites for each state. While it's convenient to do this all in one place, particularly if you are researching an issue in more than one state, you can probably find these various statutes other ways, at no cost.

FastCase

Another lower-cost online option for primary law materials is FastCase (www.fastcase.com), which features federal and state cases, statutes, court rules, regulations, and more. FastCase offers a variety of methods for sorting search results, and a feature that indicates the most-cited case among your search results. A number of subscription options are available (including month to month). FastCase also operates the Public Library of Law, which is billed as the "largest free law library in the world." Judge for yourself at www.plol.org.

Cheat Sheet of Legal Websites (Primary Sources)

- **The Federal Judiciary,** www.uscourts.gov: to find cases and other legal information from federal courts nationwide
- **Public Access to Court Electronic Records (PACER),** www.pacer.gov.: to view documents filed in federal cases throughout the country
- **GPO,** www.gpo.gov/fdsys: to search federal statutes and the Code of Federal Regulations
- **Justia,** http://law.justia.com: to find state or federal case law, statutes, regulations, and other materials
- **FindLaw,** caselaw.findlaw.com: to find state or federal case law or statutes
- **VersusLaw,** www.versuslaw.com: to purchase a low-cost system for searching federal and state case law and statutes, including subsequent history

Identifying Your Legal Issue

Now that you understand the basics of the law and have a sense of where to find legal resources, you're ready to go, right? Well, almost. To maximize the effectiveness of your research, we suggest you first spend some time framing your research question or questions. In this chapter, we'll help you do that, by covering:

- how to approach your research
- locating the resources that will help you find what you need, and
- framing your legal research question.

How to Approach Your Research

Before beginning your legal research, you'll find it helpful to break the project down into small, manageable steps. We propose thinking about your legal research this way:

Step 1: Is this a civil issue, a criminal issue, or both?

Step 2: What area of the law should I focus on?

Step 3: What are the resources that will help me solve my problem?

Step 4: What do I need to do with the information I find?

We'll presume, for purposes of explaining how to do your research and what to do with the results, that you'll approach research this way. We think you'll find it makes the most sense, and will help you stay organized and focused.

For example, let's say you're a landlord trying to figure out whether you can evict a tenant who hasn't paid rent in over three months. You start by identifying the area of law you're researching: it's a civil issue, meaning you're not trying to throw the tenant in jail, you're just trying to get him out of the apartment. And you know that it's an issue of landlord-tenant law. That means it's probably an issue of state law (because, as we explained in Chapter 1, it is almost exclusively state law that deals with landlord-tenant issues), and you can focus your research on sources that cover landlord-tenant issues. Next, you can look to the resources that will help you solve your problem, including the primary law of your state, and secondary sources like court-provided resources. Finally, you know that you can take the information you find and figure out whether it means that you should write a letter to the tenant, file an eviction suit, or pursue some other measure.

The rest of this chapter gives you more information on how to answer the four steps mentioned above.

Step 1: Is the Issue Civil or Criminal?

Understanding whether your issue is a matter of civil law or criminal law is the first broad step in narrowing your research. You might know the answer to this question very clearly. For example, if you or someone you know has been arrested, you know that your issue is one of criminal law. Or if you want to sue a creditor, that is a civil matter. Below, we'll explain how you can tell the difference between civil and criminal cases when you aren't exactly sure.

The issue of whether a matter is civil or criminal also has two subparts. You need to figure out whether the matter is substantive (are you asking about what the law is?), procedural (is your question about the court process?), or both; and whether it is an issue of state law, federal law, or both. We'll discuss those issues in further detail too.

Criminal Law

Generally, if a certain type of behavior is punishable by imprisonment (in a jail or prison), then criminal law is involved. Because crimes are considered "offenses against the people," charges are usually initiated in court by a government prosecutor. If you are involved in a legal dispute with a nongovernmental individual or corporation, then the matter is not criminal. If the government is involved, it might be criminal—but the government is involved in many civil matters, too.

Substantive Criminal Law

Within criminal law, there are two separate subcategories that will also help you narrow your search. These are substantive law and criminal procedure. Substantive law is the rules themselves—the definition and punishment of crimes. For example, the substantive criminal law tells us the difference between burglary (breaking and entering into the premises of another with the intent to commit a theft or felony) and larceny (taking personal property rightfully in the possession of another with intent to steal). It also specifies how each of these crimes is punished. Below is a list of common criminal substantive law categories. You might research substantive criminal law to better understand what you or someone you know is being accused of doing, for example, and what the punishment is if found guilty.

Criminal Law Substantive Categories		
Assault and battery	Juvenile offenses	Rape
Breaking and entering	Kidnapping	Robbery
Burglary	Larceny	Shoplifting
Conspiracy	Lewd and lascivious behavior	Smuggling
Disorderly conduct	Malicious mischief	Tax evasion
Drug and narcotics offenses	Marijuana cultivation	Trespass
Drunk driving	Murder	Weapons offenses

Criminal Procedure

Criminal procedure is the process the government must follow when bringing charges against someone. For example, criminal procedure involves such things as what kinds of evidence can be used in a criminal trial, when an accused must be brought to trial, when a person can be released on bail, and so on. You might be researching criminal procedure because you think you or someone else is not being treated fairly by the criminal justice system. For example, if you were entitled to a hearing in a criminal case and did not receive it, that would be an issue of criminal procedure. Below is a list of common criminal procedure categories.

Criminal Procedure Topics		
Arraignments	Jury verdicts	Right to counsel
Arrests	*Miranda* warnings	Search and seizure
Confessions	Plea bargaining	Sentencing
Cross-examination	Pleas	Speedy trial
Extradition	Preliminary hearings	Suppression of evidence
Grand jury	Probation	Trials
Indictments	Probation reports	Witnesses
Jury selection		

When researching criminal law, it's common to have questions of both substance and procedure. For example, let's say your house was searched by the police, without a warrant, and an illegal drug was found inside. You might want to research whether police had the right to search your house—an issue of procedure. You might also want to know whether the law requires the government to prove that the drug belonged to you, not your roommate. That's a matter of substantive law.

Civil Law

When you sue or are sued by someone else (other than the district attorney), it's a matter of civil law. In a civil action, the court can't usually imprison anyone (except in rare circumstances—for example, when a court orders a parent to pay child support and the parent willfully refuses). And that's not what the person bringing the lawsuit (the plaintiff) is looking for. Instead, they're hoping the court will compensate them for their "damages"—the loss caused by the defendant's alleged action; or order the defendant to do something. When a plaintiff asks for damages, they're asking for money. Asking the court to order the defendant to do or not do something can involve, for example, prohibiting an ex-employee from using a company's trade secrets, or requiring a person to honor a previous agreement. If you are involved in a dispute with a person, not the government, that is a good indicator that the issue is a civil one. (However, governments can also be involved in civil suits, so don't assume a government's involvement means it's an issue of criminal law.)

Substantive Civil Law

Like criminal law, research questions about civil law can be either substantive or procedural. Substantive law is the law that establishes our rights and duties—either written down in statutes or in case law. For example, when someone involved in a car accident damages property and injures people, a set of principles called "tort law" determines who is liable to whom and for what. It might not appear in a statute anywhere (tort law developed in case law over many years), but it is still part of law and the driver can be held liable for damages.

Most legal research involves substantive civil law. To help you fit your problem into the correct category, we have provided a large list of categories with definitions for each. These are found in "Figuring Out the Area of Law You're Researching," below.

Another way to find common civil actions is to review your state's civil jury instructions (many states post the jury instructions online). The instructions explain the law in simple terms that someone without legal training can understand. They're used by judges at the end of a trial. The judge tells the jury the law that applies to the case by reading the appropriate jury instructions. Then the judge instructs the jury to apply the facts heard at the trial to the law read from the jury instruction. Not only does an instruction exist for all common causes of action, but you'll get a good idea about the types of civil actions available by reading through the table of contents. The actual jury instruction explains what must be proven at trial (called the "elements") and in many cases, each instruction contains citations to important statutes and cases.

Another reason to pull the applicable jury instruction at the very outset of your case is that the instructions give you a template to follow when conducting your research. The instruction will list each element that you'll need to prove in a straightforward manner. You'll then make sure that you have adequate evidence to prove each element (if you can't prove each element with evidence, you will lose the case—which is why it is essential to clearly understand the pertinent law). We discuss how the court uses jury instructions at trial in further detail—as well as how to find them online—in Chapter 9.

Civil Procedure

Civil procedure is the set of rules that govern how our civil justice system works. It controls such matters as which courts have the authority to decide different kinds of lawsuits, what kinds of documents must be filed, when they need to filed, who can be sued, what kinds of proof can be offered in court, and how to appeal to a higher court. For example, if you want to sue the local grocery store because you slipped and fell in the store, civil procedure will tell you where you can file your lawsuit (preventing you from suing from Arkansas if you and the grocery store are located in Michigan, for example), what document or documents you must file to start the lawsuit (perhaps a simple "complaint" that explains the basis of the suit), when you must file these documents by (such as within two years after the incident occurred), and how you must notify the grocer that you've filed the lawsuit (usually, by having an unrelated third party personally hand the notification over).

Each state has its own set of procedural rules. However, many states have procedures that are very similar to the Federal Rules of Civil Procedure, used in all federal courts. We will explain more about how to find and use the rules that apply to you in Chapter 5.

State Law or Federal Law?

When thinking about the area of law you need to research, also think about whether the issue you're researching is a matter of state law, federal law, or both. This can help you narrow your research. For instance, it might help you identify whether you you should look in a secondary source that specifically deals with federal tax issues, or online for your state court's small claims procedure. It won't be immediately obvious in every case, but you can refer back to Chapter 1 for more help. If you can't figure it out yet, don't worry—as you start your research, this will probably become clear.

Step 2: Figuring Out the Area of Law You're Researching

Once you determine whether the area of law you're researching is criminal or civil and state or federal, you'll want to get a little more specific. That's because many of the secondary sources we discussed in Chapter 2 will be organized by subject area, or might even be limited to a specific area of the law. You'll want to learn the lingo for that area. For example, if you want to find out the legal requirements for incorporating in your state, you will be able to look at sources under "corporations" or "incorporating," but also search indexes for "business entity" law or formation.

Common Civil Law Categories

The task of narrowing the area of law will be slightly easier if you are dealing with a substantive criminal issue—you can look at the crime involved and start from there. But it is a little harder to classify substantive civil law issues. The list set out below contains some of the common substantive civil law categories used in many indexes. Knowing where your subject falls might help narrow your search. Many legal issues fall into more than one category. The categories:

- **Administrative law** refers to the law regulating government agencies.
- **Bankruptcy** covers the process that allows a debtor to liquidate assets and be relieved of further liability. It is governed primarily by federal law but also involves state property law.
- **Business and professions law** deals with restrictions and license requirements placed on professionals (for example, doctors and lawyers) and other occupational groups.
- **Business entity law** relates to the creation of business entities such as corporations, limited liability companies, and partnerships. It can involve both state and federal laws on how these entities can operate and be taxed, the rights of shareholders, the rights and duties of the entity's officers and directors, and more.

- **Civil rights law** means provisions that protect individuals from discrimination on the basis of such legally recognized characteristics as race, sex, ethnic or national background, or color.
- **Commercial law** involves federal and state regulations governing commercial relations between borrowers and lenders, banks and their customers, wholesalers and retailers, and mortgagors and mortgagees. Generally, this area involves disputes between businesspeople rather than between a businessperson and a consumer.
- **Constitutional law** covers issues applying to federal or state constitutions.
- **Consumer law** deals with the requirements governing transactions between a seller and a buyer of personal property in a commercial setting (for example, when individuals buy products like cars or furniture from a retailer).
- **Contracts** is the area of law dealing with written and oral agreements and what to do if they are broken or canceled.
- **Corporation law** deals with how corporations are formed and the requirements for how they operate.
- **Creditor/debtor law** covers how debts are collected and handled (for example, whether they can be cancelled or reorganized in bankruptcy).
- **Cyberlaw** refers to how the Internet affects copyright, trademark, libel, pornography, contracts, privacy, and court jurisdiction.
- **Education law** covers the rights of students and the restrictions placed on them by schools.
- **Elder law** encompasses issues relevant to seniors, such as Social Security, Medicare, Medicaid, nursing homes, and special needs trusts.
- **Employment law** means the rights of employees and the restrictions placed on employers by law.
- **Energy law** includes the state and federal laws governing the production, distribution, and utilization of energy sources like coal, natural gas, oil, electrical and nuclear power, and alternative energy.

- **Environmental law** deals with the regulation of the use of the environment by business, government, and individuals. For example, this includes issues of air and water pollution, the environmental impact of new construction projects, the preservation of endangered species, and similar matters. It is an area regulated by both federal and state governments.
- **Estate planning** means how people arrange for the distribution of their property after they die; includes such subjects as living trusts, joint tenancies, wills, testamentary trusts, and gifts.
- **Evidence** covers what kinds of items and testimony can be introduced as proof in a trial or hearing.
- **Family law, divorce law, domestic relations law** all refer to matters relating to families and family division, such as marriage, divorce, child support, and child custody.
- **Health law** relates to issues affecting health, like the type and quality of medical treatment received from hospitals or occupational health and safety requirements.
- **Housing law** covers programs involving government subsidies for construction and rental assistance, public housing, state and local planning requirements related to the type and amount of housing in different areas, and discriminatory housing practices.
- **Insurance law** encompasses problems arising under any kind of insurance contract, such as life insurance, car insurance, homeowners' insurance, fire insurance, and disability insurance.
- **Intellectual property law** is the laws and procedures governing copyrights, trademarks, trade secrets, and patents.
- **Juvenile law** deals with juvenile delinquency (when a child commits an act that would be a crime if he or she were an adult), or dependency (when a child is abused or neglected and becomes a ward of the state).
- **Labor law** broadly covers issues surrounding unions.
- **Landlord/tenant law** is concerned with all issues arising out of the landlord-tenant relationship, such as evictions, leases and rental agreements, rent control, and similar matters.

- **Military law** relates to all matters under the authority (jurisdiction) of the military, including discharges, enlistment, mandatory registration laws, court martials, and benefits.
- **Municipal law** includes zoning, ordinances, land-use planning, condemnation of property, incorporation of cities, contracting for public improvements, and other matters of local concern.
- **Prison law** covers prison conditions, disciplinary procedures, parole, constitutional rights of prisoners, and adequate access to legal information and medical treatment.
- **Property law** encompasses the purchase, maintenance, use, regulation, and sale of real estate.
- **Public benefits law** means the administration and distribution of federal and state benefits such as TANF (Temporary Assistance for Needy Families), Social Security (SSA), Social Security Disability (SSDI), Supplemental Security Income (SSI), food stamps, school lunches, foster homes, Medicaid, Medicare, and state disability.
- **Public utilities law** covers the duties, responsibilities, and rights of public utilities that provide water, telephone service, sewage and garbage disposal, and gas and electricity.
- **Tax law** includes all issues related to federal and state taxation of such items as income, personal property, business profits, real estate, and sales transactions.
- **Tort law (personal injury law)** deals with any injury to a person or business that is directly caused by the intentional or negligent actions of someone else. Many lawsuits involve torts; the most common is "negligence." This involves behavior that is considered unreasonably careless under the circumstances and that directly results in injury to another. Medical malpractice, legal malpractice, and most automobile accidents are examples of negligence.
- **Unemployment insurance** covers all matters relating to unemployment insurance benefits.
- **Workers' compensation** concerns the rights of workers who are injured or killed in work-related accidents.

Understanding Indexes and Topical Searches

Knowing which area of law you are researching is very important not only because it will help you narrow your legal questions, as we'll discuss below, but because you'll need to have some idea of where to start looking when you actually begin researching.

When you go to a law library without knowing any details on a particular topic, you will almost always need to look in an index first. Like the indexes you find in the back of books, indexes to legal texts are usually alphabetical lists of subjects, with references that tell you where within the text you can find information on those subjects. To find secondary sources, statutes, and even cases (using a special system created for this purpose, described in Chapter 6), you'll need to have some general idea of what key subjects to look for. Because no two indexes will be exactly alike, you might find one index uses one phrase, while another excludes it completely but has a different phrase that covers the same or a similar topic.

The same is true if you conduct an online search. The results you'll get from typing words or phrases into a search engine will vary depending on many factors, like how common the words are, whether they have more than one meaning, or whether they are legal terms only, applicable to narrow subject matter.

Understanding the area of law you're researching will help you in conducting searches either online or in books or printed materials. That's because you'll be able to think, as broadly as possible, about the types of words and phrases that might be relevant to your search. You can use one or all of the methods below to find the words with relevant information on your legal topic.

The Statsky "Cartwheel" Approach

The Statsky approach uses a diagram—called the Cartwheel—that prompts the reader for different categories of words. For example, suppose that the research problem involves determining who is authorized to perform a wedding and what ceremony, if any, need be conducted. The structure of the Cartwheel is shown below:

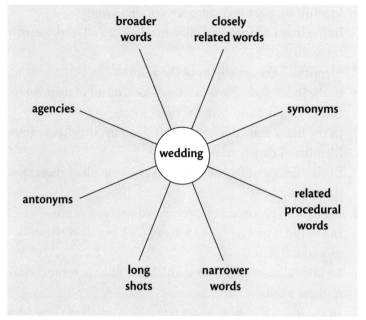

Reproduced by permission from *Domestic Relations*, by William P. Statsky, copyright © 1978 by West Publishing Company (out of print). All Rights Reserved.

The first step in using the index and table of contents in any law book is to look up the keyword—in this example, "wedding"—in that index and table. If that's not successful, either because the word is not in the index or table or because the page or section references after the word in the index and table do not lead to relevant material in the book, the next step is to think of as many different phrasings and contexts of the word "wedding" as possible.

The Cartwheel method has 18 steps to help you come up with terms to look up in an index or table of contents, as follows:

1. Identify all the major words from the facts of the research problem. Place each word or small set of words in the center of the Cartwheel.
2. In the index and table of contents, look up all of these words.
3. Identify the broader categories of these major words.
4. In the index and the table of contents, look up all of these broader categories.

5. Identify the narrower categories of these words.
6. In the index and table of contents, look up all of the narrower categories.
7. Identify all the synonyms of the words.
8. In the index and table of contents, look up all of these synonyms.
9. Identify all the antonyms of these words.
10. In the index and table of contents, look up all of these antonyms.
11. Identify all closely related words.
12. In the index and table of contents, look up all of these closely related words.
13. Identify all procedural terms related to these words.
14. In the index and table of contents, look up all of these procedural terms.
15. Identify all agencies, if any, which might have some connection to these words.
16. In the index and table of contents, look up all of these agencies.
17. Identify all long shots.
18. In the index and table of contents, look up all of these long shots.

If we were to apply these 18 steps of the Cartwheel to the word "wedding," here are some of the words and phrases that you would check in the index and table of contents of every law book that deals with family law:

- **Broader Words:** celebration, ceremony, rite, ritual, formality, festivity
- **Narrower Words:** civil wedding, church wedding, proxy wedding, sham wedding, shotgun marriage
- **Synonyms:** marriage, nuptial
- **Antonyms:** alienation, annulment, dissolution, divorce, separation
- **Loosely Related Words:** matrimony, marital, domestic, husband, wife, bride, anniversary, custom, children, blood test, premarital, spouse, relationship, family, home, consummation, cohabitation, sexual relations, betrothal, minister, wedlock, oath, contract, name change, domicile, residence

- **Procedural Terms:** application, petition, authorization
- **Agencies:** Bureau of Vital Statistics, County Clerk, License Bureau, Secretary of State, Justice of the Peace
- **Long Shots:** dowry, common law, single, blood relationship, fraud, religion, license, illegitimate, remarriage, antenuptial, alimony, bigamy, pregnancy, gifts, chastity, community property, impotence, incest, virginity, support, custody, consent, paternity.

Perhaps you might think that some of the word selections in the above categories are a bit farfetched. But you simply will not know for sure whether a word will be fruitful until you try it. To be successful, you must be imaginative.

Understanding Index Jargon

Indexes themselves use jargon that can be confusing. Here are definitions of some of the more commonly used indexing terms:

- *Generally, this index.* When a term is followed by a "Generally, this index," it means that the term can be located as a main entry in its alphabetical place in the index. For instance, if you find "child support" under the larger heading of "Minors," and it is followed by "Generally, this index," look for it as a main entry.
- *See also.* The terms following the "see also" may produce related subject matter.
- *See.* The material you are seeking will be found directly under the term following the "see" rather than under the original term.
- *See ____ infra.* The entry is found under the same main entry but further down alphabetically. Basically, it's Latin for "below."
- *See ____ supra.* The entry is found under the same main entry, but further up alphabetically. Latin for "above."

An Informal Approach

If you don't want to follow the Cartwheel method, there are other ways to approach legal indexes. The one that we use most of the time has six steps:

Step 1: Select several key plain-English terms that define the research problem, and several alternatives to these terms.

Step 2: Use these words to select one or more probable legal categories.

Step 3: Search the index for a main entry relevant to your problem and be prepared to follow up cross-references.

Step 4: Search for relevant subentries under the main entry.

Step 5: Bounce back to another main entry if your first choice doesn't work out.

Step 6: Once you find a good main entry and subentry, think even smaller and more detailed.

For instance, suppose your research question is whether a drunk driving conviction results in the loss of a driver's license. The first step is to determine some key terms. You might start with drunk driving and such variations as "operating a motor vehicle under the influence of intoxicating beverages" or "driving while intoxicated." The same process would hold true for "driver's license." Possible alternative terms for driver's license are "operator's permit" or "operator's license."

The second step is to determine whether these terms logically fit under one of the general civil or criminal law substantive categories. Vehicle law would be the most appropriate category, so you would probably start with vehicles.

The third step is to search the index and be prepared to follow up cross-references. For instance, in this example, if you started with vehicles, you would probably be referred to "motor vehicles."

The fourth step is to search for subentries under an appropriate main entry. For instance, if you looked for drunk driving under motor vehicles, you might find an alternative term, such as "operating under the influence."

287   **MOTOR VEHICLES**

Pennsylvania Index

TRAFFIC

The fifth step is to go back to another main entry if your first choice doesn't pan out. For example, if you found no reference to drunk driving or its equivalent under motor vehicles, consider looking under "alcohol," "traffic offenses," "alcoholic beverages," or "automobiles." You also might come up with some more variations of your specific terms.

The sixth step is to conceptualize even more detailed entries that are likely to refer you to material on your specific question. For instance, once you find an entry that covers drunk driving under the main entry "motor vehicles," you might consider looking for such specific terms as "license," "suspension," "revocation," "restriction," and "forfeiture."

Using the Informal Approach to Write Research Queries

Using the informal categorization method explained above is useful even if you don't ever see yourself looking through any legal indexes, because it can also help you use Boolean logic (discussed in the previous chapter) to write relevant research queries. If you don't write a search that's narrow enough, you risk getting too much information, much of it possibly irrelevant. On the other hand, if you exclude similar terms from your query, you risk losing out on possibly relevant results.

Using the example above about researching who is authorized to perform a wedding, you can write a Boolean search to include either the words wedding or marriage, by writing: (wedding or marriage). And if you wanted to be located near the word "ceremony" or a synonym, you could write it like this: (wedding or marriage) near/3 (celebration or ceremony or rite or ritual or formality or festivity).

In researching something like this, you might find yourself continually adjusting your search terms to try and narrow in on your specific topic. But it's much easier to do this if you have a list of relevant terms with which to start. As you can see, thinking of alternative words can open up your searches, while still giving you only relevant results.

If you run up against a brick wall, take a deep breath and start over. Restructure your question, come up with new terms, and find a different substantive category. We can't emphasize strongly enough that the reason most research fails is that the researcher runs out of patience at the index-searching stage.

Above are three examples from index listings to demonstrate the different ways indexes can be organized. The one thing they all have in common is that they are organized from general terms in the main entry to specific subentries. The samples show the different ways that indexes can treat the topic of license revocation for drunk driving.

We'll show you how to find the specific indexes you need later in the book. For now, just make sure that when you get there, you're ready to start researching based on some of the terms you're thinking of now.

Online Legal Indexes

Looking online is often significantly simpler and quicker than using a print index. While you might have to spend hours trying to find relevant words in a print index as you try phrase after phrase, with the help of a search engine, you can just type a phrase and see what it brings from a variety of sources instead of just one. If it doesn't work, it doesn't take long to find another phrase. And if you get relevant results that aren't detailed or reliable enough, you can often quickly look at them just to get ideas for other words or phrases.

However, if you've already found an online resource, your options might be limited the following:

- **Menus.** The typical menu approach works like a nested table of contents. Click on the largest category and get a list of sub-categories. Click on a subcategory for a third level of entries. This can go on for any number of levels—depending on the material—until you find a link that is appropriately specific.
- **Keywords.** This is the method discussed above—it lets you search for materials that contain the words you enter in a search or "query" box.

- **Keyword menus.** This method presents you with a drop-down menu of keywords. Once you select a keyword, you will be taken to materials that have been associated with the keyword by the publisher of the material.

Although none of these tools works exactly like a print index, you should keep the same principles in mind when using them. If you don't find what you are looking for at first, keep trying. If your initial keywords don't produce anything helpful, change them. If your choice of terms in a drop-down menu doesn't work, select some new ones.

Step 3: What Resources Will Help You Find What You Need?

Once you have a sense of what you're looking for, you can start identifying the possible resources that will help you find it. In the following chapters, we'll discuss how to locate the right resource. For now, answer these questions:

- **Are you looking for a general overview of the law on a specific subject?** In that case, you probably want to start with a secondary source. This might be a legal text or a court website, even an online article or summary—anything that isn't primary law counts. We'll explain how to do background research using secondary sources in Chapter 4.
- **Are you looking for a specific statute on a subject?** If you know that you need to look at a specific statute, administrative regulation, or local ordinance—for example, the definition of a crime someone has been charged with—go directly to the source. As we explain in Chapter 5, a single statute is usually just the start to finding many other resources.
- **Are you looking for a case that applies the law to a situation similar to the one you're researching?** Case law uses factual scenarios to help explain how the law works in different situations. This is a good way to learn how courts interpret laws, and makes particular

sense if you are writing a legal document or research paper. Read Chapter 6 to learn how to find cases.

We recognize this approach won't cover every situation. For example, if you're exploring an area of international law, you might be looking to other sources. (International legal research is beyond the scope of this book.) But for the vast majority of cases, answering these questions will get you started. As you explore, you might quickly find yourself needing to look at other sources. Just use these questions to decide where to begin.

Step 4: Figure Out Your Legal Research Question

The last step in the process of planning your legal research is framing your issue. That is, you want to have a clear idea about *why* you are researching and what you hope to accomplish. This might seem silly, but if you begin researching without taking this critical step, you'll soon see that it's very easy to become overwhelmed. It's rare that you won't find enough information on a subject to get you started; in most cases, you'll find that there's simply too much there to even know where to begin. Without a centering question, it's easy to get sidetracked. Framing your legal research question helps avoid this problem.

Why Are You Conducting Legal Research?

To frame your legal research question, think about why you are conducting the research. This question is important because it will help you target the types of legal resources you need to look at and how deep you need to dig to get your answers. Are you going to be filing a lawsuit? If that's the case, you'll need to spend a good deal of time looking at the legal requirements for doing so. (We'll explain how in greater detail in Chapter 9.) You'll also need to look at the law to figure out what law you believe was violated, and what appropriate damages or relief you should be granted.

On the other hand, your research will take a very different level of detail if you are planning on meeting with a lawyer, and want to know what questions to ask to make use of the lawyer's time most efficiently. In that case, you'll probably want to start with a general lay of the land, then focus in on key areas if they seem relevant. For example, if you're going to see an estate planning attorney about drafting a will, you might learn a little about the concept of wills generally. But your research might lead you to other areas of special interest—for example, placing your assets in a living trust. While you might learn about wills and estate planning generally, you might focus your research on living trusts. You probably won't read your state's statutes on living trusts, however, because your lawyer will already be familiar with those laws, and will also probably be the person who will draw up necessary documents. Instead, you're looking for information that will tell you what to ask, to help you figure out if it's the right planning tool for you.

We recommend writing down what your goal is. For example, in a case like the first one, you might write, "My goal is to file a lawsuit against the furniture store that damaged my hardwood floor when they delivered my dresser, then refused to pay for repairs." Or in the second case, you might write, "My goal is to find out what estate planning strategies are available to me that will avoid probate and minimize hassle and expense for my family."

What Questions Do You Need Answered?

With a target goal in mind, you can start to create a list of questions you need answered to help you reach your goal. As we explained above, your legal issue might contain both legal and procedural components, so you might have questions that relate to both fields.

Here are some sample questions based on the examples above.

"My goal is to file a lawsuit against the furniture store that damaged my hardwood floor when they delivered a dresser, then refused to pay for repairs."

- What law did the furniture store break by damaging the floor?
- Where do I file a lawsuit against the furniture store?
- When do I have to file my lawsuit by?
- What kind of paperwork do I need to submit to file my lawsuit?

As you can see, these are very basic questions. They might lead to new questions too. For example, once you figure out what law the furniture store broke in damaging the floor (most likely, they acted negligently), you might have to research how to calculate or prove the amount of damage caused by the mishap. Or, if you determine that you must file a lawsuit in superior court, you might find out whether the court has any standard forms to help you do this.

"My goal is to create a list of questions so I can discuss with my attorney the estate planning strategies available to me that will avoid probate and minimize hassle and expense for my family."

- What is a living trust?
- Do I need a living trust if I have a will?
- What options other than a living trust avoid probate and help minimize hassle and expense?

In the second case, you will not even have to find the answer to most of these questions. Instead, these questions will serve as the basis for the discussion you'll have with your attorney.

Your list of questions is an important starting point for conducting your legal research, keeping you focused on your task. In the next chapter, we'll talk about how you can find some background materials to get started.

Finding and Using Secondary Sources

Once you've classified your problem and settled on the terms and keywords that define your issue, you're ready to begin your actual research. But where do you start?

As we've explained, the number of available resources can seem overwhelming. And if you go straight to the text of the law itself, you might find it difficult to understand or too obscure or "lawyerly" to make much sense of it.

That's why we recommend that you start by using secondary sources. In Chapter 2, we explained that secondary sources are those that describe primary sources (like statutes, cases, and regulations)—the text of the law itself. Using secondary sources can help you familiarize yourself with the legal area you're researching. Once you understand the basic concepts, you'll usually find that primary sources aren't as difficult to understand as they first seem.

But not all secondary sources are created equal. In this chapter, we'll discuss where to find secondary sources, and how to use them.

Online Resources

Today, it's simple to go online and use a search engine to search almost any topic. Type "driving under the influence" into Google, for example, and you'll get approximately 116 million results. And these results will include many different sources—government websites, individual lawyers' websites, and more.

Below, we explain some ways to decide how reliable an online source is and how to eliminate results you don't want. For instance, one way to limit your results is to use an online search engine designed for legal resources, such as Google Scholar (http://scholar.google.com; select "Case law") or LexisWeb (www.lexisweb.com). Of course, if you're looking for general overview materials, you might not want to limit yourself this way, but as your search advances, it should help you narrow things down a little.

RELATED TOPIC

Need to figure out how to narrow your online search? Go back to Chapter 2, where we explained how you can use Boolean searching. Also recognize that search engines have their own formulas for making sure you get the most relevant results first. (These methods are proprietary, however, which means you won't know how they're calculated.) You will almost certainly find that a particular search engine gives you one set of results, while another gives you different results, so you might try rerunning the same search in more than one place, just to see what pops up.

Deciding Whether Information Is Reliable

The hard part about getting secondary information from a lot of different online resources is that it's hard to tell how reliable any of it is. After all, you don't know if a lawyer who posts information on his or her website is a legal expert in the field, or right out of law school and hoping to get that first client. Here are some indicators to help you decide when and how to rely on information you find online:

- **Does it cite primary sources?** This is the most crucial factor, because it allows you to verify things directly. If they're in sync, the source you're using is more reliable than one that does not have cites at all, or cites inaccurately. (We'll discuss more on using primary source materials in Chapters 5 to 7.)

- **What is the website's motive?** A government website (usually ending in .gov) rarely has an interest in selling you something. And a nonprofit with the goal of educating the public might be focused on just providing information. So do your best to determine the publisher's purpose. A website trying to entice you to buy legal services, for example, is likely to yield less helpful information than a website that a state bar organization provides to help self-represented litigants. And a political organization might present the issues in a way that favors its position, but probably won't be the best place to learn about the opposing position.

- **What can you tell about the author?** The more information you can get, the better. Also consider the reason the author is writing. An academic paper might include a lot of cites to primary sources, for example, but provide very little practical information about how things operate in the "real world."
- **Can you tell how old it is?** Obviously, the older the information, the more likely it is to have changed. That means you'll want to do additional research for verification purposes. A copyright date can be a good clue, but isn't conclusive when it comes to the accuracy of the content.
- **Do other reputable websites cite it?** In the course of your research, you will probably find websites that are accurate and reliable. If that's the case, the websites they refer you to are more likely to be as well—after all, the website you trust probably got to be trustworthy by carefully vetting the sites it uses, too.
- **Can users change the information?** While users' input might not necessarily be inaccurate, there's no promise of accuracy, either. In these cases, you'll want to be certain you have primary law citations to verify what you're reading.

RESOURCE

Nolo has easy-to-understand materials online. As a publisher dedicated to making legal concepts understandable for nonlawyers, Nolo's commitment extends to providing accurate, up-to-date, free legal information in articles across a variety of areas including small business, wills and estate planning, employment, patent and copyright, debt and credit, and more. Visit www.nolo.com.

Where to Look Online

As we've already explained, it won't take too long—and it will be practical and easy—to use a search engine to get started on your research. But you can also target specific websites with relevant legal information.

One of the best places to start looking for online background materials is the Cornell University Law site's Wex, a free legal dictionary and encyclopedia. It provides comprehensive, easy-to-read summaries in many areas of law. To access this information:

- Go to www.law.cornell.edu/wex.
- Click the "Browse" button on the middle of the page. This will produce an alphabetical list of all legal terms and topics.
- Find the area of your research on the alphabetical list.

For legal terms, you will find a definition. For legal topics, you will find a brief overview and a list of resources. For most topics, the list of resources follows the same pattern: federal legislative and case law materials come first, then state legislative and case materials, and finally, after you scroll down a bit, a list of links to other sites related to that topic. The list of resource links will lead you to the background materials you seek.

If you are looking for additional background materials on a specific area of law, we suggest you use the list in the appendix in the back of this book. And for general online searches—which will often lead you to helpful background resources—refer back to Chapter 2.

Self-Help Legal Books

Today, many publishers provide guides to help nonlawyers understand perplexing legal concepts. The publisher of this book, Nolo, has the longest list. Nolo has titles ranging from *How to File for Chapter 7 Bankruptcy* and *How to Form a Nonprofit Corporation* (both nationwide) to *Patent, Copyright & Trademark*. A complete list of Nolo publications is available at its website at www.nolo.com. Most of Nolo's books are written or edited by attorneys and are updated frequently, to stay current with the law.

The reliability of other self-help books varies greatly. Online book sellers, like Amazon (amazon.com), have review systems that will allow you to see how others have reviewed a book—particularly helpful if you have a lot of choices. And many of the questions written above will help you evaluate how helpful a source is likely to be.

To find these materials, look first in a law library or large public library. Many of them carry complete sets of Nolo books as well as self-help books by other publishers. If you want to buy a self-help book, you can look in a bookstore or go online. Some publishers sell their books directly on their websites; in other cases, you'll have to go to a bookseller like Amazon.

Some publishers (including West and Foundation Press) also publish books specifically for law students, called hornbooks. While a little more "legal" than self-help books, these are still intended to help readers grasp the general principles and concepts in a particular area. You can find most of these books in any law bookstore (usually near law schools) or law library.

Other good background resources are the concise law summaries intended primarily as study guides for law students. Titles such as *Gilbert's Law Summaries, Black Letter Series, Emmanuel Law Outlines, Legalines,* and *Law in a Nutshell* can be found in legal bookstores and law libraries. All provide an up-to-date framework or overview of a legal subject area, making it easier to understand the law you are researching.

Legal Encyclopedias

In addition to the books and resources developed specifically for self-help researchers and law students, many legal books are published primarily for use by attorneys. Most of these books provide a broad overview of a legal topic, often with cites to primary sources. As a result, they're not only a great resource for learning information about your legal topic, they're a great way to bridge to the next phase of your research—looking at the law itself. The most common of these are legal encyclopedias.

Legal encyclopedias contain detailed discussions of virtually every area of the law. The most helpful are those that are created for your specific state, because that will be the law that will actually apply. More general encyclopedias usually focus on broad overviews of the law, explaining the general consistencies and differences between states.

These encyclopedias are usually multivolume sets, organized alphabetically by subject matter like regular encyclopedias, but with broader main entries and a lot more subentries. In addition, they contain thorough indexes, so you can find relevant sections by using the keywords you identified in the previous chapter.

Legal encyclopedias are often a good place to start your research. Because they cover the entire range of law and their entries are broken into small segments, you are very likely to find material relevant to your research problem. Each entry provides a solid treatment of the particular topic, gives you a good idea of the all-important variables associated with your issue, and refers you to specific statutes and cases (the stuff the law is made of) to help you get to the next research phase.

The main drawback to these legal encyclopedias is that, because they're large and comprehensive, they're more difficult to access. You won't find them in a bookstore or on a free website. In fact, these books are usually located only in law libraries or large legal databases like Westlaw or Lexis. As we explained in Chapter 2, using Westlaw or Lexis is usually prohibitively expensive, so if you want to access these sources, you'll probably need to trek to the local law library.

National Legal Encyclopedias

Two encyclopedias, *American Jurisprudence* (commonly called "*Am. Jur.*") and *Corpus Juris Secundum* (abbreviated "*C.J.S.*"), provide a national overview of American law. The entries are generalized and don't necessarily provide state-specific information. However, they do contain footnoted references to court decisions from many different states and from federal courts, where relevant.

To give you an idea of how these books are set up, the table of contents and discussion employed by *Am. Jur.* on the law concerning firearms are shown below.

Which legal encyclopedia should you use if your law library has both? Many researchers favor *Am. Jur. 2d* over *C.J.S.* because they feel that *C.J.S.* tends to have too much unnecessary information. Although these two encyclopedias used to compete with each other, they're now both published by the same parent company (Thomson Reuters, which also owns Westlaw). These encyclopedias use the "Key Number" system to organize, or tag, the legal issues they discuss. To learn about the Key Number system, see Chapter 6.

State Encyclopedias

In addition to national encyclopedias, there are at least 15 state-specific encyclopedias. State-specific encyclopedias are organized the same way as the national ones. When researching a question that deals with the law of your particular state, it is almost always best to start with the state-specific encyclopedia, if one exists. That way you can avoid sifting through a discussion on the law in all the states to find the law of your state.

RESOURCE

Some state-specific legal encyclopedias (alphabetized by state):

- *California Jurisprudence 3d* (West)
- *Florida Jurisprudence 2d* (West)
- *Illinois Jurisprudence* (Lexis Publishing)
- *Indiana Law Encyclopedia* (West)
- *Michigan Law and Practice* (Lexis Publishing)
- Strong's *North Carolina Index 4th* (West)
- *New York Jurisprudence 2nd* (West)
- *Ohio Jurisprudence 3rd* (West)
- *Pennsylvania Law Encyclopedia* (Lexis Publishing)
- *Tennessee Jurisprudence* (Lexis Publishing), and
- Michie's *Jurisprudence of Virginia and West Virginia* (Lexis Publishing).

WEAPONS AND FIREARMS   79 Am Jur 2d

III. PUBLIC REGULATION
 A. Carrying or Possessing Weapons (§§ 7–28)
 B. Use of Weapons (§§ 29, 30)
 C. Registration and Licensing (§§ 31, 32)
 D. Manufacture, Transport, and Disposition (§§ 33, 34)
IV. CIVIL LIABILITY
 A. In General (§§ 35–37)
 B. In Particular Instances (§§ 38–43)
 C. Contributory Negligence (§§ 44, 45)

I. IN GENERAL
§ 1. Definitions; dangerous or deadly weapon
§ 2. —Particular weapons as dangerous or deadly
§ 3. —Unloaded firearm

II. POWER TO REGULATE
§ 4. Constitutional right to bear arms
§ 5. Basis of state regulatory power
§ 6. Source of federal power to regulate

III. PUBLIC REGULATION

A. Carrying or Possessing Weapons

1. In General
§ 7. Generally

2. Concealed or Dangerous Weapons
§ 8. Generally
§ 9. What amounts to carrying a concealed weapon
§ 10. What constitutes concealment; generally
§ 11. Concealment on person or in personal luggage
§ 12. Concealment in vehicles
§ 13. —Presumptions as to possession
§ 14. Permit to carry concealed weapon
§ 15. Criminal intent
§ 16. Carrying disabled weapon
§ 17. Carriage of weapons by travelers
§ 18. Carriage of weapons upon one's own premises
§ 19. Effect of apprehension of attack
§ 20. Peace officers
§ 21. Indictments
§ 22. Penalty
§ 23. Forfeiture

2

Am. Jur. 2d, Part of Table of Contents for Topic "Weapons and Firearms"

§ 3. —Unloaded firearm.

Generally, it is held that an unloaded gun, used as a firearm and not as bludgeon, is not a dangerous weapon within the contemplation of statutes punishing assaults made with dangerous or deadly weapons, although there is substantial authority to the contrary.[36] It is generally, but not universally, considered to be a matter of defense to show that the weapon was unloaded, rather than a substantive part of the state's case to aver and prove that it was loaded.[37] There also is authority that an unloaded revolver or gun merely pointed at the person is not a dangerous weapon within the meaning of statutes defining assault and robbery while armed with a dangerous weapon, although many courts hold that an unloaded gun or pistol is a dangerous weapon within the meaning of such statutes;[38] and generally, an unloaded pistol or revolver is regarded as within the meaning of statutes against carrying concealed "dangerous or deadly weapons"[39] or denouncing the carrying "of any concealed and dangerous weapon."[40] It has been held that a statute prohibiting the carrying of a weapon capable of inflicting bodily harm, concealed on or about the person, did not apply to an unloaded pistol found in the glove compartment of the defendant's automobile, no ammunition having been found on or about the defendant's person or in the vehicle.[41] In a few cases the courts have recognized that if the gun was unloaded, that fact would have a bearing on the determination as to whether it was carried as a weapon.[42]

Generally an unloaded gun or pistol used to strike with is not necessarily a dangerous weapon, but is such, or not, according to its size, weight, and the manner of using it.[43] Accordingly, to resolve the factual question whether a

36. See 6 Am Jur 2d, ASSAULT AND BATTERY § 54.

As to whether a simple criminal assault may be committed with an unloaded firearm, see 6 Am Jur 2d, ASSAULT AND BATTERY § 34.

As to civil action for damages for an assault by pointing unloaded firearm, see 6 Am Jur 2d, ASSAULT AND BATTERY §§ 109, 123.

37. See 6 Am Jur 2d, ASSAULT AND BATTERY § 93.

As to presumption as to whether gun was loaded, see 6 Am Jur 2d, ASSAULT AND BATTERY § 94.

38. See 67 Am Jur 2d, ROBBERY § 5.

39. Asocar v State, 252 **Ind** 326, 247 NE2d 679; Mularkey v State, 201 **Wis** 429, 230 NW 76.

Annotation: 79 ALR2d 1430, § 8.

40. Mularkey v State, 201 **Wis** 429, 230 NW 76.

. A pistol mechanically capable of being fired is a deadly weapon within the meaning of the statute prohibiting the carrying of a concealed "deadly weapon," even though it was unloaded and no ammunition was on the carrier's person or was readily available. Commonwealth v Harris **(Ky)** 344 SW2d 820.

41. State v Haugabrook, 31 **Ohio** Misc 157, 57 Ohio Ops 2d 322, 272 NE2d 213.

42. State v Larkin, 24 **Mo** App 410.

Annotation: 79 ALR2d 1432, § 8.

In Carr v State, 34 **Ark** 448, in reversing a conviction under a statute making it a misdemeanor to wear any pistol concealed as a weapon unless upon a journey, the evidence being that defendant was carrying two unloaded pistols, the court said that it must be shown that the pistols were carried as weapons, for the purpose of convenience in a fight, and that in the instant case the pistols were useless for that purpose.

43. State v Mays, 7 **Ariz** App 90, 436 P2d 482; State v Jaramillo (App) 82 **NM** 548, 484 P2d 768; Hilliard v State, 87 **Tex** Crim 15, 218 SW 1052, 8 ALR 1316.

Annotation: 79 ALR2d 1423, § 6[a]; 8 ALR 1319.

Am. Jur. 2d, "Weapons and Firearms"

American Law Reports

This series of books has two titles: *American Law Reports* (*A.L.R.*) and *American Law Reports, Federal* (*A.L.R. Fed.*). *A.L.R.* covers issues primarily arising under state statutes and in state cases, as well as federally oriented issues that arose before 1969, the year *A.L.R. Fed.* was first published. *A.L.R. Fed.* covers issues that arise primarily under federal statutes or in federal cases. Both publications are multivolume sets that contain discussions of narrow issues that have been suggested by newly decided court cases. Each discussion comments on the case itself and then discusses other cases that have considered the same or similar issues.

A.L.R. and *A.L.R. Fed.* are different from the legal encyclopedias described earlier in that they don't attempt to cover every subject. This means you might not find what you're looking for, but if you do you'll be well rewarded. Fortunately, *A.L.R.* has an excellent index that allows you to find out very quickly whether the news is good or bad for you.

A.L.R. comes in six series (*A.L.R.–A.L.R. 6th*). Unlike the legal encyclopedias, the newest series does not replace previous ones. *A.L.R. 6th* might contain an almost entirely new set of topics not covered in *A.L.R. 4th*, for example. The older series are kept up to date with "pocket parts" (inserts in the back of each hardcover volume) and hardbound volumes called the Later Case Service. *A.L.R. Federal* is still in its second series.

Form Books

Form books are a surprisingly helpful secondary source. Form books are pretty much what their name suggests: collections of legal forms, usually in a fill-in-the-blanks format. They're handy if you're looking for a form, but also because they usually discuss the procedural rules that are relevant to the use of each form. In other words, when you find the form you need, chances are you'll also find an overview of the procedure itself and instructions on how to make the most common modifications.

A typical form book entry, taken from *American Jurisprudence Legal Forms, Second Series,* is shown below. We show the form as well as the accompanying material provided about the law governing the procedure.

TIP

Are you actually looking for forms? If you are, form books are a great resource, but so are:

- **Court websites.** If you need a document you're going to file with a specific court, we suggest you start at the court's website. Many courts have standard forms for this purpose.
- **Reliable publishers.** Notice we said "reliable." Anyone can create a form, shrink-wrap it, and sell it in a stationery store. We recommend browsing www.nolo.com for helpful forms; if you find forms elsewhere, make sure you know how they were developed—that is, who created them, whether they are state specific, and so forth.

The forms in *Am. Jur. Legal Forms* are national in scope and often lack the specificity found in a form book prepared for a particular state. When looking for an appropriate form or the procedure that goes with it, it is best to start with a publication that is specific to your state or topic, if there is one. As in the case of state encyclopedias, state form books have been published only in the more populous states.

RESOURCE

Most states and individual courts have websites that contain or link to all the forms required to file claims. You can also obtain many federal court forms at www.uscourts.gov/services-forms.

Practice Manuals

Practice manuals, like form books, contain lots of forms and instructions for how to use them. However, form books tend to cover the entire spectrum of legal practice; practice manuals usually cover a specialized area of practice.

NAME   § 182:52

of __19_____, State of __19_____, and since such time has resided with her husband at the above address.

4. Applicant desires to change her name to __20_____, her maiden surname, for the following reasons: __21_____ *[specify reasons, such as* to continue her professional or business use of her maiden name *or* to avoid confusion between her professional or business relations with those of her husband *or* to assert her equal partnership with her husband in the marital relation *or* to assert her ethnic heritage, of which she is proud, *or other legally permissible reason].*

5. __22_____ *[State information as to publication of notice of intent to change name, if required by statute.]*

Dated: __23_____, 19_24_.

                                                                    [Signature]

[Jurat]

☑ **Notes on Use:**

   See also Notes on Use following § 182:43.

   Annotations: Right of married woman to use maiden surname. 67 ALR3d 1266.

   Circumstance justifying grant or denial of petition to change adult's name. 79 ALR3d 562.

   Cross references: For other change of name forms, see § 182:54 et seq.

V. CHANGE OF NAME

§ 182:51 Scope of division

Material in this division consists of forms related to change of name. Included are such matters as application to a court of record for change of name and relevant affidavits and notices.

§ 182:52 Introductory comments

Unless applicable statutes provide otherwise, a person may change such person's name at will, without any legal proceedings, merely by adopting another name. In most states, however, statutes set forth specific procedures and requirements for change of name; such procedure usually includes filing a petition or application with a court of record. The court hearing a petition or application for change of name has discretion to either grant or deny it, the general rule being that there must exist some substantial reason for the change.[8]

8. *Text references:* Change of name, generally. 57 AM JUR 2d, Name §§ 10–16.

Annotations: Circumstances justifying grant or denial of petition to change adult's name. 79 ALR3d 562.

(For Tax Notes and Notes on use, see end of form)

13A Am Jur Legal Forms 2d (Rev)   **323**

Form and Explanation From *Am. Jur. Legal Forms, 2d Series*

§ 182:53   NAME

---

§ 182:53 Annotation references

ALR annotations treating the subject of change of name by an individual are set forth below.

ALR annotations:

Circumstance justifying grant or denial of petition to change adult's name. 79 ALR3d 562.

Change of child's name in adoption proceeding. 53 ALR2d 927.

§ 182:54 Application for change of name

To: __1____ *[court of record]*

APPLICATION FOR CHANGE OF NAME

Applicant states:

1. Applicant resides at __2____ *[address]*, City of __3____, County of __4____, State of __5____, __6____ *[ZIP]*, and has resided there for more than __7__ *[number of months or years]* prior to filing this application.

2. Applicant was born __8____ *[in the City of __9____, County of __10____, State of __11____ or set forth foreign address]* on __12____, 19__13__. Applicant was named __14____ and has always been known by that name.

3. The name of applicant's father is __15____, and the name of applicant's mother is __16____. They reside at __17____ [__18____ *(address)*, City of __19____, County of __20____, State of __21____, __22____ *(ZIP) or set forth foreign address]*.

4. Applicant __23____ *[is or is not]* married. __24____ *[If married, give information as to date and place of marriage, spouse's name, and date and place of spouse's birth.]*

5. Applicant desires to change applicant's name to __25____ for the following reasons: __26____.

6. __27____ *[State information as to publication of notice of intent to change name, if required by statute.]*

7. __28____ *[State information required by statute as to financial matters, any criminal records, and pending actions or other proceedings in which the applicant may be a party.]*

Dated: __29____, 19__30__.
[Jurat]   [Signature]

☑ **Notes on Use:**

Text references: Statutory regulation of change of name, generally. 57 Am Jur 2d, Name §§ 11–16.

(For Tax Notes and Notes on use, see end of form)

Form and Explanation From *Am. Jur. Legal Forms, 2d Series*

There are practice manuals for torts, contracts, family law, real estate transactions, search and seizure questions, and a myriad of other issues. Some are state specific while others are national in scope. For example, a publication called *Defense of Drunk Driving Cases*, by Richard Erwin and Marilyn Minzer, tells you everything you need to know when handling a drunk driving offense.

Many of these books are well written and well organized. They can give you a good understanding of the procedural and substantive law, as well as the hands-on instructions necessary to file and prosecute or defend your own case. These resources are generally available in law libraries.

Continuing Legal Education Publications

Some publishers are dedicated to providing practicing lawyers with continuing education. Two of these—Continuing Education of the Bar (CEB) and the Rutter Group—direct their materials toward California lawyers, and one, the Practising Law Institute (PLI), focuses on New York lawyers. Publishers in some other states produce analogous resources, often called "CLE" (continuing legal education) books.

Continuing legal education publishers produce detailed practice guidelines, instructions, and forms for many different areas of law and practice, both state and federal. They also publish written materials used in continuing legal education seminars that they sponsor. Continuing education materials are usually available in the law libraries in the states for which they are published.

To find these publications, ask the law librarian, or go online to the publisher's website, to see what's even available (the books will probably be too expensive to buy, but then you'll at least know what you're looking for). A list of popular publishers appears below.

RESOURCE

Popular CLE publishers:

- CEB, https://ceb.com
- Rutter Group, www.ruttergroup.com
- PLI, www.pli.edu, and
- West LegalEdcenter, http://westlegaledcenter.com.

Law Reviews and Other Legal Periodicals

Because the law is always developing and changing, legal professionals are constantly analyzing its evolution. You can find articles about new legislation, current legal theories and viewpoints, and important cases in law journals published by law schools, commercial publishers, and professional legal societies, such as bar associations.

The articles in journals produced by law schools are written by law students, professors, and even practicing attorneys, and sometimes present a whole new view of an area of the law. They tend to focus on where the law is going as opposed to where it is or where it's been, although they might provide some history to set the stage for the discussion. Even if articles are more academic than practical, they still might contain valuable descriptions of the state of the law in the specific area being discussed and can provide you with research leads.

On the other hand, journals produced by bar associations and other professional groups tend to be much more practical, with an emphasis on recent developments. Many law reviews and journals are general, covering subjects across the legal spectrum. But increasingly, legal periodicals are starting to specialize in such fields as taxation, environmental law, labor, entertainment and communications, and women's studies.

Because these publications are so often academic or esoteric, in most cases we'd recommend you first try to find a basic summary or another practical publication. Even if you don't find the answer you're looking for, you'll at least have a good understanding of the subject, making it easier to digest the more difficult and specific law review articles.

Finding Law Review Articles in the Library

Most law libraries contain the more influential journals and law reviews, and some libraries (especially in large law schools) have virtually a complete set. You can find articles by using an electronic index, called LEGALTRAC, or either of two printed indexes, the *Index to Legal Periodicals* (tan cover) or the *Current Law Index* (red and black cover).

All indexes are organized by subject, author, and title, and contain an abbreviated reference to the review or journal in which the article is located. The printed indexes contain numerous volumes, which are organized according to the years in which the contents were published.

The LEGALTRAC computerized index to legal periodicals is part of a larger database called Infotrac, which contains information on a number of additional resources such as business and general periodicals. Instructions for using LEGALTRAC are shown on the screen and are very easy to follow. If you get confused, ask a law librarian for help. Incidentally, LEGALTRAC might be connected to a printer so that you can print out the information instead of copying it longhand.

Finding Law Review Articles Online

Probably far preferable, if you're researching from your home or office, is to find law review and journal articles online. The American Bar Association allows you to access over 400 law review and journal articles at no cost, including *Harvard Law Review, Stanford Law Review, Loyola Law Journal, University of Pennsylvania Journal of Constitutional Law, UCLA Law Review,* and *Yale Law & Policy Review.* To get started, go to www.americanbar.org/aba.html and enter "Free Full-Text Online Law Review/Journal Search" in the search box.

Specialized Loose-Leaf Materials

As we've already explained, there are many different areas of law. This practically forces attorneys to specialize in certain fields, because otherwise, there's simply too much out there to learn. Several publications cater to this need by offering loose-leaf compilations of recent developments in particular fields and weekly or monthly loose-leaf supplements. These materials provide information about new legislation, regulations, and judicial and administrative decisions that might affect the field of law covered by a publication.

Unless your research topic falls squarely within one of these special categories, you will probably find these resources too specialized for your purposes. If it does, locate the appropriate service, read the instructions on how to use it at the front of the first volume, and check the index. You might solve your problem almost immediately. All the loose-leaf services listed here can be found in a good law library.

Selected Loose-Leaf Services

Commerce Clearing House (CCH)
  Bankruptcy Law Reports
  Consumer Credit Guide
  Employment Safety and Health Guide
  Labor Law Reporter
  Medicare and Medicaid Guide
  Standard Federal Tax Reports
  State Tax Guide
  Unemployment Insurance Reports
  Worker's Compensation Business Management Guide
Bureau of National Affairs (BNA)
  Environment Reporter
  Family Law Reporter
  Labor Relations Reporter
  Occupational Safety and Health Reporter
  Product Safety & Liability Reporter
  United States Law Week (U.S. Supreme Court decisions)
West Group
  Social Security Law and Practice

18   INDEX TO LEGAL PERIODICALS

Constitutional theory—United States—*cont.*
Twentieth century Jeffersonian: Brandeis, freedom of speech, and the republican revival. H. Garfield. 69 *Or. L. Rev.* 527-88 '90
Construction industry
    See also
    Architects and engineers
The Kentucky no action statute: down for the count?. 79 *Ky. L.J.* 159-75 '90/'91
The qualification of arbitrators for construction disputes. M. F. Hoellering. 45 *Arb. J.* 34-41+ D '90
Construction of statutes *See* Statutory interpretation
Constructive trusts *See* Implied trusts
Consumer credit *See* Credit
Consumer protection
    See also
    Advertising
    Credit
    Health
    Loans
    Prices
    Products liability
    Unfair insurance settlement practices
Advanced Hair Studio Pty Ltd. & Anor v. TVW Enterprises Limited ([1987] 77 A.L.R. 615]. 17 *Melb. U.L. Rev.* 527-32 Je '90
Consumer problems and ADR: an analysis of the Federal Trade Commission-ordered General Motors mediation and arbitration program. A. Best. 1990 *J. Dis. Res.* 267-92 '90
Leases of personal property: a project for consumer protection. J. J. A. Burke, J. M. Cannel. 28 *Harv. J. on Legis.* 115-66 Wint '91
Shysters, sharks, and ambulance chasers beware: attorney liability under CUTPA. 11 *U. Bridgeport L. Rev.* 97-125 '90
Contempt
Current problems in the law of contempt. J. Laws. 43 *Current Legal Probs.* 99-114 '90
A new perspective on the judicial contempt power: recommendations for reform. L. Raveson. 18 *Hastings Const. L.Q.* 1-65 Fall '90
Continental shelf
    See also
    Exclusive economic zone
    Territorial waters
The EEC's continental shelf: a "terra incognita". J. E. Harders. 8 *J. Energy & Nat. Resources L.* 263-79 '90
Secured transactions affecting the federal outer continental shelf. M. C. Maloney. 34 *Inst. on Min. L.* 47-78 '87
Contracts
    See also
    Conflict of laws—Contracts
    Government contracts
    Sales
Contract versus contractarianism: the regulatory role of contract law. J. Braucher. 47 *Wash. & Lee L. Rev.* 697-739 Fall '90
Contractual concerns for hospitals and other health care organizations. M. L. Malone, R. C. Beasley. 32 *S. Tex. L. Rev.* 77-104 D '90
The myth that promises prefer supracompensatory remedies: an analysis of contracting for damage measures. A. Schwartz. 100 *Yale L.J.* 369-407 N '90
Reconsidering the reliance rules: the Restatement of Contracts and promissory estoppel in North Dakota. T. C. Folsom. 66 *N.D.L. Rev.* 317-447 '90
Strategic bargaining and the economic theory of contract default rules. J. S. Johnston. 100 *Yale L.J.* 615-64 D '90
Unconscionable conduct and small business: possible extension of section 52A of the Trade Practices Act 1974. G. Q. Taperell. 18 *Austl. Bus. L. Rev.* 370-88 D '90
    Acceptance
    See Contracts—Offer and acceptance
    Consideration
La opcion de compra en Puerto Rico. M. J. Godreau. 53 *Rev. Jur. U.P.R.* 563-608 '84
    Covenants
Flats: mutual enforceability of covenants. Two views. J. E. Adams, S. Baughen. 134 *Solic. J.* 1504-5 D 14 '90
    Offer and acceptance
    See also
    Options
Liability for mistake in contract formation. M. P. Gergen. 64 *S. Cal. L. Rev.* 1-49 N '90

The strategic structure of offer and acceptance: game theory and the law of contract formation. A. Katz. 89 *Mich. L. Rev.* 215-95 N '90
    Performance
La clausula penal. P. F. Silva-Ruiz. 54 *Rev. Jur. U.P.R.* 89-112 '85
Expectations, loss distribution and commercial impracticability. S. Walt. 24 *Ind. L. Rev.* 65-109 '91
Punitive damages for breach of contract—a principled approach. F. J. Cavico, jr. 22 *St. Mary's L.J.* 357-453 '90
Contributory negligence
    See also
    Comparative negligence
Controlled substances *See* Narcotics
Conversion
Commercialization of human tissues: has biotechnology created the need for an expanded scope of informed consent?. 27 *Cal. W.L. Rev.* 209-30 '90/'91
Moore v. The Regents of the University of California: balancing the need for biotechnology innovation against the right of informed consent. M. S. Dorney. 5 *High Tech. L.J.* 333-69 Fall '90
Tort law—informed consent—California Supreme Court recognizes patient's cause of action for physician's nondisclosure of excised tissue's commercial value.—Moore v. Regents of the University of California, 793 P.2d 479 (Cal.). 104 *Harv. L. Rev.* 808-15 Ja '91
Conveyancing *See* Title to land
Convicts *See* Prisons and prisoners
Cook, Rebecca J.
International human rights law concerning women: case notes and comments. 23 *Vand. J. Transnat'l L.* 779-818 '90
Cooperative federalism
    See also
    Federalism
    States' rights
Cooperatives
    See also
    Condominium and cooperative buildings
IRS expands availability of patronage dividend deductions and tax-exempt status for cooperatives but restricts benefit of package design expenditures. D. W. Butwill. 12 *J. Agric. Tax'n & L.* 342-51 Wint '91
Copyright
    See also
    Authors and publishers
The 101st Congress: a review of amendments to the Copyright Act. 37 *J. Copyright Soc'y U.S.A.* 462-98 '90
Accounting for profits gained by infringement of copyright: when does it end?. L. Bently. 13 *Eur. Intell. Prop. Rev.* 5-15 Ja '91
Applying the merger doctrine to the copyright of computer software. 37 *Copyright L. Symp. (ASCAP)* 173-214 '90
Computer protection against foreign competition in the United States. 10 *Computer L.J.* 393-412 O '90
The continuing battle over music performance rights in television programming. 36 *Copyright L. Symp. (ASCAP)* 167-91 '89
Contribution of the Bar to the development of copyright law. S. Rothenberg. 37 *J. Copyright Soc'y U.S.A.* 453-61 '90
Copyright and computer databases: is traditional compilation law adequate?. 37 *Copyright L. Symp. (ASCAP)* 85-125 '90
Copyright law—Fifth Circuit interprets Copyright Act to allow copying of software for any legitimate reason—Vault Corp. v. Quaid Software Ltd., 847 F.2d 255. 23 *Suffolk U.L. Rev.* 905-12 Fall '89
Copyright ownership of commissioned computer software in light of current developments in the work made for hire doctrine. 24 *Ind. L. Rev.* 135-59 '91
Copyright protection of computer "interfaces" in Japan. O. Hirakawa, K. Nakano. 7 *Computer Law.* 1-16 D '90
Copyright wrong: the United States' failure to provide copyright protection for works of architecture. 47 *Wash. & Lee L. Rev.* 1103-27 Fall '90
Copyrighted software and tying arrangements: a fresh appreciation for per se illegality. 10 *Computer L.J.* 413-52 O '90
Copyrighting "look and feel": Manufacturers Technologies v. CAMS [706 F. Supp. 984]. 3 *Harv. J.L. & Tech.* 195-208 Spr '90
Copyrights and copyremedies: unfair use and injunctions. J. L. Oakes. 18 *Hofstra L. Rev.* 983-1003 Summ '90

Listings in the *Index to Legal Periodicals*

Treatises and Monographs

Like experts in every field, legal experts publish books. When a book attempts to cover an entire area of the law, it is called a treatise. Typically, law treatises have titles like *Prosser on Torts, Powell on Real Property,* and *Corbin on Contracts.* When a book covers just a small portion of a general legal field, or introduces a new concept into the legal realm, it is called a monograph. Whatever they are called, hundreds of these books can be found in the stacks of the normal law library, and might be helpful in providing an overview of a subject.

There is a big difference between these resources and the textbooks discussed earlier in this chapter. While textbooks cover entire legal topics with the intent to teach, treatises and monographs exist to provide in-depth reference materials. Generally, they delve much deeper into an area than you would care to go. They also become dated more quickly despite periodic supplementation.

Restatements of the Law

Legal scholars are always trying to pinpoint exactly what the law "is" on a particular subject. In some cases, groups of scholars have convened under the auspices of an organization called the American Law Institute (ALI) for the purpose of putting into writing definitive statements of the law in various areas. These statements are termed "Restatements" and they have been produced for such topics as contracts, torts, and property.

While these tomes cover their subjects exhaustively, they are usually of little help to the beginning researcher looking for a good background resource. To begin with, they are not in a narrative form, but rather consist of very terse summations of legal principles and longer comments explaining them. The language in these comments is generally arcane, and the various restatements are not well indexed or organized for efficient retrieval of information. Because these publications are trying to reconcile often unreconcilable contradictions in the law, they tend to produce more confusion than enlightenment. They're not a good place to start your research, and you'll probably find you don't need them once you get going.

Finding and Using Constitutions, Statutes, Regulations, and Ordinances

At some point during your legal research, you will probably have to look at legislatively or administratively created materials, such as statutes, regulations, or ordinances. These are at the heart of what most of us think of when we think of "the law." In this chapter, we'll explain how to find those resources, then how to use them once you have them.

Finding and Using Constitutions

As a legal researcher, in most cases we doubt you'll spend much time looking at constitutional issues. That's because, as the supreme law of the land, the U.S. and state constitutions are very broad, structural documents that lay out the basic framework of how our law operates, without getting into the details. As a result, they don't cover the issues most of us need answers to—like how to calculate how much child support is owed, or whether you're entitled to be paid the vacation you've accrued when you quit your job. Instead, you'll often find the answers to these types of questions in statutes and regulations.

Constitutional research can be very time-consuming. Most constitutions use extremely broad language that creates the possibility of differing interpretations. And even if the language appears precise, many judges are willing to reach beyond the literal words to figure out what the constitution's framers really intended. These factors mean that you can't understand how a constitutional provision might affect your situation unless you:

- are already familiar with the constitution and how it has been applied to similar fact situations, or
- devote significant time and energy to constitutional research.

If you are going to do your own constitutional research, we strongly suggest you first do some background reading, using the secondary sources described in the last chapter. Because a constitution has usually been around a very long time and has been interpreted by courts over the years, in many cases, the meaning of the document itself extends far beyond the literal words on the page. You'll want to read about this history when trying to understand the context of the area of law you're researching.

It is easy to find the federal and your state's constitution online. The federal Constitution can be found on the National Archives Web page at www.archives.gov/founding-docs/constitution. This site provides multiple links to additional resources, organizes the Constitution by article and amendment, and discusses each separately. The site also has links to places in the cases that discuss the text. You can also find information on the Constitution on the Library of Congress's website.

To find state constitutions, start at The NBER/Maryland State Constitutions Project (www.stateconstitutions.umd.edu/index.aspx) or WashLaw (www.washlaw.edu), a service of Washburn University Law School. Of course, the federal and state constitutions will also be available in a law library.

The Bill of Rights

First Amendment: freedom of speech, freedom of religion, freedom of association, separation of church and state

Second Amendment: right to bear arms

Third Amendment: right not to have soldiers quartered in homes

Fourth Amendment: right of privacy, right against unreasonable searches and seizures, right to confront adverse witnesses

Fifth Amendment: right to trial by jury, right to due process of law (life, liberty, property), right against self-incrimination, freedom from double jeopardy

Sixth Amendment: speedy and public trial, right to representation by counsel, right to confront witnesses (cross-examination), right to subpoena witnesses

Seventh Amendment: right to trial in civil cases

Eighth Amendment: right to reasonable bail, ban on cruel and unusual punishment

Ninth Amendment: people retain rights in addition to those granted in the Constitution

Tenth Amendment: everything not prohibited is allowed

Finding Federal Statutes

If you are researching an area of federal law, you will most certainly have to look at a federal statute or two. These are the laws that Congress has enacted, signed by the president (or passed over a veto). But before you figure out how to interpret and use federal statutes, you need to know where to find them.

Where Federal Statutes Are Found

Federal statutes can be found in law libraries or online. If you are looking online, you will be able to find them for free on the U.S. Government Printing Office website (www.gpo.gov/fdsys) You'll have the option of searching for specific sections, or searching using keywords.

Federal statutes can also be found in law libraries. These are published in several different places, the most popular being a series of books called the *United States Code (U.S.C.)* or another called the *United States Code Annotated (U.S.C.A.)*. The difference between the two is that the second set is "annotated." We'll explain what that means later—for now, it's enough to simply know that if all you need to see is the statute itself, going to the *U.S.C.* will probably meet your needs, but you can use the *U.S.C.A.* to help you find additional resources, such as other statutes or relevant cases. Statutes available for free online are not annotated.

How Federal Statutes Are Organized

Federal statutes are organized by subject into 50 separate numbered titles that each cover a specific subject matter. For instance, Title 35 contains the statutes governing patent law while Title 11 contains the bankruptcy statutes. In the print copies you'll find in the library, these titles can span multiple volumes or only take up part of one volume—it all depends on how long the title is, and there's no rule or set structure.

Ways to Find a Federal Statute

There are several approaches to finding statutes in the U.S. codes, depending on how much information you have. We'll discuss all these options further below:

- **Do you know the citation?** If so, you can look it up directly, either by typing it into a search box, or by finding the appropriate volume. You'll search for the title number, then flip to the correct section.
- **Do you know the "popular name"?** Sometimes, you might only know the name of the act or statute, but not the specific citation—for example, the Economic and Housing Recovery Act of 2008. You can look it up in the *Popular Names Index*.
- **Do you know the subject area?** If you can pinpoint the title you need, you can use the subject index for the specific title.
- **Do you have keywords?** If you followed the advice we gave you in Chapter 3, you should have them. At the end of the entire series is a general subject index that allows you to search by keyword. If you're searching online, typing the right combination of words into a Boolean search should also yield relevant results.

Using Citations

The reference to any primary law source—including a federal statute—is called a "citation." Once you understand how to read a citation, you'll recognize them in the future, because they're written in a standard form to tell you precisely where the law is located. Citations to federal statutes contain the title of the U.S. Code where the statute is found and the section number.

EXAMPLE: The citation for the Civil Rights Act of 1964 is:

42	U.S.C.A	§ 2000	a-h
title number	United States Code Annotated	section number	subsection letters

Sample Federal Statute Citation

If you are looking for this statute online, you can simply type it into the search box (you probably won't need the "§" sign, which means "section"). Finding this statute in the law library is also easy. Locate the set of books labeled *U.S.C.A.* (maroon) or *U.S.C.* (black and blue). Look at the spine of the volumes marked 42 to find the one that includes § 2000a-h. Within the title, you'll find sections arranged numerically.

Using the Popular Name

You might hear a federal statute referred to by its popular name—for example, the Civil Rights Act, the Taft-Hartley Act, or the Marine Mammal Protection Act. You can find such a statute by using the *Popular Names Index* that accompanies the *United States Code Annotated* (*U.S.C.A.*), the "popular names table" volume that accompanies the *United States Code Service, Lawyers' Edition* (*U.S.C.S.*); or *Shepard's Acts and Cases by Popular Names: Federal and State.* This last publication is particularly useful for finding both state and federal statutes and cases through their popular names.

The *U.S.C.A. Popular Names Index* is included with the *U.S.C.A.* set of books, directly following it on the shelves. This index gives a citation that refers you to the correct title and section (for example, Title 20, § 607) of the named statute. Below are the popular names index entries for two of the three acts mentioned above. As you can see, the Civil Rights Act of 1964 is contained in Titles 28 and 42, and the Marine Mammal Protection Act is found in Title 16 of the federal code.

POPULAR NAME TABLE

Civil Rights Act of 1957
Pub. L. 85–315, Sept. 9, 1957, 71 Stat. 634 (See Title 5, § 5315(19); Title 28, §§ 1343, 1861; Title 42, §§ 1971, 1975, 1975a, 1975b, 1975c, 1975d, 1975e, 1995)
Pub. L. 86–383, title IV, § 401, Sept. 28, 1959, 73 Stat. 724 (Title 42, § 1975c)
Pub. L. 86–449, May 6, 1960, title IV, title VI, 74 Stat. 89 (Title 42, §§ 1971, 1975d)
Pub. L. 87–264, title IV, Sept. 21, 1961, 75 Stat. 559 (Title 42, § 1975c)
Pub. L. 88–152, § 2, Oct. 17, 1963, 77 Stat. 271 (Title 42, § 1975c)
Pub. L. 88–352, title V, July 2, 1964, 78 Stat. 249 (Title 42, §§ 1975a–1975d)
Pub. L. 90–198, § 1, Dec. 14, 1967, 81 Stat. 582 (Title 42, §§ 1975c, 1975e)
Pub. L. 91–521, §§ 1–4, Nov. 25, 1970, 84 Stat. 1356, 1357 (Title 42, §§ 1975a, 1975b, 1975d, 1975e)
Pub. L. 92–64, Aug. 4, 1971, 85 Stat. 166 (Title 42, § 1975e)
Pub. L. 92–496, Oct. 14, 1972, 86 Stat. 913 (Title 42, §§ 1975a–1975e)
Pub. L. 94–292, § 2, May 27, 1976, 90 Stat. 524 (Title 42, § 1975e)
Pub. L. 95–132, § 2, Oct. 13, 1977, 91 Stat. 1157 (Title 42, § 1975e)
Pub. L. 95–444, §§ 2–7, Oct. 10, 1978, 92 Stat. 1067, 1068 (Title 42, §§ 1975b, 1975c, 1975d, 1975e)
Pub. L. 96–81, §§ 2, 3, Oct. 6, 1979, 93 Stat. 642 (Title 42, §§ 1975c, 1975e)
Pub. L. 96–447, § 2, Oct. 13, 1980, 94 Stat. 1894 (Title 42, § 1975e)

Civil Rights Act of 1960
Pub. L. 86–449, May 6, 1960, 74 Stat. 86 (Title 18, §§ 837, 1074, 1509; Title 20, §§ 241, 640; Title 42, §§ 1971, 1974–1974e, 1975d)

Civil Rights Act of 1964
Pub. L. 88–352, July 2, 1964, 78 Stat. 241 (Title 28, § 1447; Title 42, §§ 1971, 1975a–1975d, 2000a–2000h–6)
Pub. L. 92–261, §§ 2–8, 10, 11, 13, Mar. 24, 1972, 86 Stat. 103–113 (Title 42, §§ 2000e, 2000e–1 to 2000e–6, 2000e–8, 2000e–9, 2000e–13 to 2000e–17)

• •

Manpower Development and Training Amendments of 1966
Pub. L. 89–792, Nov. 7, 1966, 80 Stat. 1434 (Title 42, §§ 2572b, 2572c, 2582, 2583, 2601, 2603, 2610b, 2611, 2614)

Marihuana and Health Reporting Act
Pub. L. 91–296 title V, June 30, 1970, 84 Stat. 352 (Title 42, § 242 note)
Pub. L. 95–461, § 3(a), Oct. 14, 1978, 92 Stat. 1268 (Title 42, § 242 note)

Marihuana Tax Act of 1937
Aug. 2, 1937, ch. 553, 50 Stat. 551

Marine Corps Personnel Act
May 29, 1934, ch. 367, 48 Stat. 809

Marine Insurance Act (District of Columbia)
Mar. 4, 1922, ch. 93, 42 Stat. 401

Marine Mammal Protection Act of 1972
Pub. L. 92–522, Oct. 21, 1972, 86 Stat. 1027 (Title 16, §§ 1361, 1362, 1371–1384, 1401–1407)
Pub. L. 93–205, § 13(e), Dec. 28, 1973, 87 Stat. 902 (Title 16, §§ 1362, 1371, 1372, 1402)
Pub. L. 94–265, title IV, § 404(a), Apr. 13, 1976, 90 Stat. 360 (Title 16, § 1362)
Pub. L. 95–136, §§ 1–4, Oct. 18, 1977, 91 Stat. 1167 (Title 16, §§ 1372, 1380, 1384, 1407)
Pub. L. 95–316, §§ 1–4, July 10, 1978, 92 Stat. 380, 381 (Title 16, §§ 1379, 1380, 1384, 1407)

Finding Statutes by Chapter, Section, or Title Number

Sometimes statutes are commonly known by a title, chapter, or section number that refers to how the statute itself is organized, not to the book in which it can be found. For instance, many people might have heard of Title VII, the statutes that address discrimination in the workplace. But it's not part of Title VII of the U.S. Code—it's actually in Title 42.

Where did the "Title VII" come from? When bills are written, they are assigned internal organizing labels for legislative purposes. A bill isn't assigned to a title of the federal code until it actually passes and becomes a law.

If you are researching a statute that you know only by one of its internal organizing designations—such as Title VII, Chapter 7 (Bankruptcy Code), or Section 8 (Low-Income Housing Assistance)—first see whether it is listed that way in a popular names index. If not, focus on the subject of the statute—for instance "civil rights" or "job discrimination"—and use one of the code indexes discussed above.

Using Indexes

If you don't have the name or citation of the statute, start with the index. Each title of the codes has a separate index located at the back of the last book of the title. There is also a general index for all the titles as a whole. If you know what title your statute is in—or likely to be in—start with the index for that title. If you aren't sure which title your statute is in, use the general index. Work from the keywords list you created in Chapter 2.

Some titles contain a variety of subject matter. For instance, Title 42 contains statutes relating to water resources, water planning, voting rights, civil rights, and the National Science Foundation, in addition to its general topic of public health and welfare. If you looked up any of these subjects individually in the general index, they'd all refer you to Title 42.

Making Sure Federal Statutes Are Current

Once you've found the statute or statutes you need, you will want to make sure that they are still current. After all, the series of books that publish statutes are only published occasionally, and Congress can change or update those statutes all the time. Indeed, many laws are totally changed by amendment and deletion in just a few years.

Fortunately, there's a simple way to stay up to date. This is called the "pocket part system." Pocket parts are paper supplements that fit inside each hardcover volume, usually at the back. They are published once a year and contain any statutory changes occurring in the interim. When the pocket parts get too bulky because of legislative changes, either a new hardcover volume is published that incorporates all of the changes since the last hardcover volume was published, or a separate paperback volume is published that sits on the shelf next to the hardcover book.

Always check the pocket part to see if a statute you're reading has been amended or repealed. Usually, the pocket parts will reprint the sections of any statutes in the hardcover version that have been amended. Sections of the statute that have not been amended are not reproduced in the pocket part; instead, you are referred to the hardcover volume for the text. If you don't check the pocket part, you might find that the statute you discovered in the hardcover volume has long since been amended or even repealed. If a book doesn't have a pocket part and was not published in the current year, ask the librarian if there is one.

 TIP

If you're working online, find out how up-to-date the statutes are. Even on the most advanced systems, statutes aren't updated as soon as they're passed. You might have to check the congress.gov website for any recent changes (see below).

After you do this, there will be another step in the process, commonly called "Shepardizing." Using a volume called *Shepard's Citations for Statutes*, you'll look up each time a case has mentioned a particular statute and provides a reference (citation) to the case. In addition, *Shepard's* provides references to amendments that have been made to the statute and instances when attorney general opinions and some secondary sources have mentioned the statute. We'll explain how to use this resource in Chapter 8.

Finding Recently Passed Federal Law

Sometimes, the statute you are looking for will not be in the code, because it has passed only recently. Federal statutes start out as "bills" introduced in a session of Congress. They are assigned labels and numbers depending on which house of Congress they originate in. For example, a bill introduced in the U.S. Senate might be referred to as Senate Bill 2 (S. 2).

You can search bills using the congress.gov website (www.congress. gov). On the home page, top and center, you see a box with the heading "Current Legislation" where you can search for a pending bill by sponsor (the Congress member responsible for introducing the bill), a word or phrase contained in the bill, or the bill number. The list your search produces briefly describes the bill and its current status—for example, in committee, passed from the Senate to the House, engrossed (in its final form), enrolled (sent to the president), and so on.

If you want to search for a previous bill that has recently become law, use the advanced search feature and select "Laws" in the "Legislative Actions" menu.

Few of the many bills introduced in Congress become law. To do so they have to be passed by both houses and signed by the president, or passed over his or her veto. Once a bill becomes law, it is assigned a new label. The basic label is Public Law (Pub. L.). Following the Pub. L., the statute will have one number that corresponds with the number of the Congress (for example, 94th) that passed it, followed by a second number that is simply the number assigned to that specific bill by the Congress. So Pub. L. No. 94-586, for example, refers to Public Law 586 passed by the 94th Congress.

Bill drafters are aware that their handiwork will end up in codes. Much of the new law organized in Public Laws is parceled out into various parts of the U.S. Code, because each law might amend different statutes or add new sections to different titles. For example, a new tax provision might also affect the education system; in that case, both might be part of one bill (and one Public Law), but once "codified," will go into two different titles (the tax title, Title 26, and the education title, Title 20).

Finding Out-of-Date Federal Statutes in the Law Library

If you are looking for a specific statute that has been amended or deleted and no longer appears in the United States Code, you can find it in two publications: the *Statutes at Large*, and the *U.S. Code Congressional and Administrative News*.

The *Statutes at Large* series contains statutes organized by their public law numbers instead of their federal code citations. The *U.S. Code Congressional and Administrative News* publication also carries statutes by their public law number, but is annotated and generally an easier resource to use.

Finding State Statutes

You can use many of the principles that apply to researching federal statutes when dealing with state statutes. However, there are some differences in federal and state legislative processes and in the resources that you use to find and interpret state statutes.

Ways to Find a State Statute

As with federal statutes, you can find state statutes in different ways. If you are starting from square one, you can use an index (or online keyword search) to find relevant statutes. If you have the citation for the statute, you can look it up that way.

Almost every state maintains its statutes online. The websites vary in their format, but almost all of them allow you to search for statutes by topic, by keyword searches, and by specific code numbers. You can start your research by visiting your state's legislative website. Another approach is to search in FindLaw's "Cases and Codes" section (caselaw.findlaw.com). Simply click your state and you will be taken to a page with links to your state's constitution and statutes.

> CAUTION
> **The Cornell LII index is not exhaustive.** Sometimes statutes within a particular category are found in different parts of a code and even in different codes. The LII topical index might get you to some of the statutes you seek, but might miss other relevant statutes. Make sure you browse the statutes surrounding the particular statute pulled up in this topical search. Also, when possible, do a keyword search of the entire code to pull up any additional statutes appearing in other parts.

Of course, you can still use the law library to look up state statutes, if that's your preferred choice. Just recognize that not every law library will have every state's statute. For example, if you're located in California and you want to look up a statute in Arizona, your law library might not have Arizona's state statutes.

Using State Statute Indexes

Many collections of state statutes have indexes for each subject (that is, for each title, code, or chapter) and for the collection of laws as a whole. As with indexes to the federal code, you will probably find a general index at the end of the series, with indexes to each title distributed throughout the volumes, at the beginning or end of each title.

If your state's statutes are found in two or more publications, use either index. For example, the California statutes are published both in *West's Annotated Codes* and in *Deering's Annotated Codes* (Lexis Publishing). Because both publications index the same statutes and use the same citations, a citation you find in the *Deering* index can be looked up in the *West* code, and vice versa.

If you are working online, you might not have access to this type of index. However, you should be able to search by keyword. For more on keyword searching, go back to Chapter 2.

Using State Statutory Citations

You can also use a citation to find a state statute. Citations to state statutes normally refer to the title (or volume) and section numbers. The three examples shown below are typical.

23   Vt. Stat. Ann.   § 1185

title (volume   Vermont Statutes   section
number)   Annotated   number

N.J. Stat. Ann.   2A: 170-90.1

New Jersey Statutes   volume   section
Annotated   number   number

Mich. Comp. Laws Ann.   421.27   (c)(2)(ii)

Michigan Compiled Laws   section   subsection
Annotated   number   letter

Sample State Statute Citations

In the states that have codes, like New York and California, citations look like those shown below.

P.C.   § 518

Penal   section
Code   number

Penal Law   § 14025

Collection of   section
Penal Statutes   number

Sample California and New York Citations

If you are looking for a statute online and have located the state's statutes, you can usually just type the citation into the search box. In some cases, you might have to select the right title or section from a list, then select the code from within the title. This works much like it does if you're looking in the law library. First, locate the correct title (by looking at the first number of the citation); then turn to the correct section number.

Making Sure State Statutes Are Current

As with federal statutes, you will want to make sure state statutes are current, using the pocket part system. Functionally, this will happen the same way it does when dealing with federal statutes—you'll check the back of the volume for a pocket part, then ask the librarian if there isn't one.

Pocket parts show updates in one of two ways. In most states, the part of the statute that has been amended is shown in the pocket part, with additions underlined and deletions marked by asterisks. For example, a California statute in its original form as it appeared in the hardcover volume, and the amended version as it appeared in the pocket part, are both shown below. As you can see, words that have been added to the statute are underlined and words that have been taken out are represented by asterisks.

§ 1942. **Repairs by lessee; rent deduction; limit**
If within a reasonable time after notice to the lessor, of dilapidations which he ought to repair, he neglects to do so, the lessee may repair the same himself, where the cost of such repairs do not require an expenditure greater than one month's rent of the premises, and deduct the expenses of such repairs from the rent, or the lessee may vacate the premises, in which case he shall be discharged from further payment of rent, or performance of other conditions. (Enacted 1872. As amended Code Am.1873–74, c. 612, p. 246, § 206.)

Main Volume Statute

§ 1942. **Repairs by tenant; rent deduction or vacation of premises; presumption; limit; nonavailability of remedy; additional remedy**

(a) If within a reasonable time after <u>written or oral</u> notice to the * * * <u>landlord or his agent, as defined in subdivision (a) of Section 1962,</u> of dilapidations <u>rendering the premises untenantable</u> which * * * <u>the landlord</u> ought to repair, * * * <u>the landlord</u> neglects to do so, the * * * <u>tenant</u> may repair the same himself where the cost of such repairs does not require an expenditure * * * <u>more</u> than one month's rent of the premises and deduct the expenses of such repairs from the rent <u>when due,</u> or the * * * <u>tenant</u> may vacate the premises, in which case * * * <u>the tenant</u> shall be discharged from further payment of rent, or performance of other conditions <u>as of the date of vacating the premises.</u>

Pocket Part Statute

In some states, the pocket parts reprint the sections of any statutes that have been amended. Sections of the statute that have not been amended are not reproduced in the pocket part; instead, you are referred to the hardcover volume for the text. Note how the pocket part refers the reader back to the hardcover volume for sections that have not been changed.

Finding Recently Enacted State Legislation

As we've already discussed, if your research involves a statute that is newly passed, repealed, or amended, it might not be reflected in the version of the statute you are looking at. If you're online, you can usually find the updated version by going to the state legislature's website and looking up the bill number, if you have it. If you don't, you might have the opportunity to search by statute or use a keyword search. If you can't find the state legislature's website, we suggest you start by going to FindLaw (www.findlaw.com) or WashLaw Web (www.washlaw.edu), both of which have state-by-state legal resources.

Of course, if you are using the hard-copy volumes, the changes might not yet be reflected in the pocket parts, which come out only once a year. Fortunately, most states publish newly passed statutes in legislative update publications, which appear more frequently than the pocket parts. These update publications go by different names, such as

McKinney's Session Law News of New York or *Vernon's Texas Session Law Services.* Advance legislative update services are usually shelved next to the annotated state statutes. If you can't find them, ask the law librarian.

All update publications are organized pretty much the same way, and there are several ways to get to the statutes you seek. First, the statutes appear in numerical order according to the number given them by the state legislature. In many states, statutes appear according to their "chapter" number. In others they are listed by "session law" number. If you already know which number statute you're looking for, you can get to it directly.

Using the annotated code or collection citation is another way to use the advance legislative service. If you know, for example, that Labor Code § 560.5 has been amended, a table at the front or back of each legislative service volume will convert your "code" citation to the appropriate chapter number.

Finally, all advance legislative services have a detailed alphabetical table of contents in the front and a cumulative subject index in the back.

Finding Pending State Legislation

As with newly enacted legislation, in most states, the easiest way to find pending state legislation is go online and look at the state legislature's website. If you know what bill you're looking for, you can usually look it up by bill number. If you don't, you might be able to look up the citation for a statute you know has changed, or you might do a keyword search box to perform the same function.

 TIP

If you don't use online resources, the alternatives are time-consuming and will probably require you to have a bill number or know the subject being considered. Rather than spend your time figuring this out in a law library, we suggest you call your local elected representative's office and ask for a copy of the bill.

Understanding and Using Federal and State Statutes

Most legal research projects involve finding out what the law "is" in a particular circumstance. This usually means finding a statute and then deciding how a court would interpret it given the facts in your situation. If a statute is unclear—and many are—the court will try to figure out what the legislature intended. Only if the legislature exceeded its powers or intended something unconstitutional will courts ignore the dictates of a statute—and that doesn't happen very often.

Trying to determine what the legislature intended is often challenging, however. This is partly because the legislation might have been poorly drafted in the first place, and partly because legislators compromise, delete words, and add more words in an attempt to get enough votes to pass the bill. What might have begun as straightforward and clear language often becomes so riddled with exceptions and conditions that the result presents serious difficulties to anyone who wants to understand what was intended. In the words of one frustrated judge:

I concur in the opinion of the majority because its construction of Code of Civil Procedure Section 660 seems plausible and hence probably correct, although—given the cosmic incomprehensibility of the section—one can never be absolutely sure.

It occurs to me that Section 660 illustrates poignantly the maxim so useful in statutory construction—that if the Legislature had known what it meant, it would have said so.

It seems to me shameful, however, that large sums of money should change hands depending upon one's view of what this dismal, opaque statute means.

(Bunton v. Arizona Pacific Tanklines, 141 Cal.App.3d 210, 190 Cal. Rptr. 295 (1983).)

Interpreting Statutes

Understanding what a statute says and what it means is your first goal. To get a grasp on understanding statutes, we suggest you follow these eight rules.

Rule 1: Read the Statute at Least Three Times, Then Read It Again

Often a different and hopefully more accurate meaning will emerge from each reading. Never feel that somehow you are inadequate because despite a number of readings you aren't sure what a particular statute means. A great many lawsuits result from the fact that lawyers disagree about confusing statutory language.

Rule 2: Pay Close Attention to "Ands" and "Ors"

Many statutes have lots of "ands" and "ors" tucked into different clauses, and the thrust of the statute often depends on which clauses are joined by an "and" and which by an "or." When clauses are joined by an "or," it means that the conditions in at least one of the clauses must be present, but not all. When clauses are joined by an "and," the conditions in all the clauses must be met.

Rule 3: Assume All Words and Punctuation in the Statute Have Meaning

Often, statutes seem to be internally inconsistent or redundant. Sometimes they are. However, courts presume that every word and comma in a statute means something, and you should do the same. If you're unsure about what a word or phrase means, look it up in a law dictionary or a multivolume publication titled *Words and Phrases*, discussed further below.

Rule 4: Interpret a Statute So That It Is Consistent With All Other Related Statutes, If Possible

Although it might appear one statute conflicts with others on the same subject, a judge who examines the statutes will make an attempt to reconcile the meanings so that no conflict exists. Ask yourself whether any interpretation of the statute will make it consistent rather than inconsistent with other statutes.

Interpreting "Ands" and "Ors"

Consider the following provision taken from 42 U.S.C.A. § 416:

An applicant who is the son or daughter of a fully or currently insured individual, but who is not (and is not deemed to be) the child of such insured individual under paragraph (2) of this subsection, shall nevertheless be deemed to be the child of such insured individual if:

> (A) *in the case of an insured individual entitled to old-age insurance benefits (who was not, in the month preceding such entitlement, entitled to disability insurance benefits)—*
>
> > (i) *such insured individual—*
> >
> > > (I) *has acknowledged in writing that the applicant is his or her son or daughter*
> > >
> > > (II) *has been decreed by a court to be the mother or father of the applicant, or*
> > >
> > > (III) *has been ordered by a court to contribute to the support of the applicant because the applicant is his or her son or daughter,*
> >
> > *and such acknowledgment, court decree, or court order was made not less than one year before such insured individual became entitled to old-age insurance benefits or attained retirement age (as defined in subsection (l) of this section), whichever is earlier ...*

Interpretation: To be considered a child of an insured individual, a person must satisfy at least one of the three conditions under Section (A) (i)—because of the use of the word "or"—and the condition must be met within one year of when the insured individual became entitled to old-age insurance benefits or attained retirement age, because of the "and."

Rule 5: Interpret Criminal Statutes Strictly

Courts apply a doctrine called "strict interpretation" to criminal law, to further the policy that no person should be held accountable for a crime without adequate notice that his or her behavior would be considered criminal. The only way to provide this type of notice is to insist that criminal laws be interpreted literally, interpreting any ambiguities in favor of the defendant. For example, to convict somebody of "breaking and entering a building belonging to another with the intent to commit theft or a felony therein" (a common definition of burglary), a prosecutor has to prove each element of the crime—that the person broke and entered and intended to commit a felony inside.

> **EXAMPLE:** A young man in Vermont was charged with breaking and entering into the county courthouse, a felony. He had been found in the morning passed out under the judge's desk with some rare coins in his pocket that had been taken from the desk.
>
> At his trial, the young man testified that he thought the courthouse was a church and that he simply broke in to get some sleep. However, once inside, he decided to look around and ended up stealing the coins. He didn't remember passing out. The trial judge (not the coin collector, but a more disinterested jurist) instructed the jury that unless they found beyond a reasonable doubt that the young man actually intended to commit the theft or another felony at the time he entered the courthouse, they could not convict him of breaking and entering. He was acquitted.

Rule 6: Interpret Ambiguities in Statutes in Ways That Seem to Best Further the Purpose of the Legislation

Much legislation is designed to either protect the public from ills or to provide various benefits. When ambiguities exist in these types of statutes—commonly called social welfare legislation—the courts tend to interpret them so that the protection or benefit will be provided, rather than the other way around.

EXAMPLE: A statute allows welfare recipients to "earn" up to $500 a month without losing any benefits. The purpose of the statute is to provide an incentive for those on welfare to find work. Tom's father gives him $500 a month to stop drinking. Tom reports this to the welfare department, which promptly reduces Tom's monthly grant by $500. Tom goes to court, arguing that he is "earning" the money by not drinking and is therefore entitled to the $500 exemption. The welfare department contends that since the statute was intended to stimulate employment, the term "earns" means income from employment. The welfare department's argument will probably win, since its interpretation is more consistent with the statute's underlying objective.

Rule 7: Interpret the Statute So That It Makes Sense and Does Not Lead to Absurd or Improbable Results

Courts are sometimes called on to interpret statutes that, if taken literally, would lead to a result that the legislature could not (in the court's opinion) have intended. In such an instance, a court will strain to interpret the statute so that it does make sense or leads to a logical result.

EXAMPLE: A California statute literally imposed a $100 daily penalty on landlords who interfered with a tenant's utilities with an intent to evict the tenant. The California Supreme Court ruled that the legislature could not have intended this harsh result, and instead interpreted the statute as allowing a penalty of *up to* $100 per day.

Few things are harder for a layperson to take than when the judge rejects a literal interpretation of a statute because "the legislature couldn't have intended it." The moral? When reading a statute, ask whether your interpretation is grounded in common sense and in the way the law was probably intended to work.

Rule 8: Track Down All Cross-References to Other Statutes and Sections

People who draft statutes are very fond of including references to other statutes and sections of the same statute. When faced with such a statute, the human tendency is to ignore the cross-references and hope that they don't pertain to your situation. Our advice, quite simply, is to track down each and every cross-reference and make sure you understand how it relates to the main body of the statute you are analyzing. If you don't, you could overlook something crucial.

Tools for Interpreting Statutes

Although we recommend you start by reading a statute multiple times so you understand it as best you can, other resources are available to you to help you interpret statutes.

Reading Cases That Interpret Statutes

It would be nice if research into the meaning of statutes began and ended with reading the statutes themselves. But as we've explained, the judiciary is charged with the task of interpreting statutes when a dispute over their meaning comes up in a lawsuit. Court interpretations of statutes are every bit as much a part of the law as the words of the statutes themselves.

For example, the California statute mentioned earlier provided that landlords were liable to tenants in the amount of $100 for each day the utilities were shut off by the landlord for the purpose of forcing the tenants out. When a landlord appealed a judgment against him under this statute, the California Supreme Court decided that it would be unconstitutional to penalize a landlord $100 per day regardless of circumstances (*Hale v. Morgan*, 22 Cal.3d 388, 149 Cal.Rptr. 375, 584 P.2d 512 (1978)). The Court interpreted the statute to allow a penalty of up to $100 per day, depending on circumstances. Immediately after this court decision, the law of utility shutoffs in California could be determined only by reading the statute and the court case together. (The California legislature later amended the statute to comply with the Court's ruling.)

It can be difficult to read and understand case law. We'll discuss how to do that in the next chapter.

Using Attorney General Opinions to Interpret Statutes

Attorneys general, the highest legal officers in government, are often asked by government agencies to interpret the meaning of statutes. When they do, they often issue written opinions. These attorney general opinions are not binding on the courts, but they have influence, especially when there is no precedent (relevant case law) to the contrary. And they can be very helpful in deciphering an otherwise hopelessly complicated statute.

You can find these opinions online by visiting the National Association of Attorneys General (NAAG) website (www.naag.org), which links to each state attorney general's website and provides information such as bios and phone numbers. FindLaw is also a good starting place for finding attorney general opinions—or just try using a search engine to search for your state attorney general's website.

Using *Words and Phrases* to Interpret Statutes

To properly interpret a statute, you might need to know how courts have interpreted one or more of the specialized words and phrases it contains. One tool to help you do this is a multivolume set called *Words and Phrases* (West). It contains one-sentence interpretations of common words and phrases that have been pulled from cases and organized alphabetically. This publication allows you to find out whether courts have interpreted or used any particular word or phrase you are interested in and, if so, how.

In a real sense, *Words and Phrases* is a kind of dictionary that offers contextual definitions instead of the abstract and disconnected entries found in most law dictionaries. Below is part of the *Words and Phrases* entry for "Landlord and Tenant."

As with other hardbound legal resources, don't forget to check the pocket part in the back of each book for the newest entries.

LANDLORD AND TENANT

In general

The relation of "landlord and tenant" depends upon agreement. Estes v. Gatliff, 163 S.W.2d 273, 275, 291 Ky. 93.

A "landlord and tenant relationship" will be implied from occupancy of premises with owner's consent. Crawford v. Jerry, 11 A.2d 210, 211, 111 Vt. 120.

The relation of "landlord and tenant" arises only where one in possession of land recognizes another as his landlord. Hoffmann v. Chapman, Tex.Civ.App., 170 S.W.2d 496, 498.

A contract establishing "landlord and tenant relationship" does not include principal and agent or master and servant relationships. Butler v. Maney, 200 So. 226, 228, 146 Fla. 33.

The relation of "landlord and tenant" may arise by express or implied contract and on slight evidence. Delay v. Douglas, Mo. App., 164 S.W.2d 154, 156.

Words and Phrases

You can also find these opinions in the library, collected in publications usually called something like *Opinions of the Attorney-General of the State of [State].* Each state and the federal government has its own set. If a statute is the subject of an attorney general's opinion, the citation to the opinion citing the statute will appear after the case citations in *Shepard's Citations for Statutes.* (See Chapter 8 for more on how to use this valuable tool.)

Using Legislative History to Interpret Statutes

You might be uncertain about the meaning of a statute no matter how much you study it. For instance, many statutes provide that certain government employees are entitled to an administrative hearing if they lose their jobs. What such statutes often don't say is whether the hearing must be provided before the discharge or after it.

In all likelihood, if it's confusing to you, it was previously confusing to someone else too, and that means you'll be able to find a case discussing it. But if not, how should you proceed? In those rare cases, one common way (and in many cases the only way) is to find out what the legislators intended at the time they passed the statute. Their intent can be inferred from legislative committee reports, hearings, and floor debates—what is called the statute's "legislative history."

When you investigate legislative history, keep a couple of points firmly in mind. As mentioned earlier, what the legislature intended in a statute is supposed to be gleaned from the "plain words" of the statute itself. So if a judge believes the words of a statute are reasonably clear, no inquiry into the legislative intent will be considered.

The second point is that, much of the time, despite your best efforts to unearth it, you won't find clear legislative intent. Typically, a few legislators know what's intended by the words of any particular statute, while the great majority who haven't even read it vote for or against the bill for reasons unrelated to how it's worded. For that reason, some judges stick to the words of the statute, no matter how difficult it is to understand.

Finding Federal Legislative History

Most legislative history for federal statutes is reported in committee reports. You can use the congress.gov website to find legislative history for the last several sessions of Congress. Just keep in mind that you'll get the history session by session—that is, each history will discuss only the change or changes made in that session.

To find federal legislative history in the library, look at the annotated federal code for the statute in question. Most are followed by a reference to the *U.S. Code Congressional and Administrative News*, which contains federal legislative history. If the federal statute you are investigating does not have a citation to its legislative history, you can check the subject index, popular names table, and statutory reference table in each volume of the *U.S. Code Congressional and Administrative News*. There is one major limitation to the value of these indexes and tables, however: They are not cumulative. In other words, they index only materials from the legislative session covered by that volume.

If you have the public law number of a statute, find the volume containing the public laws for the Congress indicated in the public law number. For instance, if the number is 94-584, find the volume containing material for the 94th Congress. Then use the statutory reference table to locate the committee reports. If you don't know the public law number, the *U.S. Code* citation, or the approximate year the statute was passed, you will have difficulty finding the appropriate committee reports. Your best bet is to search for the *U.S. Code* citation.

It is important to remember that the typical statute is amended many times over its lifespan. Each amendment has its own committee reports. The legislative history of a statute, therefore, generally refers to a collection of legislative histories. Each of these legislative histories must be separately researched, because any given volume of the *U.S. Code Congressional and Administrative News* contains only the committee reports for the session covered by that volume.

Finding State Legislative History

State legislative history is usually more difficult to uncover than federal legislative history. However, many states have legislative analysts (lawyers who work for the legislature) whose comments on legislation are considered by the state legislators in the same way as committee reports are considered by Congress. These comments are sometimes published in the advance legislative update services as an introduction to the new statute.

Statutes and accompanying comments that are printed in these advance legislative services are later bound and retained in volumes called *Session Laws*, according to the year they were passed. It is sometimes possible to discover the legislative history of an older state statute by finding these legislative analysts' comments with the statute in the bound *Session Laws*. To find a statute in the *Session Laws*, you need the chapter number assigned it by the legislature. That number appears directly after the text of the statute as printed in a code.

It is also common for legislative committees to have their own staff lawyers draft memoranda to guide them in their deliberations. These memoranda are normally not available in law libraries, but they might be kept on file with the legislature. The best course for a researcher is probably to ask a law librarian what kinds of legislative history for state laws are available in that state.

Using Uniform Law Histories to Interpret Statutes

Since 1892, there has been an effort to make a number of substantive areas of the law uniform among the states. A group of lawyers, judges, and law professors called the Uniform Law Commission drafts legislation covering certain areas of law, and then tries to get as many states as possible to adopt the "uniform" legislation. The packages drafted by the National Conference are not law and have no effect on our legal system until they are adopted by one or more state legislatures. And the fact that the package is adopted in one or more states does not make it law in any other state that has not adopted it.

Uniform Laws Adopted by Many States

- Uniform Commercial Code
- Uniform Controlled Substances Act
- Uniform Gifts to Minors Act
- Uniform Transfers to Minors Act
- Uniform Partnership Act
- Uniform Child Custody Jurisdiction Act

If the statute you are researching was a uniform law adopted by your state (you'll find this information in the annotations to the statutes, explained below), you can get some help interpreting its meaning by looking at a series of books called the *Uniform Laws Annotated (U.L.A.)*, published by West. It contains all of the uniform laws, the original comments accompanying them, a listing of the states that have adopted them, notations of how states have altered each provision in the course of adopting it, summaries of case opinions that have interpreted each statute, and references to pertinent law review discussions. If your annotated state statutes are published by West (almost all are), the annotation following the statute will tell you. In addition, the annotation will reproduce the National Conference comment that accompanied the statute as it was originally proposed, and will also contain comments about how the state version of the statute differs from the original.

States seldom adopt uniform law packages lock, stock, and barrel. Usually they change, add to, or delete some of the statutes in the package. So by the time uniform laws have been adopted by the various states, they are no longer, strictly speaking, "uniform." Still, for the most part, if you have an overall understanding of the package as it was produced by the National Conference, you will have a good grasp of the final result in any given adopting state.

The Cornell Legal Information Institute provides online links to state statutes that implement various uniform laws as well as provides the actual text of the uniform law for each state. You can find this information at www.law.cornell.edu/uniform.

Using Statutes to Conduct Additional Research

Up to this point, we've referred you to other resources to help you understand the statute or statutes you're reading. But statutes serve another important function: They help you conduct additional research.

Reading the Statutory Scheme

Statutes are not arranged haphazardly. Usually, legislatures arrange them into clumps called "statutory schemes." If you are interested in a particular area of law (small claims court, for example), you will usually find that the statutory scheme appears in one central location, and you can read that entire scheme at once. You might find that you can sue for up to $10,000 in one statute and then learn in another one that a lower limit has been set for cases involving evictions, for example.

Reading the statutory scheme will help you not only answer the direct question in front of you, but understand the legal principles in the field more generally. And it might also lead you to additional information you need. We suggest you browse or read the scheme anytime you are looking at a statute for the first time.

Using Annotations

Statutes can either be "annotated" or "unannotated." Unannotated statutes have only the text of the statute itself. This is usually what you'll find online, and in some volumes in the library (which will be clearly marked). If all you need to see is what the statute says, an unannotated version will suffice.

However, if you are using the statute to conduct additional research, the annotated code is very helpful. Annotated codes contain additional information, including information about other resources—like cases and secondary sources—that interpret or explain the statute in question. For example, two versions of the U.S. Code are published in annotated form: the *United States Code Annotated,* or *U.S.C.A.* (West), and the *United States Code Service,* or *U.S.C.S.* (Lexis Publishing). These annotated codes include:

- one-sentence summaries of court cases that have interpreted the statute
- notes about the statute's history (such as amendments)
- cross-references to other relevant statutes
- cross-references to administrative regulations that might be helpful in interpreting the statute
- citations to the legislative history of the statute, and
- research guides (references to relevant materials by the same publisher).

Finding and Using Regulations

Legislatures often pass laws that need active enforcement. For example, a complex series of federal statutes govern the collection of the federal income tax. However, the federal government wouldn't be solvent very long if it relied on everyone to pay their tax bill voluntarily. Accordingly, Congress created the Internal Revenue Service (IRS) to resolve questions about how the tax laws should be interpreted, provide specific guidelines to help people prepare their own tax return, and keep a close watch on us all to make sure we pay our share.

The IRS is but one of many of the "administrative agencies" created by Congress over the years to implement its programs. State legislatures have created a similar host of agencies to carry out their programs. Legislatures give such agencies the power to make rules and guidelines to carry out the goals of the statutes that authorized the creation of the agencies and the programs over which they have authority.

These rules and guidelines are collectively termed "regulations." Some are directed at the general public, some at business entities, and some at the agency itself. As long as they are consistent with the legislation that created them, they are just as binding and enforceable as statutes. Courts are willing to overturn an agency's regulations only when they conclude that the agency misinterpreted the law or issued a regulation when it didn't have the authority to do so.

Finding Federal Regulations in a Law Library

Most federal regulations are published in the *Code of Federal Regulations (C.F.R.)*, a multivolume and well-indexed paperbound set organized by subject. The *C.F.R.* is organized into 50 separate titles, each covering a general subject. For instance, Title 7 contains regulations concerning agriculture, Title 10 contains energy regulations, and so on. *C.F.R.* titles often, but not always, correspond to the *U.S.C.* titles in terms of their subject matter. For example, Title 7 of the *United States Code* covers statutes relating to agriculture, while Title 7 of the *C.F.R.* contains agriculture regulations. But Title 42 of *U.S.C.* contains statutes on the Medicaid program, while the Medicaid regulations are found in Title 45 of the *C.F.R.*

Along with each regulation, the *C.F.R.* provides a reference to the statute that authorizes it and a reference to where (and when) the regulation was published in the *Federal Register*. (All regulations are supposed to be published first in the *Federal Register*, discussed below.)

The best way to find a federal regulation published in the *C.F.R.* if you don't already have the correct citation is to start with the general subject index that comes with this series. If you already know which title your regulation is likely to be in, use the table of contents at the end of each individual title.

Once you've found a regulation, you need to be sure it's still current. A new edition of the *C.F.R.* is published each year on a staggered quarterly basis. Titles 1–16 are published on January 1, Titles 17–27 are published on April 1, Titles 28–41 are published on July 1, and Titles 42–50 are published on October 1. Each year the *C.F.R.* covers change colors.

When a new annual edition is published, the regulations in it are current as of that date. But how can you make sure you're up-to-date if the *C.F.R.* volume that contains the regulation you are interested in was published January 1, 2018, and you are doing your research in July 2018? First, consult the latest monthly pamphlet called *C.F.R.-L.S.A.*, which stands for "List of *C.F.R.* Sections Affected." Find the title and section number of the regulation you are interested in. Then see if there have been any changes between the last published *C.F.R.* volume (January 1 in our example) and the date of the pamphlet (July 2018). Below is a typical page from *C.F.R.-L.S.A.*

Suppose now that you are doing your research on July 15, and the July version of the *C.F.R.-L.S.A.* has not yet hit the library shelf. You would first use the *C.F.R.-L.S.A.* for June. Then you can use a publication called the *Federal Register*, where all new federal regulations are originally published. The *Federal Register* also contains proposed regulations, schedules of government agency meetings, presidential documents, and lists of bills that have been enacted.

 Summing Up ...
How to Find Federal Regulations in the Law Library

✓ Consult either the general subject index to the *Code of Federal Regulations (C.F.R.)*, or the *Index to the Code of Federal Regulations* (commercially published by the Congressional Information Service).

✓ After you find the regulation, read the latest monthly issue of the *List of C.F.R. Sections Affected (C.F.R.-L.S.A.)* to see whether changes in the regulation have been made since the *C.F.R.* volume was published.

✓ Consult the *List of C.F.R. Sections Affected* in the latest daily issue of the *Federal Register* for the most current status of a regulation.

✓ For regulations that have been issued since the latest *C.F.R.* volume was published, consult the cumulative index to the *Federal Register* under the appropriate agency.

The *Federal Register* can be hard to use because it contains many pages of very small type on newsprint. It is published daily, and a cumulative monthly index is available to help you find the regulation you're after. However, this index is generally organized according to the agency that initiated the action, so unless you know which agency you're dealing with, it's of little help.

92   **LSA—LIST OF CFR SECTIONS AFFECTED**

CHANGES APRIL 1, 1991 THROUGH NOVEMBER 29, 1991

TITLE 19 Chapter I—Con.   Page
171.33 (b)(1) and (d) heading
   revised.. 40780
  (b)(1) and (d) corrected............. 48823
172.22 (e) added.............................40780
  (e) corrected................................ 48823
172.33 (b)(1) revised.................... 40780
177 Interpretive rule.................... 46372
177.22 (b) introductory text
  amended...................................46115
178.2 Table amended...................32087
191.10 (e)(1)(i) amended............. 46115
191.21 (c) and (d) amended........ 46115
191.27 (c) amended...................... 46115

Chapter II—United States International Trade Commission (Parts 200—299)

200 Authority citation revised......................................36726
200.735-102 (g) removed.............36726
200.735-103 (a) and (c) introductory text amended; (b)
  and (c)(2) revised......................36726
200.735-114 Nomenclature
  change.......................................36726
200.735-115 Nomenclature
  change.......................................36726
200.735-116 (b) revised................ 36726
200.735-121 Nomenclature
  change.......................................36726

Chapter III—International Trade Administration, Department of Commerce (Parts 300—399)

356 Revised.................................. 37804

Title 19—*Proposed Rules:*

4.............................40283, 48448, 51762
10.......................................48448, 51762
19.......................................22833, 33733
24..31576
101...21111,
   22369, 55102, 56179
102.....................................48448, 51762
113.....................................22833, 33733
118..33734
134.....................................48448, 51762
142..42568
141..56608
142..56608
144.....................................22833, 33733
162..25363
177.............................46134, 48448, 51762

Note: **Boldface entries indicate November changes.**

TITLE 20—EMPLOYEES' BENEFITS

Chapter I—Office of Workers' Compensation Programs, Department of Labor (Parts 1—199)
                              Page
10.305 Revised............................. 47675
10.306 (a) revised.........................47675
10.311 (c) revised.........................47675

Chapter II—Railroad Retirement Board (Parts 200—399)

200.8 (b) amended; (d)(1), (2),
  (3), (f), (g) and (h) redesignated as (d)(2), (3), (4), (g),
  (h) and (i); (d)(1), (f) and (j)
  added....................................... 50247
216 Revised................................. 28692
236 Removed...............................55073
240 Removed...............................55073
323 Added...................................26328
330 Revised................................. 28702
367 Added...................................46375

Chapter III—Social Security Administration, Department of Health and Human Services (Parts 400—499)

404.362 (b)(1) revised; (b)(2) removed; (b)(3) redesignated
  as (b)(2)....................................24000
404.367 Introductory text and
  (b) revised.................................35999
404.401—404.499 (Subpart E)
  Authority citation revised..... 41789
404.401 (d) revised....................... 41789
  Technical correction...................50157
404.402 (d)(1) revised................... 41789
  Technical correction...................50157
404.469 Added.............................41789
  Technical correction...................50157
404.501—404.515 (Subpart F)
  Authority citation revised...... 52468
404.520 Added.............................52468
404.521 Added.............................52468
404.522 Added.............................52469
404.523 Added.............................52469
404.524 Added.............................52469
404.525 Added.............................52469
404.526 Added.............................52469
404.621 (a)(2)(i) and (ii) removed; (a)(2)(iii) and (iv)
  redesignated as (a)(2)(i) and
  (ii)... 58846

List of C.F.R. Sections Affected (C.F.R.-L.S.A.)

If you have a *C.F.R.* citation to the new regulation, or you want to bring your *C.F.R.* search completely up to date (see above), you can consult the *C.F.R.* sections affected list in the latest issue of the *Federal Register*. This will give you a listing of all *C.F.R.* sections that have been affected during the current month of the *Federal Register*.

Finding Federal Regulations Online

The entire *Code of Federal Regulations (C.F.R.)* is available online. Also, many of the special law collections that are put together for online research (see Chapter 4) contain the federal regulations that are relevant to the collection's specific topics.

You can find the *C.F.R.* online in a number of places. First, you can try the Cornell Legal Information Institute (www.law.cornell.edu). You'll find "*C.F.R.*" under the "Legal Resources" heading. You can browse by topic, search the section headings by keyword, or search by citation (if you have one).

You can also access federal regulations at the National Archives website (www.archives.gov/federal-register/cfr). Finally, you can go directly to the specific regulatory agency's website (www.<agency acronym>.gov; for example, www.fcc.gov), or use Justia's *C.F.R.* collection at https://law.justia.com/cfr.

Finding State Regulations in a Law Library

State regulations are usually more difficult to locate than federal regulations. While at least 30 states have an administrative code containing a portion of the state's regulations, typically each agency will keep its regulations in loose-leaf manuals published by the individual agency. This means it is often necessary to know which state agency is responsible for writing a particular regulation before you can find it. Some larger law libraries carry all or most of the regulations for their state, but more often you'll have to call or visit the agency itself to get regulations.

Regulations are constantly being changed by the agencies that issue them, and it is important to always check to make sure that the regulation that you've found is up to date. The easiest way is to contact the agency directly.

Finding State Regulations Online

There are many ways to find a state's regulations online. Many of the sites we list for finding state statutes online will also provide links to state regulations. Your state's website will provide links to state agencies and regulations. You might also find relevant links on Justia's website (www. justia.com). You will likely be able to do the keyword searches or search drop-down menus for the appropriate title.

Reading and Understanding Regulations

The general rules of statutory interpretation also apply to interpreting regulations. But there are some additional factors to consider in the interpretation of regulations. The most important are these:

- Agency interpretations of a regulation should either be followed or argued against, but not ignored. Because regulations are often written to implement a general statutory scheme, they tend to be both wordy and hard to understand, even more so than statutes. Increasingly, however, regulations are written so that they can be more clearly understood.
- Regulations should be interpreted in a way that best fulfills the intent of the authorizing statute.

A typical regulation consists of the actual rule that is being put forth and a paragraph or two of agency interpretation. Sometimes examples are given on how the regulation is supposed to apply to a specific set of facts. Only the rule part of the regulation acts like a law. The interpretation and examples are designed only to explain its application.

> **Summing Up ...**
> ## How to Find State Regulations in the Law Library
>
> ✓ If your state's regulations have been collected and published in an "Administrative Code," use the subject index. If there is no index, find the place in the publication that covers the agency issuing the regulations and check the table of contents.
>
> ✓ If there is no administrative code or analogous publication, find out what agency issued the regulations. Then ask the law librarian whether the library carries that agency's regulations.
>
> ✓ If the regulations cannot be found in the law library, check with the nearest large public library.
>
> ✓ If the regulations aren't kept there, contact the agency issuing the regulations and ask how you can get a copy of them.

Finding and Using Procedural Statutes and Rules

If your research involves procedural issues—such as getting a case into court and keeping it there—you need to pay special attention to several types of laws, all of which can usually be found in a law library with the help of the law librarian. We'll discuss these further in Chapter 9.

Rules of Civil Procedure

Rules of Civil Procedure are usually statutes passed by a legislature or rules issued by a state's highest court. They govern such matters as:

- who can sue whom, for what kinds of wrongs and in which courts
- which kinds of documents must be filed with the court to initiate a lawsuit and respond to it

- time limits for filing various court papers
- what court papers must say to be effective
- what ways each side to a lawsuit can find out necessary facts from the other side and from third-party witnesses (discovery)
- how a case is actually brought to trial
- what kind of trial you are entitled to (that is, by judge or jury)
- what kind of judgment and relief you are entitled to if you win
- what happens to you if you lose
- how you can enforce a judgment
- how you can appeal a judgment if you lose, and
- what kind of appeal is available if the court does not comply with the laws in the pretrial stage of the case.

You must follow these rules exactly. While some procedural mistakes can be fixed, especially if done very promptly, many violations mean that your case is lost, just as surely as if you went to trial and the court or jury found against you.

Rules of Civil Procedure for the federal courts are found in Title 28 of the *U.S.C.A.*; Rules of Civil Procedure for state courts are usually found among the other state statutes in a code, title, or chapter titled "Civil Procedure" or "Court Rules."

Rules of Court (If Any)

Your state might have an additional publication called Rules of Court or something similar. If so, it will contain rules issued by the state's highest court and specify in more detail the procedures that must be followed. For example, a statute might specify that a certain document must be filed with the court, but the Rule of Court would specify the precise form the document must follow.

Local Rules (If Any)

Many courts have their own local rules that get even more detailed. A local rule might specify the size of the paper that must be used or where an attorney's name must be placed on the page. Although these housekeeping matters might not seem as important as the accuracy of the facts and law in your papers, many lawyers have learned the hard way that you ignore them at your peril. Some judges and clerks love to use deviations from local rules as the basis for returning your papers or even denying your motion.

Finding Court Rules Online

Like other government entities, trial courts often provide online access to virtually the same information that you could get if you walked into the clerk's office, including the daily court calendar, personnel and filing information, recent court rulings, and the local court rules.

A good list of court websites can be found at the National Center for State Courts (www.ncsc.org). Under "Information and Resources," click "Browse by State," then "Court Web Sites."

> **RESOURCE**
> **Check desk references.** It is no secret that administrative assistants and paralegals play a critical role in getting the right papers to the right courts on time. These details are commonly put into a step-by-step form and published in handbooks and "desk references." You can find information about filing fees, service of process, statutes of limitation, time limits, common motions, and similar nitty-gritty matters in these publications, which exist in most larger states. For example, in California, you can use *California Paralegal's Guide 6th*, by Mack (Lexis Publishing). Ask a legal assistant, paralegal, or law librarian if this sort of resource is published in your state.

Finding and Using Local Laws or Ordinances

Counties, cities, and special districts (for example, school districts or sanitation districts) have a good deal of power over day-to-day life. The amount of rule-making authority that is afforded these local entities is usually set out in the state constitution and statutes. Subject to these higher forms of law, cities commonly have authority to:

- divide their domain into zones of activity (called "zoning power")
- set requirements for new buildings and for the refurbishing of old buildings
- pass and enforce local parking and driving rules
- set minimum standards for health and safety in rental properties, and
- promulgate fire and police regulations.

Local laws are usually called "ordinances." Ordinances are like statutes and regulations in that they have the force and effect of law, assuming they are within the local government's lawful authority. Special districts are usually empowered to pass regulations that are also binding law.

Finding Ordinances and Local Laws in the Law Library

Because of the many different forms of local government, it is difficult to specify the exact way in which you might research these ordinances or specialized regulations. Here are some general suggestions:

- Ordinances are often divided into local codes such as the "traffic code," "planning code," "building code," and the like. These codes are usually available in your local public library or law library, and can also be obtained from the pertinent city office for free or a small sum to cover reproduction costs.
- City and county agencies keep collections of ordinances that pertain to their agency.
- Special districts usually publish their regulations in paperbound pamphlets that can be obtained free or for a low price.

Ordinances, like statutes, are occasionally interpreted by the courts. If you want to find out whether or not an ordinance you're interested in has been considered by a court, you can do an online search of case law with keyword searches. In the law library, use *Shepard's Citations for Statutes*. (For instructions on how to Shepardize statutes or ordinances, see Chapter 8.)

Finding Local Laws Online

State and Local Government on the Net (www.statelocalgov.net) is a great site for finding municipal codes. The Municipal Code Corporation (www.municode.com) also has a helpful site at www.municode.com/ Library. If you draw a blank, you might also be able to find your codes or ordinances at a city or county website. Just type the name of your city, county, or other municipality into Google or another search engine.

Many local government websites will have drop-down menus with relevant codes, or will allow you to do keyword searches.

Finding Local Laws Online

Finding Cases

U sing secondary sources, as described in Chapter 4, and statutes, as described in Chapter 5, is almost certainly going to lead you to citations or references to cases that are relevant to your topic. In this chapter, we'll explain how to locate those cases. In the next chapter, we'll cover how to read and understand the cases you find.

Using Citations to Find Cases

If you're lucky, your research by now will have led you to actual citations that are relevant to what you're researching. You might not have even recognized a citation for what it is: a shorthand way of referring the reader to the location of a case.

Citations will help you get to the case you're looking for in books called "reporters," which contain compilations of decisions by appellate courts, federal trial courts, and specialty courts (such as bankruptcy). Each set of reporters contains opinions from a particular court or group of courts. For example, state reporters contain only one state's appellate decisions (for instance, "Cal.App." contains appellate cases from California) and subject matter reporters contain decisions affecting a certain area of law (for instance, "B.R." contains federal bankruptcy opinions). In addition, federal cases are reported in their own sets, one for trial level decisions (called "F.Supp.") and one for appellate opinions from the Circuit Courts of Appeals (abbreviated as "F."). When they reach a maximum volume number (usually, 999), a new series begins and is identified as "2d" or "3d," and so on. We explain more about the different types of reporters in Chapter 7.

Every reported (published) case has a unique citation. As long as you have the citation, you can find any case published in a standard case reporter. We'll use the example below to walk through the different elements.

Lukhard v. Reed	**95**	**L.Ed. 2d**	**328**	**(1987)**
case name	volume number	name of the reporter	the page number	year of the decision

Citation Form

Citations often take slightly different forms because each state is free to develop its own citation system (check your state court's website for format information). For example, it is not uncommon to see the date immediately following the case name or different abbreviations that designate the reporter. A nationwide system of citations is contained in a book titled *A Uniform System of Citation,* 20th ed. (known as the "Blue Book" because of its blue cover). It has been developed primarily for law school use, but is used in federal courts and many state courts. We follow it here for the most part.

The elements are:

- **Case name.** The first element of a case citation is the case name; here, *Lukhard v. Reed.* There are usually two names, the plaintiff's and defendant's, on either side of a "v." (short for versus). Usually the plaintiff's name is first, but not always. In *Lukhard v. Reed,* the original plaintiff was Reed, but when Lukhard appealed a lower court decision in favor of Reed, his name was put first. Other times, there will be only one name: for example, *In re Gault* is the name of a juvenile case; the "in re" means "in the matter of." These types of case names normally appear where the proceeding is brought by the state for the individual's best interest, or where the proceeding is not considered to be an adversary proceeding that warrants the "v." Finally, cases are sometimes referred to by the subject matter of the dispute. For instance, divorce cases commonly carry such names as *Marriage of Sullivan* (last name of the divorcing couple) or *In the Matter of Schmidt.*
- **Volume number.** A case citation provides the volume number of the reporter in which the case is located. The volumes of each separate reporter are numbered consecutively.

- **Name of reporter.** Obviously a citation wouldn't be much help without the name of the reporter. That information comes immediately after the volume number. In the *Lukhard* case, the full name of the reporter is *United States Supreme Court Reports, Lawyer's Edition.* Most reporters have been published in two or more series. For example, the *Lukhard* case is published in the second series of the L.Ed. reporter (L.Ed.2d). Cases decided in the 19th and early 20th century were published in the first series (L.Ed).
- **The page number.** You have undoubtedly already figured out what the next item of a citation is for. It provides the page number the case starts on. You'll need this number to look up the case in the law library, or to cite to the case in a court document, even if you are doing your research online.
- **Year of the decision.** Citations also carry the year the case was decided. This information can be helpful because newer cases tend to reflect current legal trends better than older cases. When you're doing research, you usually want to first check the most recent cases relating to your problem or issue.

Citing Federal Cases: The Circuit, State, or District

Citations to cases decided by the federal Courts of Appeal usually include the circuit of the court deciding the case. A case decided by the Court of Appeals for the Third Circuit is cited as 654 F.2d 925 (3d Cir. 1984). A U.S. District Court citation should indicate the state and judicial district of the case; for example, in *Peter v. Jones,* 509 F.Supp. 825 (E.D. Pa. 1981), the E.D. Pa. means Eastern Judicial District for Pennsylvania.

Parallel Citations

Cases are often found in more than one reporter. For example, U.S. Supreme Court cases can be found in three separate reporters. When you see a U.S. Supreme Court case referred to (that is, "cited"), you might see multiple citations following the case name.

> EXAMPLE: *Lukhard v. Reed*
> - 481 U.S. 368: *United States Reports*
> - 95 L.Ed.2d 328: *Lawyer's Edition, 2d Series*
> - 107 S.Ct. 1807 (1987): *Supreme Court Reporter.*

These three citations are known as *parallel citations* because they parallel each other (that is, refer to the same case).

Citing to Advance Sheets

As explained in the next chapter, advance sheets are the newest cases, those that haven't yet appeared in a reporter and haven't been assigned a citation format like that described above. But functionally, they're no different. Advance sheets are numbered and paginated in accord with the rest of the reporter and serve as the reporter until a new hardcover reporter is produced. When the hardcover book containing the case is published, the volume number for the hardcover is the same as it is on the advance sheet, and the case is found on the same page.

Internet Citations

As a general rule, citations to very recent cases from online services such as Lexis or Westlaw will be accepted by a court. Also, cases published by the Lexis, Westlaw, and VersusLaw services typically include the hard copy citation, which is always acceptable. However, you might run into trouble if you want to specifically cite or quote a certain page of the official reporter in a court document (called a "pincite" because you're pinpointing the exact page), particularly if you are using a free online site. Although Lexis and Westlaw have this functionality, other free websites do not. To get the pincite, you'll have to either look at the official reporter or look in an online service that provides it, normally for a fee.

Finding Cases Online

Cases are now widely available online, and that's often the easiest way to access them, particularly if you know a few significant facts about them. Websites might allow you to limit your search by party name, location or court, and date, for example. At the same time, or instead of placing these limitations, you might be able to limit your search by using keywords. Combined with the power of Boolean searching (discussed in Chapter 2), this is a strong tool for helping you locate cases that you know about, and also new cases in a narrow subject area.

To find online cases for free, try Justia (www.justia.com), Google Scholar (http://scholar.google.com), or LexisWeb (www.lexisweb.com).

Finding State Cases Online

To find state cases online, go to one of the websites identified directly above. If you already know the address for your state judiciary's site, or another address where it maintains its cases, you can go directly there.

Not every website will have all cases for each state, from the beginning of time. Still, most websites are pretty comprehensive, going back to at least the 1950s. If you need case law older than that—which is rare—you might have to use the law library or an online service that costs money, like Westlaw or Lexis. A cheaper alternative, explained in Chapter 2, is VersusLaw.

Finding Federal Cases Online

As we'll cover in greater detail in Chapter 7, there are essentially three types of federal opinions, depending on where (by which court) the lawsuit was litigated: U.S. Supreme Court opinions, federal Circuit Court of Appeal opinions, and U.S. District Court opinions. Under the U.S. District Court category, there are several specialty courts, including bankruptcy courts.

Here is a rough description of what you can find for free online at this time:

- U.S. Supreme Court opinions going back about one hundred years
- Federal Court of Appeals opinions as far back as 1950, depending on the circuit
- recent District Court opinions, depending on the district, and
- most recent bankruptcy court opinions.

The Supreme Court has its own website (www.supremecourt.gov). The circuits, districts, and bankruptcy courts have their own sites as well. Generally, the circuit sites follow the form of www.ca<circuit number>. uscourts.gov, such as www.ca9.uscourts.gov for the Ninth Circuit. District court addresses are more variable. If you don't have your circuit, district, or bankruptcy court's direct address, you can find a link at the website for the federal judiciary (www.uscourts.gov/court-locator).

Also, as we explained in Chapter 2, most primary online legal resources can be found through a basic word search as well as by using one of the dedicated legal information sites mentioned above. For instance, if you are aware of a federal district court case that you want to read, enter the case name or keywords describing the case's subject matter into a search engine and you will likely get a direct link to the case.

Using Westlaw to Find Cases

If your law library offers free access to Westlaw, you're in luck. You can locate the case you're looking for (and all other cases that cite to that case) by entering the citation or the case name into the search box at the top of the page.

For example, if a case name is *Fisher v. Priceless*, you could enter "Priceless" in the search box and pull up all cases containing that name. You could also use "Fisher" in the search, but as a general rule it's more efficient to use one name as long as it is unusual.

Finding Cases in the Law Library

There are a number of ways to find cases in the law library, depending on where you are coming from in your research:

- If you have found a relevant statute and want to read cases that interpret the provisions you are interested in, you can probably find an appropriate citation in the case notes in the annotations (see "Case Notes That Follow Statutes," below), or in the listings for that statute in *Shepard's Citations for Statutes* (discussed below, and further in Chapter 8).
- If your research involves primarily common law (cases), you might find a helpful case citation in a background resource (see "Background Resources," below) or in the subject index to a case digest (see "The Case Digest Subject Index," below).
- If you know the name of a case that you want to find but not its citation, you can use the table of cases in a case digest (see "The Digest Table of Cases," below). If the case is very recent (within the past several months) and not yet listed in the case digest table of cases, you can find it by searching the tables of cases in the advance sheets or recently published hardcover case reporter volumes (see "The Case Reporter Table of Cases," below).
- If you have a case citation for one reporter and you need the citation for a second reporter (that is, the parallel citation), you can find it by using *Shepard's*. (See Chapter 8.)

Below we examine in more detail each of these approaches to finding an appropriate citation to that one good case.

Background Resources

Many of the background materials discussed in Chapter 4 are copiously footnoted with citations to cases that discuss specific points of law covered in the main discussion. For example, consider the page from *California Jurisprudence*, a California legal encyclopedia, shown below.

Although we generally recommend that you go directly from background reading to pertinent statutes—and then to cases—researchers also go directly to any case that appears relevant, or at least note the citation for later reference. For example, if you want to know what your constitutional rights are in the event you are accused of a zoning violation, the case of *Los Angeles v. Gage* (cited in footnote 42 on the page shown below) appears to bear directly on that point. Before you search for a statute related to this issue, you might first read this case to see what light it sheds on your problem. The case itself might discuss relevant statutes.

Finding Recent Cases That Have Interpreted a Statute

Each volume of a case reporter has a "table of statutes" that are mentioned by the cases reported in that volume. The table is usually in the front of the volume. It can be helpful if you know that a statute has been interpreted in some case within a specific period of time.

For example, suppose you hear of a 2012 Illinois court decision that interprets that state's statute governing stock issuances of small corporations. You are familiar with the statute and would like to read the case, but you don't know its name or where to find it. What to do? If you aren't going to do an online search—which is probably the quickest way— you can check the particular statute in the table of statutes in each volume of the *Northeastern Reporter* that contains 2012 Illinois cases. If the statute you are interested in was, in fact, interpreted by a case, the table of statutes will tell you precisely which one and provide its citation. Remember to check the advance sheets for the reporter if you think the case was very recent.

Case Notes That Follow Statutes

If you are searching for a case that has interpreted a relevant statute, check the listings after the text of the statute in an "annotated" version of the code. In the annotated code, one-sentence summaries of court cases that interpret the statute directly follow the notes on the statute's history. These summaries are actually headnotes (discussed below) that have been lifted from the case reporter. Some statutes have been interpreted by the courts so many times that the publisher includes a little index to the case summaries, which are organized by issues raised by the statute. The example below is taken from the *Michigan Compiled Laws Annotated.*

§ 210   ZONING AND OTHER LAND CONTROLS

additional time not exceeding a specified number of days as the court may, within the original number of days, allow, but in no event later than a designated number of days after entry of the order, petition the proper reviewing court to review such order by writ of mandate. No such order of vacation is effective, nor may it be recorded in the office any county recorder, until the time within which a petition for writ of mandate may thus be filed has expired.[41]

§ 211.   Defenses

Generally speaking, any matter that is germane to a cause of action to enforce a zoning or planning enactment and that presents a legal reason why the plaintiff should not succeed therein may constitute a good defense. It is a good defense, for instance, that the enactment under which complaint is made is unconstitutional or invalid, either in toto or as applied to the defendant's property.[42] In order to plead this defense, however, the defendant must have exhausted the administrative remedies available to him under the enactment.[43] And the partial invalidity of

---

41. *Deering's Gov C § 65908 subd (b).*

42. *Los Angeles v Gage,* 127 CA2d 442, 274 P2d 34; *People v Gottfurcht (2d Dist)* 62 CA3d 634, 133 Cal Rptr 270.

Regarding validity of zoning enactments generally, see §§ 43 et seq., supra.

Practice References: 8 POF2d p. 53, Unreasonableness of Zoning Restriction §§ 1 et seq.; 13 POF2d p. 373, Vested Right in Continuation of Zoning §§ 1 et seq.; 14 POF2d p. 117, Zoning—Nonconforming Use §§ 1 et seq.

43. *San Mateo v Hardy,* 64 CA2d 794, 149 P2d 307.

A church and a member thereof failed to exhaust their administrative remedies before defending on constitu-

tional grounds against the enforcement of an ordinance requiring a use permit as a prerequisite to operation of church on property in a residential zone, where it did not appear that the member even applied for any such permit, and the church dismissed its appeal from the planning commission's decision to the city council before decision by the council. *Chico v First Ave. Baptist Church,* 108 CA2d 297, 238 P2d 587.

Property owners whose auto wrecking yard was found to be a nonconforming use and was ordered terminated by the county board of supervisors on recommendation of the county planning commission were not denied procedural due process, where a public hearing after 15 days' notice was held by the planning commission at which hearing the property owners were represented by counsel and witnesses were

---

Page From *California Jurisprudence*

It is often difficult to tell from such a brief summary whether a case is really relevant to the problem you are researching. Fortunately, the summaries also contain a case citation that allows you to look up the case and read it for yourself. It is essential that you read the case itself and not rely solely on the annotation.

Shepard's Citations for Statutes

Several different research tools are provided by a service known as Shepard's. *Shepard's Citations for Statutes* provides a complete listing of each time a particular statute, regulation, or constitutional provision has been referred to and perhaps interpreted by a published decision of a federal or state court. We'll discuss the importance of this tool, and how to use it, in Chapter 8.

Using Digests

Digests are collections of headnotes—one-sentence summaries of how a particular case decided specific legal issues—taken from cases as reported in case reporters and grouped together by topic. These headnotes are at the beginning of cases cited in West reporters. For example, in *Nationwide Insurance Co. v. Ervin*, 231 N.E.2d 112 (1967), one of the issues is classified under "Insurance." The court's holding on that issue is summarized in Headnote 5, shown below, and has been assigned a topic key number, 435.3(1). (LexisNexis has a similar system, but it is only available online, and it is not as extensive as the West system, called the "Key Number" system.) If you are interested in cases that deal with the same subject matter, you can use that headnote to look up similar cases in a digest.

There are a number of different West digests. An overall digest groups all headnote entries from all parts of the country and from all courts. This is made up of two subdigests—the *Decennials* and the *General Digest*. *Decennial* digests were originally published every ten years, with headnotes collected in a publication called the *General Digest* in the interim. About ten of these are published each year, so about 100 will be on the bookshelves before a new *Decennial* emerges.

Historical and Statutory Notes

Source:
P.A.1931, No. 328, § 451a, added by P.A. 1969, No. 243, § 1, Eff. March 20, 1970.

C.L.1948, § 750.451a.
C.L.1970, § 750.451a.

Statute text

750.452. House of ill-fame; keeping, maintaining or operating

Sec. 452. KEEPING, ETC., A HOUSE OF ILL-FAME—Any person who shall keep, maintain or operate, or aid and abet in keeping, maintaining or operating a house of ill-fame, bawdy house or any house or place resorted to for the purpose of prostitution or lewdness shall be guilty of a felony, punishable by imprisonment in the state prison for not more than 5 years or by a fine of not more than 2,500 dollars.

Historical and Statutory Notes

Source:
P.A.1931, No. 328, § 452, Eff. Sept. 18.
C.L.1948, § 750.452.
C.L.1970, § 750.452.

Prior Laws:
R.S.1846, c. 158, § 10.
C.L.1857, § 5865.

C.L.1871, § 7700.
How. § 9286.
P.A.1887, No. 34.
C.L.1897, § 11697.
C.L.1915, § 15471.
P.A.1927, No. 37, § 1.
P.A.1927, No. 40, § 1.
C.L.1929, §§ 16826, 16860.

Cross References

Disorderly persons, see § 750.167.
Public nuisances, abatement, see § 600.3801.

Library References

Disorderly House ☜5.
WESTLAW Topic No. 130.
C.J.S. Disorderly Houses § 5.

Notes of Decisions

Mini-index

Conduct or use of house   3
Elements of offense   1
Evidence   6–8
   In general   6
   Reputation   7
   Weight and sufficiency of evidence   8
House, building or place   2
Indictment or information   5
Instructions   10
Jury questions   9
Keeping of house   4
Reputation, evidence   7
Review   12
Sentence and punishment   11
Weight and sufficiency of evidence   8

or place resorted to for the purpose of prostitution * * * shall be guilty of a felony, * * *.", it is only where the operation or maintenance of a house of ill fame is charged that the reputation of the premises is an essential element. People v. Mayes (1973) 205 N.W.2d 212, 44 Mich.App. 482.

A person who solicited a female, who was at the time a prostitute, and inmate of a house of ill fame, to become an inmate of another such house, was not guilty of a violation of How. § 9286, which provided for the punishment of any person who solicited a female to enter such house for the purpose of "becoming" a prostitute. People v. Cook (1893) 55 N.W. 980, 96 Mich. 368.

Case summaries

1. Elements of offense

Under this section providing that "Any person who shall keep, maintain or operate, or aid and abet in keeping, maintaining or operating a house of ill-fame, bawdy house or any house

2. House, building or place

Evidence that defendant kept a house to which men resorted for purposes of prostitution, that frequent acts of prostitution were there committed with her, and that the house

362

Michigan Statute

A Shortcut When Using the *General Digest*

Each volume of the *General Digest* includes all West key topics and numbers. This means that if you are chasing down the key topic and number of a particular headnote, a relevant case summary might appear in any and all volumes. To make your search more efficient, each tenth volume of the *General Digest* contains a Table of Key Numbers that tells you which volumes in the preceding ten volumes have entries under your key topic and subtopic number.

West has divided this huge digest into smaller ones:

- The *U.S. Supreme Court Digest* covers only U.S. Supreme Court cases.
- The *Federal Practice Digest* covers all federal courts (including the U.S. Supreme Court).
- State digests (for example, the *Illinois Digest* covers only the cases from that state). West Group does not publish digests for every state.
- Regional digests (the states have been grouped into four regions: *Atlantic, Pacific, Northwestern,* and *Southeastern*).

As you can see, some digests overlap. For instance, both the *U.S. Supreme Court Digest* and the *Federal Practice Digest* cover U.S. Supreme Court cases. And both the *Pacific Regional Digest* and the *California Digest* cover California cases. All of the entries in these digests are duplicated in the *Decennial* and *General Digests.*

CAUTION
Always remember to check the pocket part of any digest you use to get the most recent cases.

NATIONWIDE INSURANCE COMPANY v. ERVIN   Ill. 113
Cite as 231 N.E.2d 112

1. Insurance ⟢138(1)

Parties to insurance contract are free to incorporate such provisions into it, if not unlawful, as they see fit and it is then the duty of the court to enforce those provisions.

2. Insurance ⟢146.7(8)

Rule that all ambiguities in policy will be construed most strongly against insurance company, as the party that drafted the policy, only has application where ambiguity in fact exists and court may not distort the contract to create the ambiguity itself.

3. Insurance ⟢146.2

Insurance contract should be construed in accordance with the general contract rule of construction that the agreement should be ascertained as a whole to determine intention of parties and purpose which they sought to accomplish.

4. Insurance ⟢435.2(2)

Enumeration in automobile policy of those few situations where coverage is afforded to the insured with reference to other than named automobile serves to limit areas of risk assumed by insurer.

5. Insurance ⟢435.3(1)

Provision of automobile policy limiting coverage for additional owned automobile to 30 days after acquisition by insured permits owner adequate opportunity to acquire necessary additional insurance and is not intended to cover two automobiles for any protracted period.

6. Insurance ⟢435.2(4)

Provision in automobile policy granting coverage to insured for temporary substitute automobile, not owned by the insured, applies to those situations where the named automobile is in repair shop or withdrawn from use for short period.

7. Insurance ⟢435.3(1)

Where insured had bought second automobile in July 1964 after transmission "went

231 N.E.2d—8

out" of automobile which was named in policy and which remained inoperable in driveway of his home until repair in spring of 1966, and had accident with second automobile on September 26, 1964, the second automobile was not a "replacement" for the named automobile within policy provision extending coverage to replacement automobile.

———◆———

Barrick, Jackson & Switzer, Rockford, for appellant.

Nordquist & Anderson, Rockford, for appellees.

ABRAHAMSON, Justice.

The Nationwide Insurance Company brings this appeal from a decree of the Circuit Court of the 17th Judicial Circuit, Winnebago County, entered December 29, 1966, that found that an automobile insurance policy issued by it to Douglas Ervin "covered" an accident that had occurred on September 26, 1964, and that a certain automobile operated by Ervin at the time of the accident was a "replacement" as defined in the policy.

On August 16, 1963, Nationwide issued its policy of automobile insurance number 94–441–489 to Ervin for coverage of his 1958 Chevrolet. In July of 1964 the transmission of the Chevrolet, according to Ervin, "went out" and he purchased a 1958 Cadillac. The Chevrolet was retained by Ervin, although inoperable, and left in the driveway of his home.

On September 26, 1964, Ervin was in an automobile accident with the Cadillac that involved a truck owned by the Jones Transfer Company, an Illinois Corporation, and another automobile in which Robert Holmes was a passenger. Holmes subsequently brought suit against Ervin and Jones Transfer for injuries allegedly suffered as a result of that accident. Nationwide was called upon by Ervin to defend him in that suit pursuant to the policy.

Headnotes From *Ervin*

The Case Digest Subject Index

If you haven't found a helpful case through one of the methods discussed above, you can proceed directly to a case digest. Even without a relevant headnote, you can use the subject index (called the "Descriptive Word Index" in the West digest system) in a digest to discover "that one good case."

For example, if you want to know whether a father who doesn't support his child because he has lost his job can legally be denied visitation rights, you would be dealing with the topics of "child visitation," "child support," and "child custody." You could use the subject indexes (and tables of contents) in a case digest for your state to find a relevant case that deals with your questions.

The Digest Table of Cases

It is common to hear well-known cases referred to by name only. Lawyers might talk about *Roe v. Wade*, or a criminal defendant might claim that the police violated the *Miranda* case. If you know the name of a case but need its citation to locate and read it, it might be easy to find online. For very famous cases like those above, you can probably even type the case name into a search engine and get a relevant result. For all others, you can use features on websites like Justia (www.justia. com) that allow you to look up cases by limiting by the parties' names, the court, or the year of the case. And of course, a well-written keyword search might yield a relevant result.

If you're in the law library, the West digest system is also an option. Each digest is accompanied by a table of cases that lists all the cases referred to in that digest. By using the correct digest and accompanying table of cases, you can find the name of any case that was decided long enough ago—usually a year or more—to find its way into the table of cases. The table of cases is organized with the plaintiff's name first. If you don't find your case in the table of cases, consult the Defendant-Plaintiff table.

Summing Up ...
How to Find Federal Cases in a Law Library When the Citation Is Unknown

✓ Locate the table of cases for West's *Federal Practice Digest 5th* for the most recent cases (2003 to the present); *4th* for cases reported from 1992 to the beginning of *5th*; *3rd* for cases between 1975 and 1992; *2nd* for cases between 1961 and 1975; and *Modern Federal Practice Digest* for earlier cases.

✓ Find the case name in the hardcover volume or pocket part and note the citation.

✓ If there is more than one entry for the case name, determine from the information provided with each entry (its date and issues decided) which case is the correct one. If cases involve the same topic, note both citations and read both cases.

✓ If you don't find an entry for the case name, reverse the names and look again. If you still don't find it, look in the Defendant-Plaintiff Table of Cases under both names.

When a case starts out in the trial court, the first name is the plaintiff's, and the name after the "v." is the defendant's. However, if an appeal is brought by the defendant, sometimes the defendant's name is put first in the appeal. Because most cases are opinions issued by appellate courts, a case name might in fact consist of the defendant's name in front of the "v." and the plaintiff's name after. If you can't find a case under one name, reverse the names and try again.

Federal cases can be found in the *West Federal Practice Digest*, which has multiple series based on date; Supreme Court cases can also be found in the *U.S. Supreme Court Digest*. If, for example, you are interested in the rights of unwed fathers with respect to decisions affecting their children and have heard that a U.S. Supreme Court case called *Caban v. Mohammed* is relevant, you can use the *West Federal Practice Digest* Table of Cases (start with the *Third Series*) and look it up. In the table of cases for the *Second Series* you would find what is shown below.

82 F P D 2d—61

CALIFANO

References are to Digest Topics and Key Numbers

C., Inc. v. Brookside Drug Store, Inc., Bkrtcy.Conn., 3 B.R. 120. See Brookside Drug Store, Inc., Matter of.
Caban v. Mohammed, U.S.N.Y., 99 S.Ct. 1760, 441 U.S. 380, 60 L.Ed.2d 297.—Adop 2, 7.2(3), 7.4(1); Const Law 70.-3(1), 70.3(6), 224(1), 224(2).
Caban v. Nelson, D.C.Conn., 475 F.Supp. 865. See Velez v. Nelson.
Caban, U. S. ex rel. v. Rowe, D.C.Ill., 449 F.Supp. 360. See U. S. ex rel. Caban v. Rowe.
Cabezal Supermarket, Inc., Matter of, D.C.N.D., 406 F.Supp. 345.—Bankr 303(6), 441.5, 442, 446(8.1).

Caesars Palace Securities Litigation, D.C.N.Y., 360 F.Supp. 366.—Fed Civ Proc 161, 176.
Cafeteria and Restaurant Workers Union, Local 472, AFL-CIO v. McElroy, U.S.Dist.Col., 81 S.Ct. 1743, 367 U.S. 886, 6 L.Ed.2d 1230.—Const Law 278.-4(3), 278.6(1).
Cafferty v. Trans World Airlines, Inc., D.C.Mo., 488 F.Supp. 1076.—Fed Cts 1145; Labor 416.4, 968.
Cagle's, Inc. v. N. L. R. B., C.A.5, 588 F.2d 943.—Labor 290, 367, 379, 382.2, 388.1, 394, 574, 577, 705.

& Supply, Inc., 98 Idaho 495, 567 P.2d 1246.
Calderon v. McGee, C.A.Tex., 589 F.2d 909.—Elections 12; Fed Cts 922.
Calderon v. McGee, C.A.Tex., 584 F.2d 66, vac in part and reh 589 F.2d 909.—Schools 53(1).
Caldwell v. Board of Ed. of City of St. Louis, C.A.Mo., 620 F.2d 1277. See Adams v. U. S.
Caldwell v. Califano, D.C.Ala., 455 F.Supp. 1069.—Social S 142.30.
Caldwell v. Camp, C.A.Mo., 594 F.2d 705. —Courts 508(1), 508(2), 508(7); Fed Civ

Table of Cases in *Federal Practice Digest*

If you're looking for a citation for a state case, use the West state or regional digests. For example, suppose you want to read the landmark Oregon Supreme Court case of *Burnette v. Wahl*. To find the citation, locate the West *Regional Digest* that covers Oregon (the *Pacific Digest*) or the *Oregon Digest* and get the volume containing the table of cases.

Summing Up ...
How to Find State Cases When No Citation Is Known

✓ Locate the table of cases for the state or regional digest that covers your state's cases.

✓ Find the case name in the hardcover volume or pocket part and note the citation.

✓ If there is more than one entry for the case name, determine from the information provided with each entry (its date and issues decided) which case is the correct one. If two cases involve the same topic, note both citations and read both cases.

✓ If you don't find an entry for the case name, reverse the names and look again. If you still don't find it, look in the Defendant-Plaintiff Table of Cases under both names.

The Case Reporter Table of Cases

Each case reporter volume has a table of cases, usually at the front. This table contains a listing of all cases in that volume of the reporter and their page references. This is a very valuable tool if you are searching for a case that you know only by name and that was decided too recently to be listed in a digest table of cases (generally, within the previous six months to one year).

If the case is more recent than the dates of the cases in the latest hardcover case reporter, use the table of cases in the advance sheets. But remember that there is usually a one- to two-month lag between the decision in a case and its publication in an advance sheet. If the case is old enough to be in the hardcover volumes, start with the table of cases in the latest hardcover volume and work backward.

The Case Reporter Subject Index

Each case reporter volume has a subject index, usually at the back. If the reporter is published by West (most are), the index is in fact organized according to the key numbers that have been assigned to the cases contained in the volume. If you know that a case involving a specific topic was decided during a certain time period, but don't know its name, you might be able to find it by looking in the subject index for each volume containing cases for that time period.

For example, suppose you want to read a 1992 Illinois court decision that interprets that state's statute governing stock issuances of small corporations. You could find what you were looking for by using the subject index for the volumes containing cases decided in 1992. Simply look under "corporations," "stock," or "business" until you find what you are looking for, and the index will refer you to the proper case. (See Chapter 3 for help in using a legal index.)

Be prepared to look under more than one topic when trying to find a case through this method. Also be aware that the volume might contain the case you're looking for even though it's not described in the subject index.

The Next Step

Suppose you find a good, relevant case or cases—then what? It is at this point that your research efforts can really become productive. Once you have located even one relevant case, you have the key to all other relevant case law, using many of the tools discussed here. We'll cover one additional tool, which helps you do additional research and verify that the research you've done is still an accurate reflection of the law, in Chapter 8. But first, we're going to cover how to read and understand the cases you've now discovered.

Using Case Law

F inding the case or cases you need is only your first step. Next, you'll have to read and understand what you're looking at. In this chapter, we'll cover the basics of a case, helping you understand what you're reading and how and why it's important.

What Is a Case?

A case starts in the trial court and, if one of the litigants believes an error occurred, could end up being appealed to a higher court—an intermediate appellate court or a supreme court. It is the published opinions of these appellate or supreme courts that make up most of the cases you will find in a law library. The books they are published in are called case reports or reporters.

The Nuts and Bolts of a Case

When you look at the beginning of a case in one of the reporters, you will find certain basic information. Look at the beginning of the *Keywell* case, which we have reproduced below, and follow along as we identify the important information contained on the first page.

The Citation. The editors of the *Federal Reporter* make it impossible for you to forget what case you're reading. At the top of each page, the case name is given and you are told that you should cite the case as, for example, 33 F.3d 159 (2nd Cir. 1994).

The Parties. In a civil case, the parties are known as the plaintiff (the one who filed the lawsuit) and the defendant (the one being sued). In a criminal case, the plaintiff is "the People" of the United States government (if it's a federal case), or "the People" of one of the states (if it's a state case). The defendant is the person being charged with a crime.

Some reported cases are from the trial level. For example, all of the cases in the *Federal Supplement* (F.Supp) are from United States District Courts, and, in that case, the parties are identified as "plaintiff" and "defendant." When a reported case is from one of the appellate courts, the original parties are also identified as the appellant (the one who lost

KEYWELL CORP. v. WEINSTEIN **159**
Cite as 33 F.3d 159 (2nd Cir. 1994)

KEYWELL CORPORATION,
Plaintiff-Appellant,

v.

Daniel C. WEINSTEIN and Anthony
Boscarino, Defendants-Appellees.

No. 1208, Docket 93–7994.

United States Court of Appeals,
Second Circuit.

Argued March 7, 1994.

Decided Aug. 23, 1994.

Purchaser of metal recycling plant
brought suit under CERCLA against two
shareholders, officers, and directors of selling
corporation to recover environmental cleanup
costs. The United States District Court for
the Western District of New York, William
M. Skretny, J., granted summary judgment
for defendants, and purchaser appealed.
The Court of Appeals, Jacobs, Circuit Judge,
held that: (1) genuine issue of material fact
on reasonableness of purchaser's reliance on
seller's misrepresentations precluded summary judgment on fraud claims, but (2) purchaser was not entitled to recover cleanup
costs under CERCLA, since parties clearly
allocated risk of CERCLA liability to purchaser under terms of purchase agreement.

Affirmed in part, and reversed and remanded in part.

1. Federal Courts ⬥766

When reviewing district court's grant of
summary judgment, Court of Appeals must
determine whether genuine issue of material
fact exists and whether district court correctly applied law.

2. Federal Civil Procedure ⬥2470.1

Summary judgment is appropriate only
if, resolving all ambiguities and drawing all
factual inferences in favor of nonmoving party, there is no genuine issue of material fact
to be tried. Fed.Rules Civ.Proc.Rule 56(c),
28 U.S.C.A.

3. Federal Civil Procedure ⬥2544

Party seeking summary judgment bears
burden of demonstrating absence of any genuine factual dispute. Fed.Rules Civ.Proc.
Rule 56(c), 28 U.S.C.A.

4. Federal Civil Procedure ⬥2504

Purchaser raised genuine questions of
fact on reasonableness of its reliance on sellers' misrepresentations regarding release of
hazardous substances on property, precluding summary judgment for sellers on its
claim of fraudulent misrepresentation under
New York law, since reasonable jury could
conclude that purchaser, having conducted
environmental due diligence and received report that was consistent with sellers' representations that there had been no dumping
or other release of hazardous waste on property, had no obligation to investigate further,
despite recommendation for additional testing in environmental audit.

5. Contracts ⬥2

New York law applied to claim questioning validity of contract, though parties chose
Maryland law to govern their contract, where
contract was made in New York.

6. Contracts ⬥2

Questions concerning validity of contract
should be determined by law of jurisdiction
in which it was made.

7. Fraud ⬥3

In New York, plaintiff claiming fraudulent misrepresentation must prove that defendant made material false representation,
defendant intended to defraud plaintiff thereby, plaintiff reasonably relied on representation, and plaintiff suffered damage as result
of such reliance.

8. Fraud ⬥22(1)

When party is aware of circumstances
that indicate certain representations may be
false, that party cannot reasonably rely on
those representations, but must make additional inquiry to determine their accuracy.

9. Fraud ⬥31

Defrauded party is permitted to affirm
contract and seek relief in damages, rather
than choose remedy of rescission.

Opinion in *Keywell Corp. v. Weinstein*

10. Health and Environment ⊙25.5(5.5)

Purchaser of metal recycling plant was not entitled to recover costs of environmental cleanup from two officers, directors, and majority shareholders of selling corporation as signatories to purchase agreement, where agreement clearly allocated risk of CERCLA liability, which purchaser assumed when indemnity period expired, as shortened by the signing of release. Comprehensive Environmental Response, Compensation, and Liability Act of 1980, §§ 107(a), 113(f), 42 U.S.C.A. §§ 9607(a), 9613(f).

11. Health and Environment ⊙25.5(5.5)

Private parties may contractually allocate among themselves any loss they may suffer by imposition of CERCLA liability. Comprehensive Environmental Response, Compensation, and Liability Act of 1980, § 107(e)(1), 42 U.S.C.A. § 9607(e)(1).

Stuart A. Smith, New York City (Alfred Ferrer III, Piper & Marbury, Joseph G. Finnerty, Jr., Charles P. Scheeler, of counsel) for plaintiff-appellant.

Thomas E. Lippard, Pittsburgh, PA (Craig E. Frischman, Thorp Reed & Armstrong, of counsel) for defendant-appellee Weinstein.

Jeremiah J. McCarthy, Buffalo, NY (Phillips, Lytle, Hitchcock, Blaine & Huber, of counsel) for defendant-appellee Boscarino.

Before: WALKER, JACOBS, Circuit Judges and CARMAN,* Judge.

JACOBS, Circuit Judge:

Keywell Corporation ("Keywell") has incurred costs for environmental cleanup at an industrial facility that it purchased in 1987 from Vac Air Alloys Corporation ("Vac Air"). Defendants–Appellees Daniel C. Weinstein ("Weinstein") and Anthony Boscarino ("Boscarino") were shareholders, officers and directors of Vac Air prior to the purchase and at the time of the transaction, and were signatories to the Purchase Agreement. Keywell has brought suit against Weinstein

* Honorable Gregory W. Carman of the United States Court of International Trade, sitting by

and Boscarino, (i) alleging that they induced Keywell to buy the property by making misrepresentations bearing upon the environmental risks at the premises, and (ii) alleging that, as owners and operators of Vac Air, they are strictly liable to Keywell for their equitable share of response costs pursuant to §§ 107(a) and 113(f) of the Comprehensive Environmental Response, Compensation, and Liability Act ("CERCLA"). 42 U.S.C. §§ 9607(a) and 9613(f). Following the parties' submission of cross-motions for summary judgment, the district court dismissed Keywell's claims, finding as a matter of law that Keywell could not have reasonably relied on the allegedly fraudulent misrepresentations, and that Keywell had contractually released its right to sue defendants under CERCLA.

We affirm the dismissal of the CERCLA claims on the ground that the parties allocated the risk of CERCLA liability in their Purchase Agreement, the terms of which establish that such risk now falls on Keywell. However, we reverse the dismissal of the diversity fraud claims and remand for further proceedings.

BACKGROUND

The facts, drawing all justifiable inferences in favor of the non-movant Keywell, are as follows. Weinstein founded Vac Air in 1966 and, until the time Keywell purchased certain Vac Air assets in December 1987, was a principal shareholder, president, chief executive officer, and member of the board of directors of the company. Boscarino joined Vac Air in 1971 as an assistant to the secretary/treasurer, and by 1978 he had become a stockholder, director, and vice-president of the company. Both Weinstein and Boscarino took an active part in conducting the business of Vac Air, which included the operation of a metals recycling plant located in Frewsburg, New York (the "Frewsburg plant").

From the time Vac Air was founded in 1966 until Keywell's acquisition of assets in December 1987, the Frewsburg plant recycled scrap metal—a process that entailed the

designation.

Opinion in Keywell Corp. v. Weinstein (continued)

and is now bringing the appeal) and the appellee (the one who won and is now having to defend that victory).

In the *Keywell* case, Keywell Corporation is identified as the "Plaintiff-Appellant." This label tells you that Keywell initiated the lawsuit at the trial level and was the one to file the present appeal. Weinstein and Boscarino were the defendants at the trial level and are the appellees now.

The Docket Number. When a case is filed in the trial court, it is given a number, called the "docket number," by the clerk of the court. While the case remains in the trial court, it is referred to by that number. If the case goes to the appellate level, it will be given a different number by the clerk of the appellate court. The docket number is also the number that is attached to an opinion when it is first issued (as a "slip opinion"), before it goes into the reporter series and gets its permanent cite.

In the *Keywell* case, the docket number is "No. 1208 Docket Number 93-7994." When this case was first listed in *Shepard's*, the listing would have looked like this: "Dk2 93-7994." The "Dk2" tells you that this is a slip opinion from the Second Circuit.

The Court. This is the court that wrote the decision. In the *Keywell* case, the decision was written by the United States Court of Appeals for the Second Circuit, which heard the case. To learn which trial court had the case originally, read The Summary, discussed below.

The Dates. Many opinions include the date that the case was argued and the date the court issued the opinion. If the decision announces a new rule of law, or invalidates a statute, the issue date will be important to know. (But watch out: Opinions do not become "final" until the time for granting a rehearing has passed. The local rules for each court will specify how long that time period might be.)

The Summary. This is usually a one-paragraph summary of the decision, written by the editors of the reporter series and not part of the decision itself. This text cannot be cited. If the opinion is from a trial court (like one you would read in "F.Supp.," which is the reporter series that contains federal district court cases), it will list the issue and the decision. If the opinion is from an appellate-level court, the summary will describe the trial court's decision and will go on to explain the holding of the appellate court.

The Decision. Many summaries end with a one-line phrase describing the holding of the court. In *Keywell*, we are told that the lower court's decision was "Affirmed in part, and reversed and remanded in part." This means that the decision of the trial court was upheld as to one or more issues, but that they were reversed on other issues and the case was sent back to the trial court for further proceedings as directed by the appellate decision.

How the Opinion Itself Is Organized

As we've explained, a party can file an appeal if he or she disagrees with the outcome at trial. In most appeals, the appealing party is limited to disputing mistakes the lower court made when applying the law. Except in rare circumstances, there's no fresh look at the facts, as there was at trial. Instead, the appellate court looks at the trial court's rulings to decide whether it followed the law when it applied it to the facts. Then, the appellate court issues an opinion.

Normally, every intermediate appellate or supreme court opinion contains four basic elements:

1. **A statement of facts.** These are accepted by the court as true, and are taken from the lower court's determination of the facts, unless the lower court's determinations were clearly in error.

2. **A statement of the legal issue or issues.** Put another way, this is the legal question at issue—in what way do the parties disagree about how the lower court handled the case?

3. **A ruling or holding.** This is an answer to the issues presented for resolution. If the court agrees with the lower court's conclusions and the relief it ordered for one or both of the parties, the lower court decision is "affirmed." If the court disagrees with either or both of these aspects of the lower court's decision, the decision is "reversed."

   Sometimes lower court decisions are affirmed in part and reversed in part. If the intermediate appellate or supreme court agrees substantially with the lower court, but disagrees with some particular point, it might modify or amend the decision. Usually, in the case of a complete or partial reversal, the case is sent back to the lower court to take further action consistent with the intermediate appellate or supreme court's opinion. This is called a remand.

4. **Discussion.** This explains why the ruling was made—the court's reasoning or rationale. The court's reasoning is usually the longest part of the case and the most difficult to understand.

Many court opinions present these four components—facts, issues, decision, and reasoning—in this order. Others do not. For instance, one format used by some courts is a summary of the issue and the decision in the first couple of paragraphs, followed by a statement of the facts and the reasoning.

The actual opinion issued in a case called *Deason v. Metropolitan Property & Liability Insurance Co.* is shown below. The four elements described above are labeled.

Courts Where Appeals Are Normally Filed				
Courts Cases Appealed From	**U.S. Supreme Court**	**U.S. Court of Appeals**	**State Supreme Court**	**State Court of Appeal**
U.S. Courts of Appeals	✓			
U.S. District Courts	If issued by a 3-judge panel OR when the U.S., its agent or employee is a party, and an act of Congress is held unconstitutional on its face (not as applied)	✓		
State Supreme Courts	If a federal question is involved	✓		
State Courts of Appeal	If a federal question is involved and the State Supreme Court has denied relief OR declined to hear the case		✓	
State Trial Courts			If there's no court of appeal OR it is a special case (appeal of death penalty case)	✓

DEASON v. METRO. PROP. & LIABILITY INS. CO. Ill. 783
Cite as 474 N.E.2d 783 (Ill.App. 5 Dist. 1985)

130 Ill.App.3d 620
85 Ill.Dec. 823

Mary Kaye DEASON, Administratrix of the Estate of David A. Deason, Deceased, and Mary Kaye Deason, Plaintiff-Appellee,

and

Florence Petro, Administrator of the Estate of George Petro, deceased; Sherrill Josephson, Administratrix of the Estate of Mathew Josephson, deceased; and Michael Petro, Counter-Plaintiffs-Appellees,

v.

METROPOLITAN PROPERTY & LIABILITY INSURANCE COMPANY, a Corporation, Defendant-Appellant,

and

Auto-Owners Insurance Company, a Corporation, et al., Defendants.

No. 5–84–0073.

Appellate Court of Illinois,
Fifth District.

Jan. 10, 1985.

Action was brought against automobile insurer seeking a judgment declaring that policy issued to driver's parents afforded secondary coverage in connection with an accident which occurred while insureds' son was driving his grandmother's automobile. The Circuit Court, St. Clair County, Richard P. Goldenhersh, J., entered judgment in favor of plaintiffs, and insurer appealed. The Appellate Court, Harrison, J., held that automobile operated by driver was not a "temporary substitute vehicle" under terms of automobile policy issued to parents so as to afford secondary coverage in connection with driver's accident.

Reversed.

1. Declaratory Judgment ⚮168
   Case involving question whether coverage existed under terms of automobile insurer's policy was proper subject for declaratory judgment action.

2. Insurance ⚮435.2(4)
   Where driver's use of his grandmother's automobile was not to be temporary, but regular and permanent, and the automobile was not intended by driver's parents to be a substitute for either of two automobiles owned by driver's father, under terms of automobile policy issued to parents, the automobile operated by driver was not a "temporary substitute vehicle" so as to afford secondary coverage in connection with driver's accident.

   See publication Words and Phrases for other judicial constructions and definitions.

3. Evidence ⚮200
   In action brought against automobile insurer seeking a judgment declaring that policy issued to driver's parents afforded secondary coverage in connection with an accident which occurred while insureds' son was driving his grandmother's automobile, trial court correctly noted in its judgment that statements by certain employees of insurer to the effect that they believed driver's parents' policy afforded coverage were merely opinions and were not binding on a court in its consideration of the legal question presented.

Feirich, Schoen, Mager, Green & Associates, Carbondale, for defendant-appellant.

C.E. Heiligenstein, Brad L. Badgley, Belleville, for Mary Kaye Deason.

H. Carl Runge, Jr., Runge & Gumbel, P.C., Collinsville, for Beth Martell, a minor, by her father and next friend, John Martell, John Martell and Patsie Gott, Administratrix of the Estate of Lisa J. Gott, Deceased.

Michael P. Casey, Edward R. Vrdolyak, Ltd., Chicago, for Florence Petro & Sherrill Josephson & Michael Petro.

HARRISON, Justice:

[1] Metropolitan Property & Liability Insurance Company (hereinafter referred to as Metropolitan) appeals from a judgment of the circuit court of St. Clair Coun-

Opinion in *Deason v. Metropolitan*

784 Ill.   **474 NORTH EASTERN REPORTER, 2d SERIES**

ty declaring that a policy of insurance issued by Metropolitan afforded secondary coverage in connection with a November 30, 1980, accident involving a 1975 Mercury Comet driven by Christopher Warner. The primary issue for our consideration is whether the trial court properly concluded that, under the terms of the policy issued by Metropolitan to Christopher Warner's parents, the Comet operated by Christopher Warner was a "temporary substitute automobile". Because this case involves the question of whether or not coverage exists under the terms of Metropolitan's policy, it is a proper subject for a declaratory judgment action. *Reagor v. Travelers Insurance Co.* (1980), 92 Ill.App.3d 99, 102–03, 47 Ill.Dec. 507, 415 N.E.2d 512.

The policy in question provides coverage to the insured for accidents arising out of the ownership, maintenance or use of an owned or non-owned automobile. The terms "non-owned automobile" and "owned automobile" are defined in the policy as follows:

" '[N]on-owned automobile' means an *automobile* which is neither owned by nor furnished nor available for the regular use of either the *named insured* or any *relative*, other than a *temporary substitute automobile*, and includes a *utility trailer* while used with any such *automobile:*

  •   •   •   •   •   •

'[O]wned automobile' means

(a) a *private passenger automobile* or *utility automobile* owned by the *named insured* and described in the Declarations to which the Automobile Liability Coverage of the policy applies and for which a specific premium for such insurance is charged, or

(b) a *private passenger automobile* or *utility automobile* ownership of which is newly acquired by the *named insured*, provided (i) it replaces an *owned automobile* as defined in (a) above, or (ii) METROPOLITAN insures all *automobiles* owned by the *named insured* on the date of such acquisition and the *named in-*

sured notifies METROPOLITAN within thirty (30) days of such acquisition of his election to make this and no other policy issued by METROPOLITAN applicable to such *automobile* and pays any additional premium required therefor, or

(c) a *temporary substitute automobile:* "

The policy defines "temporary substitute automobile" in this manner:

" '[T]emporary substitute automobile' means an *automobile* not owned by the *named insured* or any resident of the same household, while temporarily used with the permission of the owner as a substitute for an *owned automobile* when withdrawn from normal use for servicing or repair or because of breakdown, loss or destruction: "

The facts relevant to a determination of whether the 1975 Comet was a temporary substitute automobile are not in significant dispute. Christopher Warner spent the summer of 1980 in Ohio with his grandmother, Vera Fry. Ms. Fry, an Ohio resident, owned the 1975 Comet, which was insured by a company other than Metropolitan. During that summer, arrangements were made whereby Christopher would take the Comet with him when he returned to his parents' Cobden, Illinois home at the end of the summer. It was further agreed that Christopher would return to Ohio at Christmas time and pay Vera Fry $100 after which she would have the title to the Comet transferred to Christopher and one of his parents. Christopher did in fact bring the Comet back to Cobden in August, 1980, and he and his parents used it regularly. On November 30, 1980, before Christopher had paid any money to Vera Fry, and before title to the Comet had been transferred, the accident in question occurred.

On the date of the accident, Andrew Warner, Christopher's father, owned a 1973 Mercury and a 1974 Dodge pickup truck. Both of these vehicles were insured by Metropolitan. Neither was operable at

Opinion in *Deason v. Metropolitan* (continued)

DEASON v. METRO. PROP. & LIABILITY INS. CO.   Ill.   78£
Cite as 474 N.E.2d 783 (Ill.App. 5 Dist. 1985)

the time of the accident; the Mercury had a defective transmission and the Dodge had a twisted drive shaft. Both vehicles were put back into operation shortly after the accident involving the Comet. During his deposition, Andrew Warner testified as follows:

> "Q. Did you have any intention if the Comet hadn't been wrecked, did you have any intention to dispose of either of these other two cars just because you got the Comet?
> A. Oh, no."

[2] In ruling that Metropolitan's policy afforded secondary coverage in connection with the accident involving the 1975 Comet, the court found that Christopher Warner was "a relative operating a temporary substitute" automobile. Metropolitan contends that this conclusion is incorrect, and we are compelled to agree. Under the terms of the policy, a temporary substitute automobile is defined as one "temporarily used with the permission of the owner as a substitute for an owned automobile when withdrawn from normal use for servicing or repair or because of breakdown, loss, or destruction." Here, the unequivocal deposition testimony of all concerned establishes that Christopher Warner's use of the Comet was not to be temporary, but regular and permanent, as it was the intention of both Vera Fry and Christopher Warner that he would pay $100 for the car at Christmas time, and would not return it to her. Moreover, the Comet was not intended by the Warners to be a substitute for either the Mercury or the Dodge; rather, it was to be kept as a third car, and the fact that the Dodge and Mercury broke down during the Warners' use of the Comet was entirely coincidental. Under these circumstances, the "temporary substitute" provision of the policy issued by Metropolitan did not encompass Christopher Warner's use of the Comet on the date of the accident. (See *Sturgeon v. Automobile Club Inter-Insurance Exchange* (1979), 77 Ill. App.3d 997, 1000, 34 Ill.Dec. 66, 397 N.E.2d 522.) This conclusion is buttressed by the holding of *Nationwide Insurance Compa-*

ny v. *Ervin* (1967), 87 Ill.App.2d 432, 436-37, 231 N.E.2d 112, wherein it was recog nized that a "temporary substitute" provi sion of the type under consideration here is to be applied to those situations where an insured automobile is withdrawn from use for a short period, and not where, as here coverage is sought to be extended to an additional automobile for a significan' length of time.

[3] *Providence Mutual Casualty Com pany v. Sturms* (1962), 37 Ill.App.2d 304 185 N.E.2d 366, relied on by appellees, is not on point. *Sturms* addresses the ques tion of whether coverage afforded on a temporary substitute automobile expires immediately upon repair of the insured's regular automobile (37 Ill.App.2d 304, 306 185 N.E.2d 366), and does not discuss the more fundamental issue of when a vehicle is considered to be a temporary substitute in the first place. While appellees also suggest that portions of Metropolitan's claim file show that certain Metropolitan employees believe that the policy in ques tion afforded coverage, the trial court cor rectly noted in its judgment that these statements are merely opinions, and are not binding on a court in its consideration of the legal question presented. 31A C.J.S *Evidence* § 272(b) (1964).

For the foregoing reasons, the judgment of the circuit court of St. Clair County is reversed.

Reversed.

JONES, P.J., and KARNS, J., concur.

Opinion in *Deason v. Metropolitan* (continued)

How Appellate Courts Decide Cases

Appellate courts comprise anywhere from three to nine justices. For example, the California Supreme Court and the New York Court of Appeals have seven justices, the Vermont Supreme Court has five, and the U.S. Supreme Court has nine. In New York (and in Texas for criminal cases), the highest state court is called the Court of Appeals rather than the Supreme Court.

Only the actual decision of the majority (or plurality) of justices and the principles of law that are absolutely necessary to that decision serve as precedent for other courts. Other discussion in the opinion might be helpful in understanding the decision, but is not binding on other courts. The court's decision and the law necessary to arrive at it are called the "holding." The rest of the decision is called "dicta."

A justice on an appellate court who disagrees with the decision of the majority on a case might issue a "dissenting" opinion, which is published along with the majority's opinion. No matter how passionate a dissent happens to be, it has no effect on the particular case. However, it might have a persuasive effect on judges in future court decisions.

A justice who agrees with the majority decision but disagrees with the reasons given for it might issue a "concurring opinion," which is published along with the majority's opinion. A concurring opinion also can have a persuasive influence on future court decisions.

If the main opinion in the case is supported by less than a majority—called a "plurality" opinion—the concurring opinion can in fact operate as a weak type of authority for future cases. For instance, in a 1985 case, the U.S. Supreme Court issued an opinion in which only four justices joined. A fifth justice, Chief Justice Burger, concurred and swung the court's holding to the plurality's view; if Chief Justice Burger had sided with the other four justices, they might have been the majority (or plurality, if he only concurred with and did not join their opinion).

For a fascinating account of how the U.S. Supreme Court decides its cases, read *The Brethren: Inside the Supreme Court*, by Woodward and Armstrong (Simon and Schuster, 1979).

Using Synopses and Headnotes to Read and Understand a Case

In addition to the court opinions, the publishers of case reports also publish a one-paragraph synopsis of the case and some helpful one-sentence summaries of the legal issues discussed in it. The synopsis and headnotes come just before the opinion itself. Below are the headnotes from *Deason v. Metropolitan Property & Liability Insurance Co.*

The headnotes are numbered in the order in which the legal issues they summarize appear in the opinion. The part of the opinion covered by each headnote is marked off in the opinion with a number in brackets. See the *Deason* opinion, above, for an example.

Headnotes can be very useful in several ways. They serve as a table of contents to the opinion, so that if you are only interested in one of the many issues raised in a case, you can skim the headnotes, find the relevant issue and then turn to the corresponding bracketed number in the opinion. As discussed in Chapter 6, headnotes also allow discussions of legal issues in one case to be cross-indexed to similar discussions in other cases by the use of "digests." Finally, headnotes are very helpful when you are "Shepardizing" a case. We'll cover that in Chapter 9.

> CAUTION
>
> **Headnotes are prepared by the publisher. They are not part of the case as such.** Because the editors who prepare the headnotes are human, don't rely on the headnotes to accurately state the issue or principle of law as it appears in the opinion. Headnotes tend to overly simplify issues, so beware— what might seem like a helpful case holding might not be what the case stands for at all. Also, never quote a headnote in any argument you submit to a court, because again, you're likely to misrepresent what the case stands for. Instead, you must read the pertinent section of the opinion for yourself and, if the case is helpful, pincite to the appropriate page.

DEASON v. METRO. PROP. & LIABILITY INS. CO.   Ill. **783**
Cite as 474 N.E.2d 783 (Ill.App. 5 Dist. 1985)

130 Ill.App.3d 620
85 Ill.Dec. 823

Mary Kaye DEASON, Administratrix of
the Estate of David A. Deason, Deceased, and Mary Kaye Deason, Plaintiff-Appellee,

and

Florence Petro, Administrator of the Estate of George Petro, deceased; Sherrill
Josephson, Administratrix of the Estate
of Mathew Josephson, deceased; and
Michael Petro, Counter-Plaintiffs-Appellees,

v.

METROPOLITAN PROPERTY & LIA-
BILITY INSURANCE COMPANY, a
Corporation, Defendant-Appellant,

and

Auto-Owners Insurance Company, a
Corporation, et al., Defendants.

No. 5–84–0073.

Appellate Court of Illinois,
Fifth District.

Jan. 10, 1985.

Action was brought against automobile
insurer seeking a judgment declaring that
policy issued to driver's parents afforded
secondary coverage in connection with an
accident which occurred while insureds' son
was driving his grandmother's automobile.
The Circuit Court, St. Clair County, Richard P. Goldenhersh, J., entered judgment in
favor of plaintiffs, and insurer appealed.
The Appellate Court, Harrison, J., held that
automobile operated by driver was not a
"temporary substitute vehicle" under
terms of automobile policy issued to parents so as to afford secondary coverage in
connection with driver's accident.

Reversed.

1. Declaratory Judgment ⬅168

Case involving question whether coverage existed under terms of automobile insurer's policy was proper subject for declaratory judgment action.

2. Insurance ⬅435.2(4)

Where driver's use of his grandmother's automobile was not to be temporary,
but regular and permanent, and the automobile was not intended by driver's parents
to be a substitute for either of two automobiles owned by driver's father, under terms
of automobile policy issued to parents, the
automobile operated by driver was not a
"temporary substitute vehicle" so as to afford secondary coverage in connection with
driver's accident.

See publication Words and Phrases
for other judicial constructions and
definitions.

3. Evidence ⬅200

In action brought against automobile
insurer seeking a judgment declaring that
policy issued to driver's parents afforded
secondary coverage in connection with an
accident which occurred while insureds' son
was driving his grandmother's automobile,
trial court correctly noted in its judgment
that statements by certain employees of
insurer to the effect that they believed
driver's parents' policy afforded coverage
were merely opinions and were not binding
on a court in its consideration of the legal
question presented.

Headnote [label for "1. Declaratory Judgment ⬅168"]

Headnotes From *Deason v. Metropolitan Property & Liability Insurance Co.*

How Cases Are Published

In Chapter 6, we explained that cases are published in volumes in the library called reporters. There are many separate reporters for different courts and for geographical areas; an opinion might be published in more than one. For example, New York Court of Appeals cases are found in a publication titled *New York Appeals* and in a regional reporter called the *Northeastern Reporter,* which contains state court cases from New York, Illinois, Indiana, Massachusetts, and Ohio.

Federal Cases

Federal court cases are published according to the court they are decided by.

U.S. District Court Cases

Only a very small percentage—those deemed to be of widespread legal interest—of U.S. District Court cases are published. This means that occasionally a case can be on the front page of your local paper for weeks and never be reported. There is no automatic connection between sensational facts and legal import. All published U.S. District Court cases are collected in the *Federal Supplement* (F.Supp.) or *Federal Rules Decisions* (F.R.D.).

Bankruptcy Court Cases

Decisions of the U.S. bankruptcy courts are reported in the *Bankruptcy Reporter* (B.R.), published by West.

U.S. Court of Appeals Cases

All published decisions by the U.S. Courts of Appeals are collected in the *Federal Reporter.* This is currently in its third series and is abbreviated as "F." or "F.2d" or "F.3d" (*Federal Reporter, Third Series*).

The U.S. Court of Appeals (the intermediate federal appellate court) is divided into 12 circuits and a special court called the Federal Circuit that hears appeals relating to patents and customs. Below is a table of the states in each circuit.

Circuits of the U.S. Court of Appeals

First Circuit
  Maine
  Massachusetts
  New Hampshire
  Puerto Rico
  Rhode Island

Second Circuit
  Connecticut
  New York
  Vermont

Third Circuit
  Delaware
  New Jersey
  Pennsylvania
  Virgin Islands

Fourth Circuit
  Maryland
  North Carolina
  South Carolina
  Virginia
  West Virginia

Fifth Circuit
  Louisiana
  Mississippi
  Texas

Sixth Circuit
  Kentucky
  Michigan
  Ohio
  Tennessee

Seventh Circuit
  Illinois
  Indiana
  Wisconsin

Eighth Circuit
  Arkansas
  Iowa
  Minnesota
  Missouri
  Nebraska
  North Dakota
  South Dakota

Ninth Circuit
  Alaska
  Arizona
  California
  Guam
  Hawaii
  Idaho
  Montana
  Nevada
  Oregon
  Washington

Tenth Circuit
  Colorado
  Kansas
  New Mexico
  Oklahoma
  Utah
  Wyoming

Eleventh Circuit
  Alabama
  Florida
  Georgia

District of Columbia Circuit
  Washington, DC

Federal Circuit
  Patent and Customs Cases

U.S. Supreme Court Cases

Last, but certainly not least, United States Supreme Court cases have three separate reporters. Each of them contains the same cases but different editorial enhancements as described below:

- *United States Supreme Court Reports (U.S.).* This reporter is the so-called "official" reporter, commissioned by Congress. Other reports that cover these cases are "unofficial" reports. This doesn't mean the opinions collected in the official reporter are more accurate or authoritative; for basic legal research purposes there is little difference among them. However, most courts require a citation to the official reporter when referring to a U.S. Supreme Court case in court documents.

- *Supreme Court Reporter (S.Ct.).* This reporter is part of the West Group series of reporters, which means it is also part of an elaborate cross-reference system known as the "key system" (explained in Chapter 6). If you are using the West research system, it is a good idea to use this reporter.

- *United States Supreme Court Reports, Lawyers' Edition (L.Ed.).* This reporter is published by Lexis Publishing and is very handy if you are using that company's research system. This reporter contains not only all of the U.S. Supreme Court cases (as do the other two reports), but also provides considerable editorial comment about the case's impact, including an annotation that relates the case to other cases on the same subject.

You might wonder why it is necessary to have three reporters for a single court. It's really not; many small law libraries only buy one, or two at the most.

State Court Cases

Each state arranges for its appellate court cases to be published in official state reporters. In the larger states, there are usually two official reporters: one for the highest court cases and another for the intermediate appellate court cases. If you are interested in using the official reporters for your state while doing your research, ask your law librarian where the official state reporter is shelved.

In addition to these official reporters, the cases of each state—both supreme court and appellate—are published by West in a series of reporters called "regional reporters." West has divided the country into seven regions, and the cases produced by the courts of each state in a region are published together. For example, cases from Alabama, Florida, Louisiana, and Mississippi are all published in the *Southern Reporter.*

West also publishes state-specific versions of its regional reporters. For this reason, the *Southern Reporter* found in an Alabama library might contain only Alabama cases.

Most academic law libraries carry both the official reporters for their own state and the regional reporters for the entire country. However, when it comes to cases from other states, they probably won't have state-specific reporters. So if you are in New Hampshire and want to look up a New Hampshire case, you will have a choice between the New Hampshire official reports and the *Atlantic Reporter* (the regional reporter for the Northeast). However, if you want to find a Florida case, you will most likely need to use the *Southern Reporter.*

Keeping Case Reporters Up-to-Date

A significant time lag usually exists between the date a case is decided and publication of a new hardcover reporter. To make new cases available during the interim, reporters have weekly update pamphlets called "advance sheets." The chances are great that if a case was decided within several months (or even years for some Supreme Court cases) of when you are doing your research, it will be found in an advance sheet rather than in the latest hardcover volumes. Obviously, this won't be nearly so problematic if you are doing your research online.

The National Reporter System

Full Name of Reporter	Abbreviation	State Courts Included
Atlantic Reporter (First, Second, and Third Series)	A., A.2d, and A.3d	Supreme and intermediate appellate courts in DC, Connecticut, Delaware, Maine, Maryland, New Hampshire, New Jersey, Pennsylvania, Rhode Island, and Vermont
North Eastern Reporter (First, Second, and Third Series)	N.E., N.E.2d, and N.E.3d	Court of Appeals in New York and supreme and intermediate appellate courts in Illinois, Indiana, Massachusetts, and Ohio
North Western Reporter (First and Second Series)	N.W. and N.W.2d	Supreme and intermediate appellate courts in Iowa, Michigan, Minnesota, Nebraska, North Dakota, South Dakota, and Wisconsin
Pacific Reporter (First, Second, and Third Series)	P., P.2d, and P.3d	Supreme and intermediate appellate courts in Alaska, Arizona, California (Sup. Ct. only since 1960), Colorado, Hawaii, Idaho, Kansas, Montana, Nevada, New Mexico, Oklahoma, Oregon, Utah, Washington, and Wyoming
South Eastern Reporter (First and Second Series)	S.E. and S.E.2d	Supreme and intermediate appellate courts in Georgia, North Carolina, South Carolina, Virginia, and West Virginia
Southern Reporter (First, Second, and Third Series)	So., So.2d, and So.3d	Supreme and intermediate appellate courts in Alabama, Florida, Louisiana, and Mississippi
South Western Reporter (First, Second, and Third Series)	S.W., S.W.2d, and S.W.3d	Supreme and intermediate appellate courts in Arkansas, Kentucky, Missouri, Tennessee, and Texas
New York Supplement (First and Second Series)	N.Y.S. and N.Y.S. 2d	All New York supreme and intermediate appellate courts
California Reporter (First, Second, and Third Series)	Cal.Rptr., Cal. Rptr. 2d , and Cal.Rptr. 3d	All California supreme and intermediate appellate courts

It is important to remember that all appellate opinions (and some at the trial level) are followed by a period of time during which the parties can request and the court can grant a rehearing before the same court. Also, most decisions are appealable by means of a petition for hearing or a writ of *certiorari* to the next higher court. Opinions might appear in the advance sheets during this time period. If either a rehearing or a petition for hearing or *certiorari* is granted, the underlying opinion is rendered null and void, and it cannot be cited. For this reason, the advance sheets have subsequent case history tables that you should consult whenever you cite to a case that is still in the advance sheets.

Most law libraries shelve advance sheets next to the hardcover volumes. Sometimes, however, they are kept behind the reference desk.

The Newest Cases

When an opinion is issued by a judge, it has a life of its own before it appears in the weekly advance sheets. Typically, the opinion is signed by the judge(s) and then sent to the clerk's office for distribution to the public. Copies go to the parties, the general press, the local legal newspapers, the case reporter services (for inclusion in the next advance sheet booklet), and *Shepard's*.

During this time, it is referred to as a "slip opinion," and it is identified by its docket number—the court number the case received when it was first filed. When it appears in the next week's advance sheets it will get a regular citation; but before that time, it might be picked up by *Shepard's* if it cites other cases. *Shepard's* will refer to the case by its docket number. If you need to see an opinion that is identified only by its docket number, your best bet is to go to an online site or use one of the computerized research services (Lexis or Westlaw).

It is risky to cite a slip opinion. As with opinions in the advance sheets, slip opinions can be wiped off the books if a rehearing is ordered or a higher court decides to take the case. Slip opinions do not become "final" and citable until the time for filing these motions has passed. If you cite a slip opinion, be sure to thereafter track its course through the advance sheets, by checking to see if it appears and whether it shows up in the subsequent case history table.

Researching California Cases

In California, unlike most other states, there is a good reason to use the official reporters—*California Reports* for California Supreme Court cases and *California Appellate Reports* for California Court of Appeal cases. This is because the California Supreme Court frequently depublishes published Court of Appeal opinions. Depublished opinions can no longer be relied on as correct statements of California law. When a case is depublished, its conclusion remains intact as far as the case's parties are concerned, but it is taken out of the official reports and replaced with a notation to that effect. It usually remains in the unofficial reports. By using the unofficial reports, you run a small risk of relying on a case that appears helpful but no longer exists from a legal standpoint.

In California, the advance sheets for the official case reports published by Lexis contain a section at the back that tells you what has happened to cases since they were published in the reports. Cases are sometimes reheard, taken for hearing by the Supreme Court, or ordered depublished. A table that appears in the advance sheets—called the cumulative Subsequent History Table—informs you when this happens. You might also use *Shepard's* (discussed in Chapter 8), to find out whether a case has been depublished.

Although the concept of depublication appears Orwellian, its purpose is to allow the Supreme Court to administratively weed out misstatements of the law without having to handle the errant case on appeal. Also, it allows a weak or divided Court to render impotent a decision by a lower court that creates new law or is controversial in nature. Depublication allows the appellate court decision to operate as far as the parties to that case are concerned, but its decision does not become a precedent upon which others can rely.

Publishing Cases Online

Cases have been available electronically for many years. However, the two large legal databases—Lexis and Westlaw—charge substantial fees for their use and have pretty much been inaccessible to the individual legal researcher.

However, many law libraries now subscribe to one or both of these services and make them available to their patrons. So, if you have access to a law library that gives you access to Westlaw or Lexis, the law librarian can get you started on your case research. After a few minutes, you'll have the hang of it.

As we explained in Chapter 2, you can access cases online for no cost, on websites like Justia (www.justia.com) or FindLaw (www.findlaw. com). While this allows you to see the actual text of the cases and will give you the citation to the official reporter, online cases don't always have "pincites"—that is, the ability to tell you on what page of an official reporter particular text appears. This isn't generally a problem, unless you're drafting a document that will be submitted to a court. In that case, you will generally need a pincite from the official reporter.

You might need to go to the library, or you might want to utilize an online service like Westlaw on a short-term basis.

How Cases Affect Later Disputes

Past decisions in appellate cases are powerful predictors of what the courts are likely to do in future cases given a similar set of facts. Most judges try hard to be consistent with decisions that either they or a higher court have made. This consistency is very important to a just legal system and is the essence of the common law tradition. (Common law— the decisions of courts over the years—is discussed in Chapter 3.) For this reason, if you can find a previous court decision that rules your way on facts similar to your situation, you have a good shot at persuading a judge to follow that case and decide in your favor.

There are two basic principles to understand when you're reading cases with an eye to using them to persuade a judge to rule your way. One is called "precedent," the other "persuasive authority."

Precedent

In the legal sense, a precedent is an earlier case that is relevant to a case to be decided. If there is nothing to distinguish the circumstances of the current case from the already-decided one, the earlier holding is considered binding on the court.

The idea of a precedent comes from a basic principle of the American common law system: *stare decisis* (Latin for "Let the decision stand"). Once a high court decides how the law should be applied to a particular set of facts, this decision controls later decisions by that and other courts.

A case is only a precedent as to its particular decision and the law necessary to arrive at that decision. If, in passing, a judge deals with a legal question that is not absolutely essential to the decision, the reasoning and opinion in respect to this tangential question are not precedent, but nonbinding "dicta."

> EXAMPLE: A Court of Appeals rules that the lesser dung beetle is protected under the Endangered Species Act. As part of his reasoning, the judge writing the opinion states that as he reads the statute, even mosquitoes are entitled to protection. Since the court was asked to rule on the lesser dung beetle, the judge's comments on mosquitoes are dicta—language unnecessary to deciding the case before the court—and not binding as to any future dispute on that point.

It is common for courts to avoid overruling earlier decisions by distinguishing the earlier one from the present one on the basis of some insignificant factual difference or small legal issue. It is much easier to get a court to "distinguish" an old case than openly overrule it. Simply put, it is sometimes difficult to tell whether an earlier case has been overruled (and is clearly no longer precedent) or distinguished (and therefore technically still operative as precedent).

On the other hand, prior decisions are sometimes expressly overruled as not being consistent with the times. When the U.S. Supreme Court decided *Brown v. Board of Education* in 1954, it held that separate educational facilities for black and white students were unconstitutional. That overruled a 19th-century case called *Plessy v. Ferguson*, which had held that such "separate but equal" facilities were constitutional.

The precedential value of the earlier case is affected by which court decided it. Here are some guidelines for determining the effect that one court's decisions has on another's:

- Appellate court cases (including supreme court cases) operate as precedent with respect to future decisions by the same courts.

    EXAMPLE: In 2020, the Indiana Supreme Court rules that county general relief grants cannot be terminated without first providing the recipient with a hearing. In 2021, a fiscally strapped county cuts everyone off general assistance without hearings. A group of recipients seeks court relief. In 2021, the issue gets to the Indiana Supreme Court, which orders the recipients reinstated on the ground of its earlier ruling.

- U.S. Supreme Court cases are precedent for all courts in respect to decisions involving the U.S. Constitution or any aspect of federal law.

    EXAMPLE: In 2020, the U.S. Supreme Court rules that under the First Amendment to the U.S. Constitution, nonlawyers may help the public use self-help law books without being charged with the unauthorized practice of law. In 2021, the Nebraska Bar Association sues a nonlawyer to stop him from telling people how to use a self-help divorce book. He claims a violation of his First Amendment rights and wins on the basis of the U.S. Supreme Court case.

- U.S. Courts of Appeals cases are precedent for U.S. District Courts within their circuits (that is, the states covered by the circuit) and for state courts in this area with respect to issues concerning the U.S. Constitution and any aspect of federal law.

(The country is divided into 12 circuits—see "Circuits of the U.S. Court of Appeals," above.)

> EXAMPLE: Let's say the U.S. Court of Appeals for the First Circuit rules that the Eighth Amendment to the U.S. Constitution requires that bail in a criminal case be set in an amount that the defendant can reasonably afford to raise. A few years later, Perry is charged in the U.S. District Court for New Hampshire with the crime of assault against a federal officer. Because the U.S. District Court for New Hampshire is within the First Circuit, it must follow the rule for bail laid down by the Court of Appeals for that circuit. However, if Perry were charged with the crime in the U.S. District Court in Vermont—which is in the Second Circuit—the First Circuit case would not be binding.
>
> If Perry were charged with a crime in a New Hampshire state court, he would still be entitled to the new bail rule, since it is based on the U.S. Constitution and New Hampshire is within the First Circuit.

- U.S. District Court case opinions are never precedent for other courts. (They might be persuasive authority; see "Persuasive Authority," below.)

> EXAMPLE: A U.S. District Court in Hawaii rules that the Federal Endangered Species Act applies to mosquitoes. A U.S. District Court in Houston is asked to stop a local development because it threatens an endangered mosquito species. The U.S. District Court in Houston is free to follow the Hawaii case or reach a different conclusion.

- State supreme court cases are precedent with respect to all courts within the state.

> EXAMPLE: The Nevada Supreme Court rules that casinos may not require female employees to wear revealing outfits. This ruling is binding on all Nevada courts that are later faced with this issue.

- State intermediate appellate court cases are precedent with respect to the trial courts in the state. In larger states (for example, California), where the intermediate appellate courts are divided into districts (for instance, the fifth appellate district or the second appellate district), any particular intermediate appellate court's decision is sometimes regarded as precedent only by the trial courts within that district.

> **EXAMPLE:** The intermediate appellate court for the Fifth Appellate District in California rules that preparing an uncontested divorce petition for another is not the practice of law. As long as this is the only intermediate appellate court ruling on this issue in the state, it is binding on all California trial courts. The following year, the intermediate appellate court for the Second Appellate District rules that preparing an uncontested divorce petition is the practice of law and can be done only by attorneys. The first ruling, from the Fifth Appellate District, is binding on the trial courts located within that district—for example, those in Fresno. The second ruling is binding on trial courts in the Second Appellate District—for instance, Los Angeles. Trial courts in other appellate districts may follow either precedent, until their intermediate appellate courts issue their own rulings.

Persuasive Authority

If a case is not precedent (binding on later courts) but contains an excellent analysis of the legal issues and provides guidance for any court that happens to read it, it is persuasive authority. For example, the landmark California Supreme Court case of *Marvin v. Marvin*, the first major case establishing the principle of "palimony," was considered persuasive authority by many courts in other states when considering the same issue, though the *Marvin* decision was not binding on courts outside California.

364 Colo.   **697 PACIFIC REPORTER, 2d SERIES**

must inevitably result in suppressing protected speech." *Id.* at 526, 528, 78 S.Ct. at 1342, 1343.

Presumptions similar or identical to the one at issue here have been invalidated as unconstitutional by various courts. In *State v. Bumanglag*, 63 Hawaii 596, 634 P.2d 80 (1981), for example, the court held that such a presumption [18] impermissibly inhibited free expression: "Its application would tend to limit public access to protected material because booksellers may then restrict what they offer to works they are familiar with and consider 'safe.' The distribution of protected, as well as obscene, matter may be affected by this self-censorship." [19] 634 P.2d at 96.

In *Davis v. State*, 658 S.W.2d 572 (Tex. Crim.App.1983), the court perceived a similar danger to the guarantees of the first amendment, noting that, especially in the case of a large establishment, "[t]he risk of suppressing freedom of expression is not negligible; ... it rises to astronomical proportions." 658 S.W.2d at 579. In addition to observing that the presumption cannot survive due process analysis, *see Leary v. United States*, 395 U.S. 6, 89 S.Ct. 1532, 23 L.Ed.2d 57 (1969), the Texas court concluded that "[f]reedom of expression is too important a right to allow it to be seriously impeded or impaired by a presumption such as the one implicated in this case." 658 S.W.2d at 580. *See also Grove Press, Inc. v. Evans*, 306 F.Supp. 1084 (E.D.Va.1969); *Skinner v. State*, 647 S.W.2d 686 (Tex.App. 1982) (presumption impermissibly shifts burden of proof and eliminates element of

scienter); Model Penal Code § 251.4(2), comment 11 (1980) ("A presumption that one who disseminates or possesses obscene material in the course of his business does so knowingly or recklessly places a severe burden of prior examination and screening on legitimate business. It seems unlikely today that such a presumption would pass constitutional scrutiny."); Note, *The Scienter Requirement in Criminal Obscenity Prosecutions*, 41 N.Y.U.L.Rev. 791, 797–99 (1966) (evidentiary presumptions similar to the one at issue here are invalid after *Smith v. California*).

The Supreme Court has, on one occasion, expressly declined to reach the issue of the constitutionality of such presumptions. *Ginsberg v. New York*, 390 U.S. 629, 632 n. 1, 88 S.Ct. 1274, 1276 n. 1, 20 L.Ed.2d 195 (1968). More recently, however, in a case in which the same issue was raised, the Supreme Court dismissed an appeal for want of a substantial federal question in *People v. Kirkpatrick*, 32 N.Y.2d 17, 343 N.Y.S.2d 70, 295 N.E.2d 753 (1973), *appeal dismissed*, 414 U.S. 948, 94 S.Ct. 283, 38 L.Ed.2d 204 (1973). In *Kirkpatrick*, the state courts upheld the constitutionality of a statutory presumption that the seller of obscene materials knows the contents of that material, and also held that there was sufficient independent evidence of scienter to support the conviction.

[23] This dismissal, in its procedural context, was equivalent to an adjudication of the federal issue on its merits.[20] *Hicks*

---

18. HRS § 712–1214 provided that:
   (1) A person commits the offense of promoting pornography if, knowing its content and character, he:
   (a) Disseminates for monetary consideration any pornographic material....
   The presumption at issue, contained in HRS § 712–1216, provided that:
   (1) The fact that a person engaged in the conduct specified by sections 712–1214 or 712–1215 is prima facie evidence that he engaged in that conduct with knowledge of the character and content of the material disseminated or the performance produced, presented, directed, participated in, exhibited, or to be exhibited....

19. Additionally, the court in *Bumanglag* implied that the challenged presumption violated due process. The court agreed that salespeople generally were less likely than not to know the contents of their entire stock: "We find this difficult to discount, for a conclusion that a person who sold a book also was familiar with its character and content does not comport with what common sense and experience tell us about booksellers, salesclerks and their knowledge of the contents of books." 634 P.2d at 96.

20. We are aware that summary affirmances have sometimes been accorded less than full precedential weight by the Supreme Court. *See Edelman v. Jordan*, 415 U.S. 651, 671, 94 S.Ct. 1347, 1359, 39 L.Ed.2d 662 (1974); *Richardson*

As a general rule, the higher the court, the more persuasive its opinion. Every word (even dicta) of a U.S. Supreme Court opinion is considered important in assessing the state of the law. Opinions written by an intermediate appellate court in a small state, however, are not nearly so influential on other courts.

> EXAMPLE: In the case partially set out above, a Colorado court used cases from Hawaii, Texas, and Virginia as guidance in arriving at its own decision.

How to Analyze the Effect of an Earlier Case on Your Issue

Reading cases and understanding how they apply to your issue can be vexing. Most law and paralegal schools offer an entire course on case analysis. Obviously this book can't replace that training. But the steps below offer one possible approach:

Step 1. Identify the precise issues decided in the case—that is, what issues of law the court had to decide in order to make its ruling.

Step 2. Compare the issues in the case to the issues you are interested in and decide whether the case addresses one or more of them. If so, move to Step 3. If not, the case is probably not helpful.

Step 3. Carefully read and understand the facts underlying the case and compare them to the facts of your situation. Does the case's decision on the relevant issues logically stand up when applied to your facts? If so, move to Step 4. If not, go to Step 5.

Step 4. Determine whether the court that decided the case you are reading creates precedent for the trial or appellate courts in your area. If so, the case might serve as precedent. If not, move to Step 5.

Step 5. Carefully read and understand the legal reasoning employed by the court when deciding the relevant issues and decide whether it logically would help another court resolve your issues. If so, the case might be persuasive authority.

8

Validating Your Research

Once you've found the relevant statutes and cases you've been looking for, you probably feel like you're in the home stretch. But wait—there's a final step to ensuring your research is complete. You need to make sure that all the primary law you've found is still "good law." That means that since you started your research, the cases and statutes you're relying on haven't been overruled, reversed, or otherwise invalidated. (As unlikely as it might seem, it happens frequently.) At the same time, you can see whether there are other cases or other legal resources that refer to your statute or case because reading these new opinions is an easy way to expand your research even further, as well as ensure that you have the most up-to-date information.

This process is informally known as "Shepardizing." It derived the name from the well-known publisher, Shepard's (Westlaw offers a similar KeyCite feature). Shepard's was acquired by LexisNexis, who continues to offer the service both online and in print. In this chapter, we'll explain how to use it and other similar resources.

Making Sure It's "Good Law"

Shepardizing serves two important functions: it ensures you're working with "good law," and it helps you do additional research. In this section, we'll focus on the first function.

What Is "Shepardizing"?

Shepardizing is fairly simple to do (we explain how later in the chapter), but behind the scenes, it's actually quite complex. It essentially involves taking a case or statute, then tracking every single time another court cites the original citation or the original citation is affected by legislative action (for example, because a legislature repeals the statute in question). When you think about the number of statutes and published cases out there, this in itself is a huge task. But *Shepard's* goes even further. It looks at how subsequent courts handle cases or statutes, including special notations about how subsequent rulings deal with particular issues in a case.

Why You Must Shepardize

Although it might seem counterintuitive, Shepardizing is every bit as important as finding a case or statute in the first place. As we've already explained, finding additional relevant cases can be the icing on the cake. But the real value in Shepardizing is making sure the case or statute you're working with is still valid.

Why is this important? Imagine you are a plaintiff in a lawsuit, and you write a legal brief to the court that focuses on a case just like yours, that says a person in your position is entitled to compensation. But before the judge hears your argument, he or she reads your brief, then follows up to discover the case you're relying on has been overruled. Since you relied fully on one case, you didn't take advantage of any similar cases. And you didn't do anything to show how your case is different from the one in question, to explain why you'd still be entitled to recover even though someone in a similar situation didn't.

Not only is your argument out the window now, but so is your credibility. The judge doubts the quality and thoroughness of your work because you didn't take the time and effort to make sure the current case was valid. And you crafted an entire legal argument based on a legal proposition that no longer exists. This scenario is every lawyer's worst nightmare. Fortunately, it's also an avoidable one.

Understanding Your Results

We'll explain in further detail below how you will Shepardize. But before you do, it's helpful to understand the basic concepts that explain what kind of information you can get from Shepardizing.

Shepardizing will essentially lead to a list of citations. At the top of the list will be the history of your case or statute, including anything that's happened since publication. For example, a higher court might have reviewed the case in the meantime and issued a new ruling that will obviate the ruling on your case.

Further down the list will be references to how other courts have dealt with your case—usually starting with federal courts (the Supreme Court, if applicable, then by circuit), and then followed by individual states' courts. At the bottom of the list are references to the *A.L.R.*, a secondary source discussed in Chapter 4.

These citations give you more information than it might seem. First of all, they'll include a set of letter codes that explain how subsequent citations dealt with your original citation. You do not need to memorize these. They are laid out in the front of every volume of *Shepard's* in the library, and we'll explain what they mean in this chapter. (If you Shepardize online, you'll use a whole different set of codes, explained further in the next section.)

Another helpful piece of information that will make Shepardizing more useful to you is a small number that appears in superscript in the middle of a citation. This superscript refers to one of the headnotes of your case. If you want to look for subsequent cases that deal with a particular headnote, this will clue you in that you can use some and avoid others. We'll discuss this in further detail below.

How to Shepardize a Case

Now that we've fully convinced you of the need to Shepardize, it's time to learn how to do it. You have two options: using the law library, or going online. We'll explain both here.

Sheparizing Cases in the Law Library

Once you have located a case that speaks to your research issues, *Shepard's* gives you a list of every later case that has referred to it. You can use this list to see if the case was affirmed, modified, or reversed by a higher court; see if other cases affect the value of the case as precedent or persuasive authority; and find other cases that might help your argument or give you better answers to your question.

Shepard's works only when the case you are interested in has actually been referred to in the later case by name. If a later case deals with the same subject but doesn't mention your case, *Shepard's* won't help. One of the happy byproducts of the adversary system (happy at least for legal researchers) is that attorneys arguing appeals usually dredge up and present to the court every possibly relevant case. These cases, and others located by the court's own clerks, are typically included in the court's opinion. *Shepard's* is therefore an extremely reliable guide to how any given case has been used by the courts.

> **TIP**
>
> **Read First, Practice Later.** As you read the next several pages, you might feel that the information is so dry and technical that you can't absorb it all at once. Don't try. Just understand the broad outline of how the system works. When you actually need to use *Shepard's*, take this book along. After the first few encounters you'll surely get the hang of it.

Shepard's: The Basics

Before learning how to use *Shepard's*, it helps to know the basics: *Shepard's* are dark red, thick, hardcover volumes with separate update pamphlets that might be gold, bright red, or white, depending on how recently the hardcover volumes were published.

Here are some more tips:

- Separate *Shepard's* are published for each state, for federal court cases, and for U.S. Supreme Court cases. Sometimes the *Shepard's* is in a separate volume; sometimes it is combined in the same volume with *Shepard's Citations for Statutes* for a state.
- The outside of each *Shepard's* volume tells whether it covers statutes, cases, or both. For example, the *Shepard's Mississippi Citations* has the following on its outside cover: "Cases, Constitutions, Statutes, Codes, Laws, Etc." *Minnesota Shepard's*, on the other hand, has case citations in one volume and everything else in another.

- *Shepard's* is organized according to the case reporters that publish cases. Each *Shepard's* volume has a box in the first couple of pages telling you the specific publications covered by that volume. Below is a sample taken from the *Shepard's* contained in the *Northeastern Reporter*.

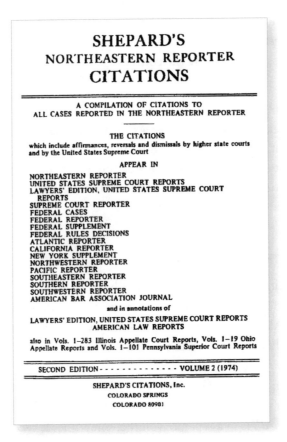

- To use *Shepard's*, you need the case citation—the name of the case reporter your case appears in, its volume number, and the first page on which the case appears.

- *Shepard's* hardcover volumes for the cases of a particular state's courts, or the federal courts, cover different time periods. For example, one hardcover volume might contain all references made by cases decided before 1980, another might contain all references made by cases decided between 1980 and 1985, and a third might contain all references made by cases decided between 1985 and 1990.
- *Shepard's* uses its own citation system. Every *Shepard's* volume has a table of abbreviations in case you get confused.

Shepard's, Step by Step

Now let's walk through how to use *Shepard's*. Remember, it's difficult to do this without being in the law library, so even if you don't understand it now, you'll probably be fine once you've actually got the right set of books in front of you. Just bring these instructions with you.

Step 1. Identify the citation of the case you wish to Shepardize. Most cases are published in at least two reporters—the official reporter and a West regional reporter. You can use *Shepard's* for either. The only parts of the citation you need are the volume, reporter abbreviation, and page number—for instance, 112 Cal.Rptr. 456.

Step 2. Find the *Shepard's* volumes that cover the reporter in the citation. If you chose the *Northwestern Reporter* citation, for example, select the *Shepard's* for the *Northwestern Reporter*.

Step 3. If a *Shepard's* volume contains citations for more than one reporter (for example, for both the official reporter and for the West regional reporter), find the part that covers citations for the reporter named in the citation you have selected. For instance, if your citation is for the *Northwestern Reporter*, locate the pages that cover this series rather than the pages that pertain to your state's official reporter.

Step 4. Note the year of the case you are Shepardizing. Select the volume or volumes that contain citations for cases decided after the case you are Shepardizing. Remember to check the update pamphlets—gold, red, and white—if you have started with a hardcover volume. Some researchers prefer to work backwards—checking the pamphlets first and then working back to the earliest relevant hardcover volume. Either way is fine.

Step 5. Find the volume number (in boldface) that corresponds to the volume number in the citation to the case being Shepardized. For example, if you are Shepardizing a case with the citation "874 F.2d 1035," search for Vol. 874 in bold print at the top of or on the page. (Each volume of *Shepard's* will cover multiple volumes of the case reporter.)

Step 6. Under the correct volume number, find the page number of the citation for the cited case. To continue the example from Step 5, search for the page number ("-1035-") in bold print.

Step 7. Under the bold page number, review the citations given for the citing cases.

Step 8. Use the letters to the left of the citation to decide whether any subsequent citation is worth reviewing.

Step 9. Use the numbers to the right of the citation to decide whether the citing case is referring to the cited case for issues you might be interested in.

Step 10. After you write down all potentially useful citations, go on to more recent *Shepard's* volumes and update pamphlets, and repeat these steps.

How *Shepard's* Works: An Example

This example shows how Steps 1 through 7 work. Steps 8 and 9 are covered above. We are searching for cases that have referred to *Nationwide Insurance v. Ervin*, 231 N.E.2d 112 (1967). We call *Ervin* the "cited case," and any case that has referred to it is called a "citing" case.

Step 1. Identify the citation for the *Ervin* case. We will use the West regional reporter citation, 231 N.E.2d 112 (1967).

Step 2. Find the volume that contains citations to cases published by the *Northeastern Reporter*.

Step 3. Use the part of the volume that contains *Northeastern Reporter* citations. The volume that contains citations for *Northeastern Reporter* cases also contains citations for the official case reporter (*Illinois Appellate Reports*).

Step 4. Find the volume for the correct period. We only want to use volumes that have citations for cases decided after 1967, the year *Ervin* was decided. In this example, all volumes of *Shepard's* that contain *Northeastern Reporter* citations have at least some citations to cases that have been decided after 1967, so we must check them all, including the pamphlets.

Step 5. Find the volume number appearing in the Northeastern Reporter citation for *Ervin*—Vol. 231.

Step 6. Find the page number. The *Ervin* page number appears as "-112-."

Step 7. Review the citations. Under the page number ("-112-") appear the citations to every case that has referred to the *Ervin* decision.

See the illustration of this example on the following page.

323FS⁶344	—107—	453NYS2d	—128—	—131—	—134—	24.Æ363n	—157—
596FS⁵784	(87Il.Æ139)	[597	Case 1	(20NY799)	Case 1		(142InA154)
650FS437	cc257NÆ233	513NYS2d72	(20NY794)	(284NYS2d	(20NY802)	—138—	241NÆ¹77
64.Æ506s	317NÆ¹631	Cir. 2	(284NYS2d | [455)	(284NYS2d	(249Ind173)	Nebr
	347NÆ¹70	d282FS⁴73	[451)	[459)	[459)	304NÆ⁴877	421NW3
—70—	360NÆ²1197	j282FS⁴82	s274NYS2d	s232NÆ652	s189NÆ620	336NÆ692	
(120S26)	378NÆ¹1157	f292FS⁴115	[392	s234NÆ840	s239NYS2d	339NÆ97	—159—
(41ϴp159)		439FS⁴975	s281NYS2d	s261NYS2d	[124	430NÆ¹787	(141InA669)
231NÆ³332	—109—	439FS⁴977	[974	[336		452NÆ1006	d252NÆ²606
370NÆ²458	(87Il.Æ82)	Cir. 4		s271NYS2d	—134—	526NÆ1229	d252NÆ³606
371NÆ⁵843	Cert Den	339FS⁴499	—128—	[523	Case 2		254NÆ²219
381NÆ²972	262NÆ¹797	Cir. 6	Case 2	s285NYS2d	(20NY802)	—140—	255NÆ¹829
414NÆ⁴438	281NÆ¹388	311FS⁴1191	(20NY795)	[621	(284NYS2d	(249Ind178)	j275NÆ¹856
453NÆ⁴664	378NÆ³606	Calif	(284NYS2d	s287NYS2d	[459)	242NÆ42	278NÆ²336
454NÆ²1389	412NÆ¹629	90CaR921	[451)	[886		f363NÆ226	278NÆ²336
488NÆ927		94CaR604	s281NYS2d	Cir. 2	—134—	e400NÆ²1111	280NÆ²865
	—112—	484P2d580	[985	9BRW824	Case 3		316NÆ¹593
—71—	(87Il.Æ432)	Colo			(20NY802)	—145—	316NÆ⁸593
(120A68)	241NÆ¹120	509P2d1272	—128—	—132—	(284NYS2d	(249Ind141)	339NÆ¹112
(41ϴp122)	241NÆ³120	Iowa	Case 3	Case 1	[460)	338NÆ¹262	340NÆ¹813
p166NÉ808	272NÆ⁷61	247NW271	(20NY796)	(20NY801)	s205NÆ879	j403NÆ811	357NÆ⁷256
c484NÆ220	274NÆ⁸879	Mich	(284NYS2d	(284NYS2d	s257NÆ879		387NÆ²1339
j484NÆ221	287NÆ¹530	164NW37	[452)	[456)	[960	—147—	433NÆ²21
18.Æ813s	289NÆ³703	N H	s281NYS2d	s219NÆ295	s282NYS2d	(249Ind144)	
	293NÆ³704	400A2d53	[864	s269NYS2d	[174	360NÆ604	—161—
—81—	305NÆ³417	468NYS2d	[368	s272NYS2d		f408NÆ620	(141InA655)
(120A87)	379NÆ266	496P2d516	[161	[782	—135—	f408NÆ⁴621	233NÆ²805
(41ϴp163)	d412NÆ⁵632	W Va		s388US41	Case 1	f408NÆ⁴621	256NÆ²923
432NÆ²212	d412NÆ⁷632	279SÆ408	—129—	s18LÆ1040	(20NY803)	f408NÆ⁴621	322NÆ⁴103
Cir. 6	e427NÆ⁷130	34.Æ155s	Case 1	s87SC1873	(284NYS2d	409NÆ⁶1272	323NÆ¹238
577FS⁴1131	474NÆ⁶785	65.Æ1069n	(20NY796)	59LÆ962n	[460)	409NÆ⁴1274	323NÆ⁸238
Md	474NÆ⁷785		(284NYS2d	37.Æ3630n	s273NYS2d	j437NÆ113	f355NÆ⁷438
513A2d938	481NÆ¹45	—126—	[452)	57.Æ3178n	[572	441NÆ⁵22	f355NÆ⁸438
	497NÆ³479	Case 1	s282NYS2d	57.Æ3201n	s282NYS2d	471NÆ⁵731	393NÆ⁸810
—85—	502NÆ²1295	(20NY792)	[438	82.Æ3376n	[639	471NÆ⁸731	417NÆ⁷338
(120A59)	510NÆ²1183	(284NYS2d		60.ÆF710n	250NÆ582	486NÆ¹662	486NÆ⁴442
(41ϴp117)	Ga	[449)	—129—		265NÆ924	Mass	9.Æ1044s
	221SÆ482	s282NYS2d	Case 2	—132—	288NYS2d	j440NÆ776	
—91—	Iowa	[664	(20NY797)	Case 2	[246	Calif	—165—
(120A83)	174NW383	242NÆ395	(284NYS2d	(20NY801)	j288NYS2d	140CaR294	(141InA672)
(41ϴp160)	N C	295NYS2d	[453)	(284NYS2d	[247	Conn	231NÆ¹863
521NÆ⁴1153	198SÆ56	[163	292NYS2d45	[457)	303NYS2d	261A2d296	j235NÆ¹99
521NÆ⁴1153	39.Æ4333n		j292NYS2d47	s229NÆ192	[524	Tex	242NÆ⁴140
31.Æ3585n		—126—	307NYS2d	s245NYS2d	317NYS2d	547SW624	261NÆ⁴602
	—115—	Case 2	[191	[353	[629	61.Æ31210n	308NÆ878
—94—	(87Il.Æ159)	(20NY793)	321NYS2d	s272NYS2d	391NYS2d	61.Æ31219n	Okla
(120hM127)	m243NÆ225	(284NYS2d	[842	[974	[220	1.Æ475n	541P2d861
(41ϴp131)	231NÆ¹³713	[449)	426NYS2d	s282NYS2d	392NYS2d28		40.Æ342n
	367NÆ²395	s238NÆ502	[843	[497	433NYS2d	—151—	40.Æ358n
—97—		s278NYS2d	432NYS2d	385NYS2d	[657	(249Ind168)	40.Æ375n
(87Il.Æ411)	—120—	[770	[156	[681	434NYS2d	241NÆ¹368	
Cert Den	(20NY417)	s291NYS2d12		39.Æ3497n	[278	309NÆ²845	—169—
269NÆ²355	(284NYS2d		—130—	65.Æ3512n	497NYS2d	309NÆ⁸847	(141InA662)
269NÆ⁸356	[441)	—127—	Case 1	44.Æ4888n	[530	316NÆ²689	f239NÆ¹173
273NÆ¹162	j437NÆ1095	Case 1	(20NY798)	44.Æ4893n	42.Æ4828n	323NÆ¹239	249NÆ516
280NÆ¹246	437NÆ⁴1095	(20NY793)	(284NYS2d	68.ÆF957n		e331NÆ¹780	j249NÆ³517
283NÆ¹⁵43	287NYS2d	(284NYS2d | [454)		—135—	399NÆ¹368	j251NÆ⁸26
318NÆ¹²122	[467	[450)		—133—	Case 2	Me	j251NÆ⁴26
326NÆ⁸468	298NYS2d	s275NYS2d	—130—	(20NY801)	(20NY804)	318A2d498	251NÆ¹34
363NÆ⁸625	[645	[960	Case 2	(284NYS2d	(284NYS2d		269NÆ³767
363NÆ¹²626	300NYS2d	s282NYS2d	(20NY798)	[458)	[461)	—154—	j269NÆ⁴770
369NÆ¹295	[397	[973	(284NYS2d	Cert Den	s275NYS2d	(141InA649)	270NÆ767
369NÆ²295	f304NYS2d		[454)	US cert den	[674	274NÆ⁸742	e272NÆ⁸629
447NÆ⁴441	[263	—127—	s282NYS2d	in390US971	527NYS2d	301NÆ¹243	e272NÆ³633
458NÆ⁵1069	318NYS2d	Case 2	[934	s229NÆ220	[585	310NÆ²279	272NÆ⁴874
f502NÆ⁶478	[653	(20NY794)		s282NYS2d		348NÆ¹81	f273NÆ²553
18.Æ633s	335NYS2d	(284NYS2d	—130—	[538	—136—	Ala	f273NÆ³553
	[749	[450)	Case 3	495NYS2d	(20NY805)	361So2d9	277NÆ606
—103—	387NYS2d	s272NYS2d	(20NY798)	[539	(284NYS2d	Minn	280NÆ³303
(87Il.Æ181)	[718	[446	(284NYS2d	33.Æ41132n	[462)	222NW80	284NÆ³735
Cert Den	e388NYS2d	294NYS2d77	[455)		s274NYS2d	4COA569§3	286NÆ¹698
323NÆ²809	[472		s242NÆ486		[850	16.Æ5192n	297NÆ¹471
323NÆ⁸809	j452NYS2d		s280NYS2d		268NÆ646	17.Æ4494n	307NÆ¹504
374NÆ²1140	[338		[952		j295NYS2d		383NÆ1085
	452NYS2d⁴				[970		
	[338				24.Æ3327n		Continued

Reviewing Subsequent History

Once you have a case in which you are interested, you first want to find out whether it has been appealed and, if so, whether the appeal affected the case as a source of law. *Shepard's* uses a code next to its citations that instantly gives you this information.

For example, suppose you read a case called *Jones v. Smith,* which is located at 500 F.Supp. 325. Because the case is published in the *Federal Supplement,* we know it was decided by a U.S. District Court. (See Chapter 7.) The District Court case might not have had the last word, however; the case quite possibly was appealed to a higher court—typically, a U.S. Circuit Court of Appeals, but in rare instances the U.S. Supreme Court.

Once a case is appealed, the published opinion of the lower or intermediate appellate court might or might not continue to be a valid expression of the law. When a higher appellate court reverses a published decision of a lower court, it usually vacates the lower court's opinion. This means that the opinion is not to be considered as law for any purpose. The underlying case might also be affirmed or modified on appeal. In these situations, the lower court's opinion will usually remain in existence to provide guidance for future courts, but sometimes also might be ordered vacated and replaced with the higher court's opinion.

When a case is directly affected by a higher court on appeal, *Shepard's* places a small letter just before the citation of the case. For instance, if the higher court vacated the cited case's opinion, a "v" will appear next to the citation, as shown below.

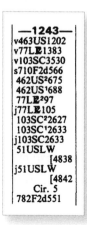

Citation Showing Vacating of Later Court

Abbreviations Showing Action by the Supreme Court

When an unsuccessful attempt has been made to take the cited case before the U.S. Supreme Court, *Shepard's* uses certain notations to tells you exactly what happened.

US cert den. This means that the U.S. Supreme Court refused to issue a writ of certiorari. When this happens, the cited case is considered to be good law, since the Supreme Court refused to review it.

US cert dis. This means that the petition for cert was dismissed, usually for procedural reasons. It's possible that the case may still be taken by the Supreme Court at a later time.

US reh den. This only appears when the cited case is a U.S. Supreme Court case, and means that the U.S. Supreme Court refused to grant a rehearing in that case.

US reh dis. This means that a request for a rehearing was dismissed.

Shepard's Abbreviations: Appeal of the Cited Case

Here are some of the most common codes you'll encounter.

Code	Short for	Meaning
a	affirmed	The higher court agrees with and validates the decision of the lower court.
cc	connected case	There is another decision with the same parties or arising from the same subject matter.
D	dismissed	The citing case dismisses an appeal of the cited case.
m	modified	This is the cited case, but the ruling has been changed in some way.
r	reversed	A higher court does not agree with the legal conclusion of the lower court, and undoes it. It cannot be relied on, at least for the principle on which it was reversed. Sometimes, when there is more than one legal issue in a case, a court may only reverse part of a decision.
s	same case	Simply, the same case as the cited case.
v	vacated	The cited case has been invalidated by a subsequent case.

Shepard's Abbreviations: Treatment of a Case

With laws constantly changing, a case you find in your research might not reflect the way current courts would decide the same issue. *Shepard's* provides a second set of abbreviations to explain why the citing case referred to the cited case. This set is used only when the citing case is unrelated to the cited case—that is, not reviewing the cited case on appeal. The most commonly used abbreviations are:

Code	Short for	Meaning
c	criticized	Another court has criticized the decision in the cited case. It's good to look at such cases to see what kinds of arguments an opponent might make or if the cited case is against you, the arguments you might make or tweak.
d	distinguished	When a case is similar but a court wants to point out the differences the court will distinguish a case (and usually, go on to explain why a different result follows).
e	explained	If a court feels the original case causes confusion—often, because two parties in a subsequent case interpret things differently—it may explain the original case in greater detail.
f	followed	Cases that follow the rule and logic of the cited case; cases with this notation will be helpful.
j	dissenting opinion	Appellate courts may have more than one judge reviewing a case. If so, they don't always agree about the decision. This notation informs you that a judge who disagreed with the majority in a later case cited the case you are looking at.
~	concurring opinion	Even if judges deciding a case agree on the final outcome, sometimes more than one judge wants to explain his or her rationale. Such a judge may write a concurring opinion. The majority opinion is what forms the law, but the concurring opinion tells you another judge's view of things.
o or op	overruled or overruled in part	When a higher court overrules the cited case, it is no longer valid.
q	questioned	An indicator that a court isn't sure about the logic or validity of the argument in the cited case. As with a decision criticizing the cited case, this can suggest what an opponent would argue. Or, if a case isn't in your favor, a case that questions the original can give you additional ammunition.
su	superseded by statute	A statute, as stated in a subsequent case, has superseded the cited case.

If you are using *Shepard's* primarily as a means of checking a case for its precedential or persuasive value, you can skim down a list of the citations under the cited case and search for these abbreviations. If none appear, or the ones that do appear indicate that the cited case is still good law, you might stop there. But if the cited case was questioned, criticized, or overruled by the citing case, you would definitely want to read that citing case. If there is no letter to the left of the citation, it usually means that the cited case was mentioned in passing and wasn't important to the decision in the citing case.

Summing Up ...
How to Shepardize State Court Cases

✓ Select one of the parallel citations of the case you wish to Shepardize.

✓ Note the year of the case you are Shepardizing.

✓ Find the *Shepard's* volumes—and if necessary the parts of these volumes—that cover the reporter in the citation.

✓ Select the volume or volumes that contain citations for cases decided after the case you are Shepardizing.

✓ Find the volume number (in boldface) that corresponds to the volume number of the case being Shepardized.

✓ Under this volume number, find the page number (in boldface) of the citation for the cited case.

✓ Under this page number, review the citations given for the citing cases.

✓ Use the letters to the left of the citation to decide whether the case has been directly affected by a higher court in an appeal.

✓ Use the numbers to the right of the citation to decide whether the citing case is referring to the cited case for issues in which you might be interested.

✓ After you write down all potentially useful citations, repeat these steps with the more recent *Shepard's* volumes and update pamphlets.

Summing Up …
How to Shepardize U.S. Supreme Court Cases

✓ Select one of the three parallel citations for the case you wish to Shepardize.

✓ Note the year of the case.

✓ Find the *Shepard's* labeled *United States Case Citations*.

✓ Select the volume or volumes that contain citations for cases decided after the date of the case you are Shepardizing.

✓ Select the part of the *Shepard's* volume that pertains to the citation you are using. For instance, if your citation is for the *U.S. Supreme Court Reporter* (S.Ct.), locate the pages that cover this report rather than the pages that pertain to the *United States Supreme Court Reports* (U.S.) or the *Supreme Court Reports, Lawyer's Edition* (L.Ed.).

✓ Find the boldface volume number that corresponds to the volume number of the case being Shepardized.

✓ Under this volume number, find the page number of the cited case.

✓ Under the page number, review the citations of the citing cases.

✓ Use the letters to the left of each citation to decide whether the case has been directly affected by a higher court in an appeal.

✓ Use the numbers to the right of the citation to decide whether the citing case is referring to the cited case for issues in which you might be interested.

✓ After you write down all potentially useful citations, repeat these steps with the more recent *Shepard's* volumes and update pamphlets.

Shepardizing Cases Online

Shepardizing cases online has very distinct benefits over doing the same thing in the law library stacks. First of all, it's much quicker. Simply by typing the citation into Westlaw (using a similar program called KeyCite) or Lexis, you can quickly pull up all subsequent citations at once. If you want to read those subsequent citations, you can click on them and get to them immediately.

Also, citations are clearly marked, using systems created by Westlaw and Lexis, to show you the effect of the subsequent case—that is, what it does in relation to your original citation. In Westlaw, there's even a graphical depiction of how subsequent cases relate to your original citation and a system to indicate how significant a discussion of the cited case is.

Finally, unlike print copies, citations can be updated almost immediately electronically—within 48 hours on Lexis and as quickly as one to four hours (if direct negative history is involved) on Westlaw. When dealing with print copies, you would have to go to several different sources to be as up-to-date as possible, and even then, you won't be able to rival that thoroughness.

On the downside, Shepardizing online is an expensive proposition, so unless your local law library provides free access to Lexis or Westlaw, you could end up paying some serious cash.

RESOURCE

Look up your cases for free. We recommend you look up cases for free on a website like Justia (www.justia.com) or FindLaw (www.findlaw.com), or use a very low-cost service like VersusLaw (www.versuslaw.com), and see if you can access KeyCite at your local law library.

If you do choose to Shepardize online, you'll find that the results look a little different than they do in print. Instead of the letter system discussed above, cases on *Shepard's Citations Online* have the following treatment indicators.

Shepard's Abbreviations: Appeal of the Cited Case

Here are some of the most common codes you'll encounter in *Shepard's Citations Online*.

Code	Short for	Meaning
⬤	**Warning**	Negative treatment is indicated—shows that the case contains strong negative history or treatment of your case (i.e., overruled or reversed)
Q	**Questioned**	Validity questioned by citing references—contains treatment that questions the continuing validity or precedential value of your case because of intervening circumstances, including judicial or legislative overruling
△	**Caution**	Possible negative treatment—contains history or treatment that may have a significant negative impact on your case (i.e., distinguished or criticized)
◆	**Positive**	Positive treatment is indicated—contains history or treatment of your case that has a positive impact on your case (i.e., affirmed or followed)
Ⓐ	**Analysis**	Citing references with analysis available—contains treatment of your case that is neither positive nor negative (i.e., explained)
ⓘ	**Information**	Citation information available—citing references are available for you to raise, but do not have a history or treatment analysis (i.e., law reviews)

Source: www.lexisnexis.com

Westlaw's KeyCite has its own system.

Westlaw's KeyCite Abbreviations	
 Red Flag	In cases and administrative decisions, a red flag warns that the case or administrative decision is no longer good law for at least one of the points of law it contains. In statutes and regulations, a red flag indicates that the statute or regulation has been amended by a recent session law or rule, repealed, superseded, or held unconstitutional or preempted in whole or in part.
 Yellow Flag	In cases and administrative decisions, a yellow flag warns that the case or administrative decision has some negative history but hasn't been reversed or overruled. In statutes and regulations, a yellow flag indicates that the statute has been renumbered or transferred by a recent session law; that an uncodified session law or pending legislation affecting the statute is available (statutes merely referenced, i.e., mentioned, are not marked with a yellow flag); that the regulation has been reinstated, corrected, or confirmed; that the statute or regulation was limited on constitutional or preemption grounds or its validity was otherwise called into doubt; or that a prior version of the statute or regulation received negative treatment from a court.
	A blue-striped flag indicates that the case has been appealed to the U.S. Courts of Appeals or the U.S. Supreme Court (excluding appeals originating from agencies).

© 2015 Thomson Reuters

KeyCite uses "Depth-of-Treatment Bars" that allow you to see, visually, how subsequent cases affect your current case. Four green bars ("Examined") means the subsequent case includes extended discussion of your case; three green bars ("Discussed") means the subsequent case includes substantial discussion of your case; two green bars ("Cited") means the subsequent case includes some discussion of your case; and one green bar ("Mentioned") indicates that the subsequent case makes brief reference to your case.

RESOURCE

Before you use either service, we recommend reading training materials both publishers provide online. This will ensure your research is as efficient as possible.

To learn more about *Shepard's Citations Online*, check out: http://law.lexisnexis.com/shepards and click on the "Resources" tab.

And for KeyCite, find out more at: https://info.legalsolutions.thomsonreuters.com/pdf/wln2/L-356347.pdf. (If you can't find what you need, we suggest typing "KeyCite" into a search engine; it's sometimes difficult to find the correct material on the Thomson Reuters website.)

An Alternative to Online Shepardizing

If you can't afford Lexis or Westlaw access and can't get it for free, it probably makes sense to spend at least one day in a law library, using the method we describe above. However, you do have an alternative. We're hesitant to recommend it, however, because it's time-consuming and prone to human error.

A few websites, like VersusLaw, offer an alternative to Shepardizing. This involves providing the user with a list of all subsequent case citations for the citation in question. VersusLaw does this only for cases (not statutes), and the subsequent citations do not specify how they deal with the cited case.

If you're dealing with a fairly new case that hasn't been cited extensively, this might work. You can review each subsequent case that might have precedential value. But if you are dealing with a case that has been around a long time or has been talked about a great deal, you could find yourself overwhelmed by extensive subsequent case history. If you don't review the cases carefully, you could miss one that does something important, like overrule or reverse the cited case. And you won't have any statutory citations either, that could have the same effect. Also, it's not always clear how often these services are updated.

For these reasons, we generally recommend you don't rely on this "shortcut." It won't necessarily save time, and it opens you up to a greater possibility for error.

Shepardizing Statutes

You can and should Shepardize statutes, too. As with case law, the quickest way to do this is online. Both Westlaw and Lexis offer this service on the same terms as citing cases.

If you are going to Shepardize in the law library stacks, here are the basics for using *Shepard's Citations for Statutes*:

- *Shepard's Citations for Statutes* are dark red, thick, hardcover volumes with separate update pamphlets that can be gold, red, or white, depending on how recently the hardcover volumes were published.

- A separate *Shepard's* exists for the statutes of each state and for federal statutes.

- *Shepard's* hardcover volumes for the statutes of a state or the federal government cover different time periods. For example, one hardcover volume might contain all references made by court decisions before 1980, another might contain all references made between 1980 and 1990, a third might contain all references made between 1990 and 1998, and so on.

- To use *Shepard's*, you need the exact number (citation) of the statute. It is very helpful to know the approximate year it was passed.

- Each *Shepard's* volume is organized in the same way as the statutes being referred to are labeled in the codes of each state or the federal government. So if you want to know whether a particular New York criminal statute has been interpreted by a court, you would first locate the place in the New York *Shepard's Citations for Statutes* that covers the New York criminal laws, and then look for the specific statute by number. In other states, where statutes are not grouped by topic but only by sequential number, you would only need to find the statute by its number.

- Once you find the statute you are Shepardizing, you will see whether or not any court decisions have referred to it. If so, the citations tell you the reporter, the volume, and the page where the reference occurred.

CAUTION

Four Warnings When You're Using *Shepard's Citations for Statutes:*

- Make sure you use the *Shepard's* that covers the state in which you are interested.

- When you look up a statute in *Shepard's,* make sure you use the part that deals with statutes (marked clearly on the front of the volume and the top of the page), and not with the part that deals with cases, regulations, or the constitution.

- Use the *Shepard's* volumes for the appropriate years. A hardcover volume that contains citations from 1980 through 1985 will not do you any good for a statute enacted in 1986. You should use only the volumes that contain citations to cases decided after the statute was passed.

- Look in all hardbound volumes and paperback supplements that might contain citations.

Summing Up ...
How to Shepardize Federal Statutes

✓ Note the year the statute you wish to Shepardize was passed.

✓ Find *Shepard's Citations for Statutes.*

✓ Select the volumes covering the years since the statute was passed.

✓ Find the title of the citation as it appears in boldface at the top of the page (for example, Title 25 U.S.C.).

✓ Under the appropriate title number, find the section number of the statute (for example, Title 25 U.S.C. § 863).

✓ Copy the citations listed under the section number. The citations refer to the exact page in the case where the statute is referred to.

✓ Follow this procedure for all volumes and pamphlets up to the most recent.

Summing Up ...
How to Shepardize State Statutes

✓ Find the *Shepard's* volume for your state's statutes.

✓ Select the volumes covering the years since the statute was passed.

✓ If your state statutes are organized into codes, find the title of the code in the upper margin in boldface (for example, *Penal Code*). If your state goes by a title system, find the title number at the top of the page. If your state's statutes are consecutively numbered without reference to a code or title, find the place in *Shepard's* where the number appears in boldface.

✓ If you are dealing with a code or title, find the section number of the statute (for example, Title 19, § 863).

✓ Note the citations under the section number. These citations are to the book and pages where the statute is referred to.

✓ Follow this process for all volumes and pamphlets up to the most recent.

Shepard's Abbreviations: History of a Statute

Shepard's Citations for Statutes has its own set of codes, and they'll be listed in the front of the relevant volume of *Shepard's* that you'll be using. Some of the most important codes are shown below.

Code	Short for	Meaning
A	amended	The statute you're looking at has been amended.
Ad	added	A new section has been added to your statute.
R	repealed	The statute has been repealed and is no longer good law.
Rs	repealed and superseded	The statute has been repealed and superseded by new legislation.
S	superseded	New legislation has been substituted for the current statute you're looking at.

Using *Shepard's* for Research

Shepard's was designed primarily as an updating tool. However, as we've pointed out, it can be used for much more than updating. Once you've found a case or statute that's relevant, *Shepard's* can be used to find other cases dealing with the same issue. Every citing case is potentially relevant; thus, if you start out with one cited case, you might find any number of useful cases that have referred to it. Then, each of these citing cases can itself be Shepardized.

Suppose, for example, *Shepard's* lists five cases that have referred to your initial case. Then you Shepardize each of these five cases and find an additional two citing cases for each one. In very little time, you have a list of over ten cases that might be relevant to your situation.

There is a catch to this, however. We have seen that *Shepard's* gives you a list of every case that has referred to the cited case. But most cited cases deal with a number of legal issues, and a citing case will usually only mention the cited case in connection with one (or perhaps several) of those issues.

For example, if a cited case touches on 20 different legal issues, a citing case might refer to it for only three of these. If the issues in which the citing case is interested are the same as the issues in which you are interested, the citing case might be helpful in your research. However, if the citing case refers to the cited case for issues in which you aren't interested, the citing case won't do you any good.

To help you separate the wheat from the chaff and avoid this time trap, *Shepard's* identifies the specific issues the citing case was interested in when it referred to the cited case. It does this by:

- identifying the issue from the cited case that is being discussed by the citing case
- selecting the headnote in the cited case that most closely states the issue being discussed in the citing case, and
- placing that headnote number just to the right of the citation to the citing case.

EXAMPLE: *Nationwide Insurance v. Ervin*, 231 N.E.2d 112 (1967) is referred to (cited) in *Deason v. Metropolitan Property & Liability Insurance Co.*, 474 N.E.2d 783 (1985).

DEASON v. METRO. PROP. & LIABILITY INS. CO.   Ill.   **785**
Cite as 474 N.E.2d 783 (Ill.App. 5 Dist. 1985)

the time of the accident; the Mercury had a defective transmission and the Dodge had a twisted drive shaft. Both vehicles were put back into operation shortly after the accident involving the Comet. During his deposition, Andrew Warner testified as follows:

"Q. Did you have any intention if the Comet hadn't been wrecked, did you have any intention to dispose of either of these other two cars just because you got the Comet?

A. Oh, no."

[2] In ruling that Metropolitan's policy afforded secondary coverage in connection with the accident involving the 1975 Comet, the court found that Christopher Warner was "a relative operating a temporary substitute" automobile. Metropolitan contends that this conclusion is incorrect, and we are compelled to agree. Under the terms of the policy, a temporary substitute automobile is defined as one "temporarily used with the permission of the owner as a substitute for an owned automobile when withdrawn from normal use for servicing or repair or because of breakdown, loss, or destruction." Here, the unequivocal deposition testimony of all concerned establishes that Christopher Warner's use of the Comet was not to be temporary, but regular and permanent, as it was the intention of both Vera Fry and Christopher Warner that he would pay $100 for the car at Christmas time, and would not return it to her. Moreover, the Comet was not intended by the Warners to be a substitute for either the Mercury or the Dodge; rather, it was to be kept as a third car, and the fact that the Dodge and Mercury broke down during the Warners' use of the Comet was entirely coincidental. Under these circumstances, the "temporary substitute" provision of the policy issued by Metropolitan did not encompass Christopher Warner's use of the Comet on the date of the accident. (See *Sturgeon v. Automobile Club Inter-Insurance Exchange* (1979), 77 Ill. App.3d 997, 1000, 34 Ill.Dec. 66, 397 N.E.2d 522.) This conclusion is buttressed by the holding of *Nationwide Insurance Compa-*

ny v. Ervin (1967), 87 Ill.App.2d 432, 436–37, 231 N.E.2d 112, wherein it was recognized that a "temporary substitute" provision of the type under consideration here is to be applied to those situations where an insured automobile is withdrawn from use for a short period, and not where, as here, coverage is sought to be extended to an additional automobile for a significant length of time.

[3] *Providence Mutual Casualty Company v. Sturms* (1962), 37 Ill.App.2d 304, 185 N.E.2d 366, relied on by appellees, is not on point. *Sturms* addresses the question of whether coverage afforded on a temporary substitute automobile expires immediately upon repair of the insured's regular automobile (37 Ill.App.2d 304, 306, 185 N.E.2d 366), and does not discuss the more fundamental issue of when a vehicle is considered to be a temporary substitute in the first place. While appellees also suggest that portions of Metropolitan's claim file show that certain Metropolitan employees believe that the policy in question afforded coverage, the trial court correctly noted in its judgment that these statements are merely opinions, and are not binding on a court in its consideration of the legal question presented. 31A C.J.S. Evidence § 272(b) (1964).

For the foregoing reasons, the judgment of the circuit court of St. Clair County is reversed.

Reversed.

JONES, P.J., and KARNS, J., concur.

Page From *Deason v. Metropolitan Property & Liability Insurance Co.*

Authority

NORTHEASTERN REPORTER, 2d SERIES

Vol. 231

323FS[8]344
596FS[6]784
650FS437
64A3506s

—70—
(12OS26)
(41Op159)
231NE[3]332
370NE[3]458
371NE[3]843
381NE[2]972
414NE[4]438
453NE[4]664
454NE[2]1389
488NE927

—71—
(12OA68)
(41Op122)
p166NE808
c484NE220
j484NE221
18A2813s

—81—
(12OA87)
(41Op163)
432NE[6]212
Cir. 6
577FS[4]1131
Md
513A2d938

—85—
(12OA59)
(41Op117)

—91—
(12OA83)
(41Op160)
521NE[4]1153
521NE[6]1153
31A3585n

—94—
(12OhM127)
(41Op131)

—97—
(87IlA411)
Cert Den
269NE[2]355
269NE[5]356
273NE[1]162
280NE[12]46
283NE[15]43
318NE[12]122
326NE[9]468
363NE[5]625
363NE[12]626
369NE[1]295
369NE[2]295
447NE[6]441
458NE[5]1069
f502NE[6]478
18A2633s

—103—
(87IlA181)
Cert Den
323NE[2]809
323NE[4]809
374NE[4]1140

—107—
(87IlA139)
cc257NE233
317NE[1]631
347NE[1]70
360NE[2]1197
378NE[1]1157

—109—
(87IlA82)
Cert Den
262NE[1]797
281NE[1]388
378NE[3]606
412NE[1]629

—112—
(87IlA432)
241NE[1]120
241NE[3]120
272NE[7]61
274NE[3]879
287NE[1]530
289NE[3]703
293NE[3]704
305NE[3]417
379NE[2]66
d412NE[5]632
d412NE[7]632
e427NE[7]130
474NE[6]785
474NE[7]785 — Deason
481NE[1]45
497NE[3]479
502NE[2]1295
510NE[2]1183
Ga
221SE482
Iowa
174NW383
N C
198SE56
39A4333n

—115—
(87IlA159)
m243NE225
231NE[13]713
367NE[2]395

—120—
(20NY417)
(284NYS2d
[441)
j437NE1095
437NE[4]1095
287NYS2d
[467
298NYS2d
[645
300NYS2d
[397
f304NYS2d
[263
318NYS2d
[653
335NYS2d
[749
387NYS2d
[718
e388NYS2d
[472
j452NYS2d
[338
452NYS2d[4]
[338

453NYS2d
[597
513NYS2d72
Cir. 2
d282FS[4]73
j282FS[4]82
f292FS[4]115
439FS[4]975
439FS[4]977
Cir. 4
339FS[4]499
Cir. 6
311FS[4]1191
Calif
90CaR921
94CaR604
484P2d580
Colo
509P2d1272
Iowa
247NW271
Mich
164NW37
N H
400A2d53
Wash
496P2d516
W Va
279SE408
34A2155s
65A31069n

—126—
Case 1
(20NY792)
(284NYS2d
[449)
s282NYS2d
[664
242NE395
295NYS2d
[163

—126—
Case 2
(20NY793)
(284NYS2d
[449)
s238NE502
s278NYS2d
[770
s291NYS2d12

—127—
Case 1
(20NY793)
(284NYS2d
[450)
s275NYS2d
[960
s282NYS2d
[973

—127—
Case 2
(20NY794)
(284NYS2d
[450)
s272NYS2d
[446
294NYS2d77

—128—
Case 1
(20NY794)
(284NYS2d
[451)
s274NYS2d
[392
s281NYS2d
[974

—128—
Case 2
(20NY795)
(284NYS2d
[451)
s281NYS2d
[985

—128—
Case 3
(20NY796)
(284NYS2d
[452)
s281NYS2d
[864
468NYS2d
[161

—129—
Case 1
(20NY796)
(284NYS2d
[452)
s282NYS2d
[438

—129—
Case 2
(20NY797)
(284NYS2d
[453)
292NYS2d45
j292NYS2d47
307NYS2d
[191
321NYS2d
[842
426NYS2d
[843
432NYS2d
[156

—130—
Case 1
(20NY798)
(284NYS2d
[454)

—130—
Case 2
(20NY798)
(284NYS2d
[454)
s282NYS2d
[934

—130—
Case 3
(20NY798)
(284NYS2d
[455)
s242NE486
s280NYS2d
[952

—131—
(20NY799)
(284NYS2d
[455)
s232NE652
s234NE840
s261NYS2d
[336
s271NYS2d
[523
s285NYS2d
[621
s287NYS2d
[886
Cir. 2
9BRW824

—132—
Case 1
(20NY801)
(284NYS2d
[456)
s219NE295
s269NYS2d
[368
s272NYS2d
[782
s388US41
s18LE1040
s87SC1873
59LE962n
37A3630n
57A3178n
57A3201n
82A3376n
60ARF710n

—132—
Case 2
(20NY801)
(284NYS2d
[457)
s229NE192
s245NYS2d
[353
s272NYS2d
[974
s282NYS2d
[497
385NYS2d
[681
39A3497n
65A3512n
44A4888n
44A4893n
68ARF957n

—133—
(20NY801)
(284NYS2d
[458)
Cert Den
US cert den
in390US971
s229NE220
s282NYS2d
[538
495NYS2d
[539
33A41132n

—134—
Case 1
(20NY802)
(284NYS2d
[459)
s189NE620
s239NYS2d
[124

—134—
Case 2
(20NY802)
(284NYS2d
[459)

—134—
Case 3
(20NY802)
(284NYS2d
[460)
s205NE879
s257NYS2d
[960
s282NYS2d
[174

—135—
Case 1
(20NY803)
(284NYS2d
[460)
s273NYS2d
[572
s282NYS2d
[639
250NE582
265NE924
288NYS2d
[246
j288NYS2d
[247
303NYS2d
[524
317NYS2d
[629
391NYS2d
[220
392NYS2d28
433NYS2d
[657
434NYS2d
[278
497NYS2d
[530
42A4828n

—135—
Case 2
(20NY804)
(284NYS2d
[461)
s275NYS2d
[674
527NYS2d
[585

—136—
(20NY805)
(284NYS2d
[462)
s274NYS2d
[850
268NE646
j295NYS2d
[970
24A3327n

24A3363n

—138—
(249Ind173)
304NE[4]877
336NE692
339NE97
430NE[1]787
452NE1006
526NE1229

—140—
(249Ind178)
242NE42
f363NE226
e400NE[2]1111

—145—
(249Ind141)
338NE[1]262
j403NE811

—147—
(249Ind144)
360NE604
f408NE620
f408NE[4]621
f408NE[5]621
f408NE[6]621
409NE[6]1272
409NE[4]1274
j437NE113
441NE[5]22
471NE[5]731
471NE[6]731
486NE[1]662
Mass
j440NE776
Calif
140CaR294
Conn
261A2d296
Tex
547SW624
61A31210n
61A31219n
1A475n

—151—
(249Ind168)
241NE[1]368
309NE[2]845
309NE[3]847
316NE[2]689
323NE[1]239
e331NE[1]780
399NE[1]368
Me
318A2d498

—154—
(141InA649)
274NE[5]742
301NE[1]243
310NE[2]279
348NE[1]81
Ala
361So2d9
Minn
222NW80
4COA569§ 3
16A4192n
17A4494n

—157—
(142InA154)
241NE[1]77
Nebr
421NW3

—159—
(141InA669)
d252NE[2]606
d252NE[3]606
254NE[2]219
255NE[1]829
j275NE[1]856
278NE[1]336
278NE[2]336
280NE[2]865
316NE[1]593
316NE[2]593
339NE[1]112
340NE[1]813
357NE[1]256
387NE[2]1339
433NE[2]21

—161—
(141InA655)
233NE[2]805
256NE[3]923
322NE[8]103
323NE[1]238
323NE[8]238
f355NE[7]438
f355NE[8]438
393NE[8]810
417NE[7]338
486NE[8]442
9A21044s

—165—
(141InA672)
231NE[1]863
j235NE[1]99
242NE[4]140
261NE[6]602
308NE878
Okla
541P2d861
40A342n
40A358n
40A375n

—169—
(141InA662)
f239NE[1]173
249NE516
j249NE[3]517
j251NE[3]26
j251NE[4]26
251NE[1]34
269NE[3]767
j269NE[4]770
270NE767
e272NE[4]629
e272NE[3]633
272NE[4]874
f273NE[2]553
f273NE[3]553
277NE606
280NE[3]303
284NE[3]735
286NE[1]698
297NE[1]471
307NE[1]504
383NE1085

Continued

Page From *Shepard's*

Therefore, in this example, *Ervin* is the cited case and *Deason* is the citing case. If you Shepardize *Ervin*, you would find the citation to the page in *Deason* where the *Deason* court cited *Ervin*, as shown above.

The little numbers (6 and 7) between the N.E.2d and the page number (785) are the numbers of the headnotes in *Ervin* that, in the opinion of *Shepard's*, best describe the issues which the case is being cited for in *Deason*. These headnotes are shown above.

Thus, *Deason* used *Ervin* when it discussed the issues summarized in these two headnotes. If the issues in these two headnotes were the reason you were Shepardizing *Ervin*, you would definitely want to read *Deason*. However, if you were not interested in the issues discussed in headnotes 6 and 7, you might wisely choose not to read *Deason*.

If there is no headnote number next to the citation—that is, the citation doesn't identify the issue for which the cited case is being mentioned—it means that the reference to the cited case appeared, to the *Shepard's* editors, to be general rather than in reference to a specific legal issue. The citing case might or might not be of interest, so you should at least skim it.

Organizing and Putting Your Legal Research to Use

After spending hours in the law library or scouring countless websites, you're probably much more knowledgeable about your chosen legal topic than you were when you started out. Congratulations! You've come a long way.

But we don't want you to lose the benefit of all your hard work. For this reason it's important that you organize your research in a usable way. How best to do this will depend, in large part, on what you intend to do with the information you've compiled. As we discussed in Chapter 3, you might plan to file a court document, meet with a lawyer, write an academic paper, or explain the results to your boss.

In this chapter, we'll give you some tools and strategies to put your research to work for you. We'll cover:

- organizing your research
- writing a legal memorandum
- the basics of going to court and preparing documents for court, and
- preparing to meet with a lawyer.

When you're done with this chapter, you'll be in a good position to take what you've learned and put it to use.

Organizing Your Research

If you are like many researchers, by the time you're done collecting everything you need, you're surrounded by a stack of books and papers. It's important that you keep track of what's in front of you. If you're disorganized, you could easily lose track of that perfect case and find yourself repeating some of your work.

How you'll organize your research will depend on what you're researching and why, but here we will present a basic plan that will work for most people. In Chapter 3, we encouraged you to think about the legal questions you needed answered to complete your research. We suggest you organize your research the same way. For example, you might want to get several folders or accordion files (sometimes called "redwells") to sort papers related to each legal question you have. In each folder or file, you can put the documents that give you your answers. (If a document goes to more than one issue, we suggest you put it in the folder or file that deals with the first or most important of those issues.) You might want to highlight or write on these documents—that's fine too. For example, in Chapter 7 we explained the important parts of an opinion (the issue, facts, decision, and rationale). You might want to notate where these appear in each case you've read so that if you need to refer to one again, the important information will be easy to find.

If you are working in a law library, we suggest you make copies of the important documents you need, and store them as we've described here. This will probably include statutes and cases, and maybe some secondary sources too. (You don't need to make copies of the pages of Shepard's you look up, unless you want to research the listed cases, or anything you can find online. As we explained in Chapter 2, you can find many legal resources online, so it's possible to access many documents you need with the click of a mouse.)

How to Write a Legal Memorandum

The words "legal memorandum" can certainly be intimidating. If so, your first step is to relax, because creating one isn't as hard as it might seem. A legal memorandum can be a couple of paragraphs long, written in plain English, and in many cases, relatively easy to prepare.

Why Prepare a Legal Memorandum?

Whether you are doing research for yourself or someone else, the main purpose of a legal memo is to force you to put the results of your search in writing. Why is this important? There are three basic reasons. The first is that you won't really know whether your research is done until you try to write it up. You might think you have answered the question you started with, but find that the answer isn't as clear once you put pen to paper, or that you have additional questions that must be answered to make the process complete. A legal memorandum serves as a "checklist" for your research, forcing you to answer all the tough questions even if you thought you already had it all sorted out.

The second important function of a legal memorandum is to provide you with an accessible record of the fruits of your research after time has erased the memories from your mind. It is unfortunately common for people to put in a day or two of research in the law library on a particular issue, neglect to take an extra hour or two to write it up, and later have to spend another day in the library because they are unable to use their notes to reconstruct what they found.

The third important function of a legal memorandum is to communicate the results of your research to someone else. This will be necessary if you are a paralegal doing research for a supervising lawyer, or if you are researching your own case and wish to inform the judge and opposing party of what you've found. No matter who will be looking at it—even if it's just you—taking the time to summarize what you've learned in a legal memorandum will not be time wasted.

How to Prepare a Legal Memorandum

In this section, we tell you how to prepare a legal memorandum. You'll also learn how to organize your legal writing using the style accepted throughout the legal community.

In Chapter 7, we stated that judicial opinions almost always have four primary elements: a statement of the facts, a statement of the issue or issues, a decision or holding on the issue or issues, and a discussion of the reasoning underlying the holding.

Like case opinions, legal memoranda should include a statement of the facts, a statement of the issue or issues, a conclusion about what the law is (equivalent to the holding), and a brief discussion of why you reached your conclusion. Laying things out this way will help you summarize and recognize the most important points in each section. For example, after reviewing the law, you will understand what facts are the most important to your case. Before we get started, however, here's a tip: Keep your emotions out of the analysis. Although you might be furious that the pizza delivery guy ran over the bike your son left in the driveway, you know your feelings aren't part of the most important facts that determine whether the pizza business must pay for the ruined bike. Instead, you'll need to focus on the elements that go to your alleged claim—that is, that the pizza delivery guy was actually the person responsible, that he admitted to doing it, and so forth.

> **CAUTION**
> **A memorandum is not the same as a brief.** In this discussion, we are talking about internal memoranda—memoranda intended solely for your own use or the use of your employer. This should be distinguished from legal documents prepared for external purposes. Commonly called "briefs" or confusingly, "memoranda of points and authorities," these documents are ordinarily submitted to the court in the course of a lawsuit to advance a particular position with the utmost vigor (or so the client hopes). That's different than your purpose here—to lay out the facts and law.

The Statement of Facts

The statement of facts in your memo is where you're going to lay out the most important and relevant facts you need to answer your legal question or questions—that is, the facts that are legally relevant. For example, if your issue is whether a new owner of an apartment house can evict a tenant for having pets even though the prior landlord allowed them, your statement of facts would have to include such items as:

- the kind(s) of pet(s) in question
- the date ownership was transferred, and
- information about any rental agreement or lease that was signed by the tenant, and so on.

As you move to writing other parts of the memo, you might recall or recognize that additional facts are important. If that's the case, make sure you go back and amend your statement of facts. You want to make sure you capture all relevant information in your statement of facts.

Many people choose to write their statement of facts under a separate heading, like "Facts" or "Statement of Facts."

The Statement of Issues

In a legal memorandum, the statement of issues is often called the "question presented." The general idea is that you want to summarize, in as succinct a way as possible, the legal issue or issues that are central to your case. If written as a question, the question is usually one that can be answered with "yes" or "no" (even though the answer might not actually be a simple yes or no). An example might be, "Can a new owner of an apartment house in California evict a tenant for having pets even though a prior landlord allowed them?"

The Decision or Holding

The decision—sometimes labeled conclusion or answer—is like a court's holding. The idea is that whatever question or questions you're researching are answered by the decision (the conclusion you anticipate the court would come to if presented with the issue). You'll explain how you arrived at that conclusion in the discussion section, covered next. Continuing the example above, the decision might read. "Probably not. The new owner takes ownership subject to the agreements, written and, in some cases, oral, that were negotiated by the prior owner. If a tenant has a lease that allows pets, the new owner cannot evict the tenant for having a pet."

A Discussion of the Reasoning

The discussion of the reasoning (sometimes referred to as the "analysis") that helped you reach your conclusion is really the most important part of your entire memo. It is where you will take what you've learned by reading the law and apply it to the facts of your case. This section is often the most challenging for new researchers, but doing it will help you identify, understand, and forward potential arguments.

To make it a little more manageable and to help organize their thoughts, lawyers have developed a way to approach writing this material that you can use, too (this is the organizational approach we initially referred to that you'll want to use in all of your legal writing). It goes by the acronym I.R.A.C. (pronounced "I rack") and stands for "issue, rule, analysis, conclusion." Here's how that plays out in practice:

- **Issue.** Start by identifying the issue you are addressing that is covered in a case or cases you'll discuss. In other words, what is the problem before you that the case will answer? For example, "In this case, we must determine whether a Louisiana employer is liable for injuries sustained by a pedestrian who was hit by an employee who was negligently driving while talking on a cell phone about work-related matters."

- **Rule.** Next, lay out the rule the case or cases you've found provides. For example, "In *Ellender v. Neff Rental, Inc.*, a Louisiana appellate court determined that an employee who was found 100% responsible for a car accident was acting in the course and scope of his employment because he was on work-related business, took a work-related call at the time of the accident on a cell phone provided by his employer, and that this contributed to or caused the accident. The court explained that because the employee was acting in the course and scope of employment, the employer could be held 'vicariously liable' for the employee's actions."

- **Analysis.** Next, take the rule from the case you are citing and apply it to the facts of your situation. While the situations might not be exactly the same, it's up to you to show how similar the situations are and why. "Here, as in the *Ellender* case, the employee admitted he did not see the pedestrian and caused the accident. At the time of the accident, he was acting in the course and scope of his employment because he was dialing a phone number to make a work-related call on his work-provided phone."

- **Conclusion.** The conclusion is where you sum up what the case and its application has led you to determine about your own case. For example, "Applying *Ellender*, the employer in this case could be held vicariously liable for hitting the pedestrian because the employee who caused the accident when making a work-related call was acting within the course and scope of his employment."

If more than one case or statute is relevant to your issue and they reach different conclusions or go to different points, you might repeat this structure several times in your legal memo.

Preparing a Memo for Someone Else

If you are preparing a legal memorandum for someone else—for example, you're a paralegal and you are putting it together for a supervising attorney, a student writing a paper, or an employee writing for an employer—two additional points might be useful. First, it is usually a good idea to list the resources that you've checked, even if some or many of them didn't pan out. This helps the reader feel secure, knowing you've covered everything out there. For example, in any research project you might check *A.L.R., Am. Jur.*, a local digest or two, and some treatises, in addition to a local encyclopedia. Even if you don't find any useful information in the local encyclopedia, the reader will feel better knowing that you've thoroughly checked each available resource.

You might also want to insert citations throughout your legal memorandum. As we explained in Chapter 6, citations are the roadmap to finding a relevant resource. In the example above, the citation for the *Ellender* case is 965 So.2d 898. Some people even like to see the "pincites"—the exact page number on which a legal principle or factual information is found. For instance, the rule in the *Ellender* case is found on page 902, so the pincite would look like this: 965 So.2d 898, 902. Recall that a standard format for citing cases can be found in The Bluebook (www.legalbluebook.com). Also, remember that if you print a case online, it might not have the page citations to the official reporter in it. If you want or need the pincite, you might have to look up the case in the reporter in the library to get them, or pay to obtain it using an online service like Westlaw.

Finally, all statements about what the law is should be supported by some primary legal authority, such as statutes, regulations, cases, or ordinances. Other legal materials generally comprise somebody else's opinion about what the law is. It's okay and even desirable to include references to these secondary or background sources, but they cannot replace primary authority.

Going to Court

Today, many individuals conduct legal research because they are representing themselves in small claims court or other legal actions. In fact, your legal research might have been conducted to determine whether you wanted to proceed with your case. If the answer is yes, your next step might require you to file a legal action.

> ! CAUTION
> **In most cases, we anticipate that if you are a self-represented litigant, it will be for a simple matter only.** If you're planning on representing yourself in a criminal matter or a civil matter where there is more than a few thousand dollars involved, we recommend you at least talk to an attorney first, because the matter is likely to be complex. As we'll explain below, you might be able to reach a mutually agreeable solution to allow the attorney to represent or advise you at low cost.

The Court Process

When someone new to the law—whether law student, paralegal, or citizen interested in a personal case—thinks of "going to court," the images that come to mind are often movie-like scenes with argumentative attorneys, stern judges, and courtrooms filled with spectators and the press. The complexity of it all can seem too much to deal with.

In fact, the great majority of court matters are handled in a quite straightforward manner—but it would be unreasonable to say that you'll be able to avoid the parts of litigation that bring on stress, such as preparing for and appearing in court. A few cases move forward without fanfare, such as cases asking a judge to appoint a guardian or conservator, approve an adoption or name change, allow the probate of a simple estate, grant an uncontested divorce, discharge certain debts in bankruptcy, or seal a criminal record. On the other hand, criminal cases are usually no picnic, and any case can get messy when a real dispute exists or lawyers have a financial incentive to string the matter out, as can often happen in complicated business disputes for which attorneys bill by the hour. (In such cases, consulting with an attorney is likely in your best interests.)

Also, keep in mind that whatever the matter, filing a case and pushing it through court always involves carefully following a number of technical court rules. The trick is to know these procedural rules in minute detail. Fortunately, these rules are, for the most part, available to all—but to be frank, they aren't always easy to master in the amount of time available to most litigants.

CAUTION
This is not a practice guide. This section talks in general terms about the steps in civil litigation, and it is not intended as a guide for the aspiring lawyer or paralegal, or for the reader who intends to represent him- or herself in court. To find out in more detail about civil and criminal procedure, start with a good background resource (as discussed in Chapter 4). You can get information about how to represent yourself in a civil court proceeding in *Represent Yourself in Court*, by Paul Bergman and Sara J. Berman (Nolo).

Court procedures and rules are substantially similar in all state and federal courts. Details vary, however, and similar procedures are often referred to by different names. For example, an eviction action is called "unlawful detainer" in California and "summary process" in Massachusetts. Yet the proceedings are basically the same.

In Chapter 6, we explained that you can learn more about how courts where you live do things by looking at any court or local rules. If you can't find such rules, contact the court to find out if they exist, and if so, how you access them. These rules might cover anything from how the legal papers you submit must look to how much it costs to file and serve papers. Obviously, it's important to know these rules when and if they apply.

The sections below describe the typical course of a civil case. Because most of you will have a lawyer if you're charged with a criminal offense, we won't present the typical course of a criminal case (for details, see *The Criminal Law Handbook*, by Paul Bergman and Sara J. Berman (Nolo)).

Small Claims Court

All states have small claims courts with simplified rules that are fairly easy to follow. Small claims court clerks are usually required by statute to help people with all procedural details. If you are the plaintiff (the one bringing the case) and can squeeze the amount of your monetary claim within the small claim limits for your state (usually from $2,000 to $10,000), you might find that small claims court is an excellent alternative to the formal legal system.

One of the nicest aspects of small claims court is that in many states, litigants are not allowed to be represented by lawyers (there's no rule against consulting with a lawyer beforehand, however). By learning to do your own research and writing, you can present a solid case and not run the risk of being overwhelmed by an experienced hired gun on the other side. Unfortunately, most small claims courts are not designed to handle problems other than those where one person has a monetary claim against the other. (For more information, see *Everybody's Guide to Small Claims Court*, by Cara O'Neill (Nolo).)

The Pretrial Process

The first phase of a contested civil case is called the pretrial phase. Here, we'll outline the typical steps you'll go through in this phase.

The Plaintiff Files a Complaint

A case begins when the plaintiff (the party who sues) files with the court a document called a "complaint." This document tells what allegedly happened and what the plaintiff wants done about it, such as asking for a monetary award, court order, or other remedy. It also tells the court the legal basis for the litigation. The plaintiff must be sure to file the lawsuit in the correct jurisdiction (see "Jurisdiction and Venue," below.)

Part of the plaintiff's responsibility will be to "serve" the complaint. That means to make sure the defendant gets a copy according to the rules set out by the court. Most often, the plaintiff must arrange for "personal service"—that is, to have a copy of the complaint (usually stamped by the court) personally handed to the defendant by a neutral third party (a person not involved in the suit). The plaintiff will have to file a document called "proof of service," signed by the person who made the delivery, to show that the document was handed over. Many courts have a standard form for this purpose.

The Defendant Responds

After the defendant (the party who is sued) is served with a copy of the complaint, he or she has a certain time to respond in writing—usually 30 days (or less depending on state law). If no response is made, a "default" judgment may be obtained by the plaintiff, which means the plaintiff wins without having to fully prove the case. There are a variety of ways the defendant might respond, including:

- **The Answer.** Most commonly, the defendant files an "answer," a statement setting out which parts of the complaint the defendant agrees and disagrees with. Under the procedural rules of most states, the defendant's answer must also contain any affirmative defenses (factual statements of the reasons or excuses for the defendant's actions) and counterclaims (claims that the plaintiff is actually legally responsible and owes the defendant something) that the defendant has. The defendant can also state that he or she doesn't have enough information about the allegations and denies the complaint on that basis.

- **Motion to Dismiss Case.** This document—also called a "demurrer" in some states—asks the court to dismiss the suit instead of requiring an answer from the defendant. There are a number of reasons why you'd want to file a motion to dismiss instead of an answer. For instance, the plaintiff has only a certain amount of time to file the action. If the case wasn't filed within this "statute of limitations" period, the judge will dismiss the lawsuit. You'd also file this type of motion if the plaintiff doesn't plead all of the elements necessary to prove a case against you within the complaint. Usually, the basis for this request boils down to this: Even if the facts in the plaintiff's complaint are true, so what?

The defendant is essentially saying that even if everything the plaintiff says is true, the plaintiff's claims don't add up to a legal violation—you simply didn't do anything wrong. To make the decision, the judge assumes that the factual allegations in the complaint are true and then decides whether the law supports the claim for relief. This is the first "dispositive motion" a party can file, because it has the potential to end the case entirely. If the judge grants the motion but allows the plaintiff a chance to fix the problem ("granted with leave to amend"), the plaintiff simply rewrites the complaint and the process starts all over again. If the judge grants the motion without leave to amend, the case ends unless the plaintiff appeals the decision. On the other hand, if the judge overrules (denies) the motion or demurrer, the defendant must file an answer.

Both Sides Engage in Discovery

From the time that the pleadings in a case are filed, the parties begin to exchange information about the case in each other's possession through a process called "discovery." While it might seem strange to ask the other side to willingly give up information that helps your case, there's often no other way to get it—and the law favors the open exchange of information.

Of course, that doesn't mean it's always willingly surrendered. For this reason, discovery often adds considerably to the time and expense of litigation. Disputes can arise over what information must be turned over—for example, one side might assert that the requested documents are protected from disclosure by the attorney-client privilege, or that a request for information isn't relevant (doesn't have anything to do with the issue being resolved), or that what's being asked for isn't clear. Often the parties try to resolve these disputes on their own, which takes time as they go back and forth (usually, writing letters to each other). If the dispute can't be resolved informally, the parties can file a motion asking the court to make a decision. If a party does not like the result, it is usually possible to take the matter to a higher court before the underlying case proceeds further; however, this rarely happens.

Jurisdiction and Venue

As you know from reading this book, there are courts all over the country, in all 50 states. But you cannot simply file a lawsuit anywhere you wish. Rules about the proper location for filing suit limit what you can do. The general idea is that it isn't fair to sue someone in a location that doesn't bear any relation to where the problems that led to the suit occurred, or where the person being sued can fairly be expected to go. For example, if you live in New York and, while vacationing in Hawaii, get hit by a motorist who lives in Hawaii, is it fair to expect that you can sue that person in California because you think the law in California favors your case? Should you be able to sue that Hawaiian in New York?

Jurisdiction and venue rules prevent both choices. Jurisdiction rules decide whether a court has the authority to hear the case, while venue rules determine where the most convenient location for a lawsuit is, based on the position of the parties. Venue rules can be waived—for example, a defendant in a lawsuit can agree to have the case heard in a neighboring county where the plaintiff resides, even if he'd normally be entitled to have the case heard in his home county, where the accident occurred.

In many cases, jurisdiction and venue will not be an issue. However, if you are planning on initiating a lawsuit against someone who lives outside your state or county and the incident giving rise to the lawsuit occurred outside your state or county, we suggest you check your court and local rules or speak with a lawyer first, to find out the proper jurisdiction and venue.

Normally, discovery consists of the following devices:

- **Depositions.** Witnesses or parties are required to go to the office of one of the attorneys and answer questions, under oath, about their knowledge of the dispute. The testimony is usually taken down by a court reporter, but sometimes by a tape or video recorder.
- **Interrogatories.** One party sends another written questions to be answered under oath by a certain date. Interrogatories are also used to ask the other party to identify the source and validity of

documents that might be introduced as evidence at trial. Most courts limit the number of interrogatories either side can ask.

- **Admissions of Facts.** Factual statements are set out that the other side must admit or deny. Anything that isn't denied is considered admitted. Parties are often reluctant to admit to facts, so they might object to the language before responding.

- **Production of Documents.** One party asks another to produce specified documents. In a complicated case, the documents exchanged can be extensive.

One or More Sides File Motions

At any time after the pleadings have been filed, but before trial, the plaintiff or defendant might ask the court to order the other side to do something or to refrain from doing something. Sometimes these types of motions are used to preserve the status quo until the case can come to trial. For example, if the circumstances are truly urgent, a party can request the court to issue a "temporary restraining order" (TRO) or "preliminary injunction," stopping the defendant from taking some action before trial. This often occurs when the plaintiff fears that the defendant will liquidate assets or make other changes that will defeat the purpose of the litigation. As mentioned, motions might also be filed to enforce discovery (that is, to require a party to answer questions or produce documents when appropriate) or to protect a party against abusive discovery (for example, requiring attendance at a week-long deposition).

In some cases, one of the parties will file a summary judgment motion. Like a demurrer, this is a dispositive motion, because it potentially ends the entire case. With this motion, a party is trying to show that there isn't a dispute about any important facts in the case (called "triable issues of material fact"). Trials serve to determine facts, so if there are no disputed facts, there's no reason to have a trial. The judge can go ahead and apply the relevant law to the undisputed facts, resolving the case entirely before it ever goes to trial, saving everyone time and money. Preparing a summary judgment motion can be costly, too, however, and it rarely occurs without the parties first engaging in extensive discovery. Why? The motion can be likened to trying the case on paper. The party bringing the motion will need to spell out all of the relevant issues, and provide evidence—or demonstrate a lack of evidence—that supports the facts that make up the factual scenario claimed by the person bringing the motion. The opposing side will also present evidence in an opposition brief that supports a different version of the facts. Once briefing is complete, the parties will argue their position before the judge deciding the matter.

One Side Requests a Trial Date

In some court systems, a case is never set for trial unless one of the parties requests it. Accordingly, a party who feels adequately prepared can file a document with the court requesting a trial and specifying whether it should be held in front of a jury. These documents are titled differently in different courts, such as "memorandum to set," "at-issue memorandum," and "motion to set for trial." Whatever their titles, they might be opposed by the other party (for a variety of reasons) or agreed to.

Alternative Dispute Resolution

Most courts require the parties to try to resolve the dispute before going to trial. For instance, it's common for litigants to submit the case to a volunteer attorney in an informal nonbinding arbitration. Either side can reject the arbitration award and continue toward trial. Additionally, most courts require the parties to appear at a settlement conference shortly before the trial date. Again, a volunteer attorney will likely encourage resolution by helping each side see the weaknesses of the case.

A Pretrial Conference Is Held

Usually, once a case is set for trial, a pretrial conference between the parties, their lawyers, and the judge is scheduled. At the pretrial conference, the judge makes sure that everyone understands what the remaining issues are in the case and gets an idea of how long the trial will take. Many judges use these conferences—often quite successfully—to pressure the parties to settle the case. If no settlement is reached, the trial date is fixed.

The Trial

Most lawsuits never go to trial. The parties usually settle their dispute beforehand—likely because trying a case is extremely expensive and the stakes can be high.

The parties can opt for a trial by jury or a trial by judge (either side can demand a jury; otherwise, the case will be tried by the judge). A jury trial is more advantageous for a defendant who believes an emotional issue might favorably pull the heartstrings of the jury. By contrast, a trial by judge might be the better choice for a defendant worried that irrelevant evidence might negatively sway the jury in some way (judges are presumed to be able to act impartially and tell reliable evidence from unreliable evidence).

Jury Trials

Jury trials begin with the selection of the jury. The judge and lawyers for both sides question potential jurors about their knowledge of the case and possible biases relating to their clients and the important issues in the case. This process is called *voir dire*.

Motions *in Limine*

Before the trial begins each side can ask the judge to handle evidence (allow it or refuse to admit it) in a certain way. For instance, the plaintiff might want to prevent the defendant from trying to prove a certain point, believing that to do so would hopelessly prejudice the jury against the plaintiff. These types of requests are called "motions *in limine*" (that is, motions on the verge of trial). They are considered by the judge in a meeting outside the hearing of the jury, usually in the judge's office.

Once a jury is selected, the attorneys address the jury in opening statements that outline what they expect to show in the upcoming trial. Then the plaintiff begins, offering testimony from witnesses and information in documents to establish a version of events. The testimony and documents are then subject to challenge by the defendant through a process called "cross-examination."

Once the plaintiff's case is presented, the defendant has the opportunity to present a defense, subject to the plaintiff's cross-examination. Commonly, the plaintiff gets the last shot (called a "rebuttal") in an opportunity to answer the defendant's case.

RESOURCE

Represent Yourself in Court, **by Paul Bergman and Sara J. Berman (Nolo), is an excellent guide to what goes on in a trial.** It is based on the Federal Rules of Civil Procedure, which many states follow, and is a good place to start if you are facing or involved in a trial. *How to Win Your Personal Injury Claim*, by Joseph Matthews (Nolo), provides a straightforward discussion on how to file, process, and settle a personal injury claim.

When the parties finish presenting their cases, both sides get to make closing arguments summarizing what they think they've proved and imploring the jury to see it their way. Then the judge explains to the jurors that it is their job to decide what the facts are in the case and to apply those facts to the law. Next, the judge reads the jury specially written versions of the law called "jury instructions." (As discussed in Chapter 3, these are the streamlined summaries of law designed to be easily understood by people who are not legal professionals. They're invaluable when researching a case because they set forth the legal elements a plaintiff must prove to win the case.)

Although it is the judge's responsibility to give the instructions, the plaintiff and defendant are first invited to give the judge a set of proposed instructions that they believe apply to the case and that will be most favorable to their side. The judge and attorneys review the proposed instructions together but the judge makes the final decision. Then the judge assembles the instructions that are to be given in a final written version and reads from it verbatim (on average, it takes the judge approximately 45 minutes to read through all of the instructions).

Researching Jury Instructions

A judge who refuses to instruct the jurors on the appropriate law creates an appealable issue that could result in the case being tried a second time. So a judge will carefully review the jury instructions offered by each side. (See "Appeals," below.)

Compilations of acceptable jury instructions are available in most states for common types of cases—for instance, auto accident cases (and many, many more). To find jury instructions online, try searching for "jury instructions" and the name of your state. For instance, searching for "jury instructions New York" brings up the New York State Unified Court System page (www.nycourts.gov) and you'll find New York's jury instructions at www.nycourts.gov/judges/cji/index.shtml.

In California, civil jury instructions are published in *California Civil Jury Instructions for Judges and Attorneys* (CACI) and criminal instructions are in *California Criminal Jury Instructions for Judges and Attorneys* (CALCRIM). You can find copies of both sets on the California Court website at www.courts.ca.gov/partners/juryinstructions.htm.

Federal jury instructions are located in either *Federal Jury Practice and Instructions* (West) or *Modern Federal Jury Instructions: Civil and Criminal* (Lexis). Try searching for the titles or visit Marquette University Law School at http://libraryguides.law.marquette.edu/c.php?g=318617&p=3806593 to access them online.

Once the jury has heard the instructions, they retire to a room to decide the case. In civil cases the plaintiff must prove its case by a "preponderance of evidence"—that is, it must be more probable than not that the plaintiff is right. The jury need not be unanimous; the normal requirement is a three-quarters vote in favor of either party (check the requirements of your state). Most civil juries consist of 12 jurors, but some states are experimenting with six-member juries.

When the jury has reached a verdict, they report it to the judge, who announces it in open court with the parties present. Any party who is dissatisfied with the verdict can ask the judge to set it aside or modify it. Usually the judge upholds the verdict and issues a judgment for the winner.

Judge Trials

Judge trials are a lot easier than jury trials. There are fewer disputes about evidence and no jury instructions to prepare. When all the evidence is in and parties have made final arguments to the judge, the judge decides the case and issues a judgment, usually accompanied by a document termed "Findings of Facts and Conclusions of Law." This document tells the parties why the judge reached the decision and gives them a basis for deciding whether to appeal.

Researching the Rules of Evidence

Any source of information that a party offers as proof of a fact is called "evidence." There is admissible evidence and inadmissible evidence, and the rules that determine what is allowed to be introduced at trial are quite complex.

Many of the disputes during a trial revolve around what evidence is admissible and what isn't, and the many bench conferences (when the attorneys and the judge huddle and whisper out of the jury's hearing) that occur during the typical trial involve whether a bit of testimony or a particular document should or should not be allowed "into evidence." Decisions by the judge on these disputes are often the subject of an appeal by the losing party.

The rules of evidence for each state are usually published as part of that state's statutes. Most states also have secondary sources designed to help you understand the rules of evidence. (See Chapter 3.)

Appeals

Any party who is dissatisfied with the judgment can appeal the issue to a higher court (but you'll need to demonstrate that some type of mistake occurred at the trial level). As we've explained, in most cases an appeal doesn't start the whole process over. Instead, the appellate court only looks to see if the trial court made any errors, such as failing to allow the jury to hear relevant evidence, allowing in evidence overly prejudicial to the defendant, failing to provide the jury with the appropriate law, and so on. The appellate court won't usually hear new evidence or conduct a new trial.

Appeals are usually allowed from final decisions in a case, such as a judgment of dismissal, summary judgment, or judgment after trial. However, sometimes decisions by the court before final judgment is entered can be reviewed by an appellate court before the trial continues. These are termed "interlocutory appeals." These interlocutory appeals are the exception to the rule; appellate courts much prefer to refrain from reviewing lower court decisions until the trial is over and they can decide all questions at once.

In an appeal, "briefs"—typewritten statements of the parties' views of the facts and law—are submitted to the appellate court. The appellate court also has a copy of the entire written "record" of the trial court. This record usually consists of all documents submitted by the parties to the trial court, exhibits and documents introduced in the trial, a transcript of exactly what was said at the trial (produced by a court reporter or a tape recorder), and all judgments and orders entered by the trial court.

In addition to considering the briefs and the trial court record, the appellate court usually hears oral arguments from the attorneys on each side. After the oral arguments, the justices (judges on courts of appeal are usually called "justices") discuss the case and arrive at a decision. A justice representing the majority (sometimes the justices who hear the case will not agree on how it should be decided) is assigned to write the opinion.

If a party disagrees with the outcome of an appeal in the appellate court, another appeal can usually be made—to a state supreme court or the U.S. Supreme Court. That requires filing a "Petition for Hearing" in a state court, or a "Petition for Writ of Certiorari"—or, as it is usually called, "Petition for Cert"—asking the Supreme Court to consider the case. If the court grants a hearing or issues a Writ of Certiorari to the court that decided the case being appealed, it will consider the case. If it denies a hearing or "cert," then it won't.

Supreme courts grant hearings or cert only in a very small percentage of cases presented to them. They usually choose cases that present interesting or important questions of law or an issue that two or more lower appellate courts have disagreed on. For example, if the federal Court of Appeals for the Sixth Circuit decides that the military registration system is unconstitutional because it doesn't include women, and the Court of Appeals for the Seventh Circuit decides that the system is constitutional, the U.S. Supreme Court might grant cert in these cases and resolve the conflict.

Filing Cases Directly in Appellate and Supreme Courts

Occasionally, cases can be brought directly in the intermediate appellate courts or supreme courts, but only when there are extremely important issues of law in the case and little factual dispute. Also, under federal and state constitutions, certain types of disputes go directly to the supreme courts; this is called "original jurisdiction," as opposed to their usual appellate jurisdiction. For example, if one state sues another, the suit is brought in the U.S. Supreme Court, not a U.S. district court.

When the U.S. Supreme Court or a state's highest court decides a case, it almost always issues a published opinion. U.S. Supreme Court cases serve as precedent and binding authority for all federal courts, and cases from a state's highest court serve as precedent and authority for all state courts in that state.

Writing and Filing Court Documents

If you are involved in a civil suit, you will go through most if not all of the steps we've outlined above. In many cases, you'll have to submit documents to the court, with copies to your opponent.

Fortunately, many courts have standard documents for this purpose. For example, your state court might have a standard complaint form you can use to initiate the lawsuit. In more complex matters, an attorney might not want to use the form, instead preferring to write a new document without any limiting language or questions. But for your purposes, these forms can be invaluable. Instead of having to figure out the exact format of any legal document you file, you can spend your time and energy filling out the form accurately, following any instructions provided with it.

To find standard forms, check your state court website, or call the clerk of the local court. Or if no forms exist, the clerk can tell you what format your legal documents can take. Pay special attention to the court's particular rules—you might need to use a certain font size and style, and if you get it wrong, could find that a court will reject your papers. If you're up against a deadline, this can be particularly stressful.

If you are going to write a legal brief or even fill out a form explaining the facts of your case to the court, we encourage you to look back to your legal memorandum. In it you will have already laid out the most important facts, which you can copy onto any other documents.

We can't tell you how to write a legal brief here—it's too complicated and varies too much depending on the type of motion you're making and what court you are in. As we've explained, if you get to that level of complexity in a lawsuit, we generally recommend you at least talk to a lawyer. However, if you're determined to do it yourself, or if you are working with your own lawyer to draft such a document, we'd like to remind you that your legal memorandum should be a good starting point for preparing a well-reasoned argument for the court. Just remember that the purpose of the brief is different. While in a legal memorandum you're laying out the basics of the law in an objective manner, in a brief you're persuading a court that your position is the correct one. For this reason, the same material in your legal memorandum can look very different in a brief.

Finding and Working With a Lawyer

Perhaps the issue of filing documents isn't applicable to you because you already have, or plan to hire, an attorney. Or, even after doing a lot of legal research on your own, you might decide that you really need an expert's help. Here are some tips for finding and working with a lawyer.

Finding a Lawyer

The best way to find a lawyer is generally to get a recommendation from someone you know who has worked with that person. Keep in mind that lawyers often specialize by subject area and limit practice to a particular geographic area. For instance, if your parents have a great estate planning lawyer in Denver, Colorado, that won't do you any good if you're looking for a family law expert in Louisville, Kentucky. The general idea is that you want to look for someone local with skills in the area of law at issue. Usually, that means finding someone with at least several years' of experience, too.

If you can't get a recommendation, consider whether any local professional organizations can help. If you're a new landlord looking for advice on how to deal with a difficult tenant, for example, a local apartment association might know local lawyers with the experience and knowledge you are looking for.

Finally, if these two methods don't work, you might want to use a lawyer referral system. For example, Nolo's Lawyer Directory provides detailed profiles of attorney advertisers, including information about each lawyer's education, experience, practice areas, and fee schedule. Go to www.nolo.com/lawyers or Nolo's main website at www.nolo.com.

With a few names, you can make some phone calls to either set up appointments with prospective lawyers. Be sure to find out whether you'll be charged for this initial consultation; some lawyers charge, while others don't. You'll want to know about the lawyer's education and experience, any history of professional discipline, and so forth. You shouldn't be shy about asking for recommendations, either—former clients have just the kind of perspective you're going to need.

When you choose a lawyer, you'll have to decide how payment will be structured. Some lawyers are willing to work on a contingency basis. That means they will not get paid unless, as the plaintiff in a lawsuit, you win or settle your case. The amount you'll pay the lawyer depends on what you agree to; in a case that settles, 25% of the recovery is typical, and in a case that the attorney wins at trial, 33% isn't uncommon.

Other lawyers might work for a flat fee, while some will charge you an hourly rate. If you have an attorney charging you by the hour, we suggest you set a time limit, after which the lawyer must call before doing additional work. This will prevent your costs from going sky-high without your input.

As we'll explain in the next section, you and the lawyer might be able to work out a more flexible work arrangement, with you utilizing some of the knowledge you've gained through the legal research you've already done.

Working With a Lawyer

Hopefully, after reading this book, the world of legal research no longer feels like a foreign place that only lawyers ever visit. Instead, you should be well-versed in the resources available to you. And if you've already researched your legal topic, you might be an expert in that as well.

These resources can be put to use if you are working with an attorney. First of all, as we've already discussed, they help you establish a list of questions you can ask your attorney. Additionally, understanding important legal concepts will help you focus on the most important facts and information you need to convey to your attorney to help make your legal case. Not only will your attorney appreciate your ability to recognize important issues, you'll save money because you won't waste time talking to your lawyer about facts that won't be considered by the court.

Also, knowing the law will allow you to assure yourself that your attorney is strongly advocating on your behalf, or, if necessary, recognize when it's time to find a lawyer who is a better fit.

Glossary

G

ab initio

Latin for "from the beginning." This term is used by lawyers intent on getting their money's worth from a liberal arts education by uttering such statements as, "The judge was against me ab initio."

abatement

A reduction. After a death, abatement occurs if the deceased person didn't leave enough property to fulfill all the bequests made in the will and meet other expenses. Gifts left in the will are cut back in order to pay taxes, satisfy debts, or take care of other gifts that are given priority under law or by the will itself.

abstract of title

A short history of a piece of land that lists any transfers in ownership, as well as any liabilities attached to it, such as mortgages.

abstract of trust

A condensed version of a living trust document that leaves out certain details, including what is in the trust and the identity of the beneficiaries. You can show an abstract of trust to a financial organization or another institution to prove that you have established a valid living trust, without revealing specifics that you want to keep private. In some states, this document is called a "certification of trust."

accessory

Someone who intentionally helps another person commit a felony by giving advice before the crime or helping to conceal the evidence or the perpetrator. An accessory is usually not physically present during the crime. For example, hiding a robber who is being sought by the police might make you an "accessory after the fact" to a robbery. Compare *accomplice*.

accomplice

Someone who helps another person (known as the principal) commit a crime. Unlike an accessory, an accomplice is usually present when the crime is committed. An accomplice is guilty of the same offense and usually receives the same sentence as the principal. For instance, the driver of the getaway car for a burglary is an accomplice and will be guilty of the burglary even though he may not have entered the building.

accord and satisfaction

An agreement to settle a contract dispute by accepting less than what is due. This procedure is often used by creditors who want to cut their losses by collecting as much money as they can from debtors who cannot pay the full amount.

acquittal

A decision by a judge or jury that a defendant in a criminal case is not guilty of a crime. An acquittal is not a finding of innocence; it is simply a conclusion that the prosecution has not proved its case beyond a reasonable doubt.

act of God

An extraordinary and unexpected natural event, such as a hurricane, a tornado, an earthquake, or even the sudden death of a person. An act of God may be a defense against liability for injuries or damages. Under the law of contracts, an act of God often serves as a valid excuse if one of the parties to the contract is unable to fulfill his or her duties—for instance, completing a construction project on time.

action

Another term for a lawsuit. For example, a plaintiff might say, "I began this negligence action last fall after the defendant, Ms. Adams, struck me while I was crossing the street at Elm and Main."

actus reus

Latin for a "guilty act." The actus reus is the act which, in combination with a certain mental state, such as intent or recklessness, constitutes a crime. For example, the crime of theft requires physically taking something (the actus reus) coupled with the intent to permanently deprive the owner of the object (the mental state, or mens rea).

ademption

The failure of a bequest of property in a will. The gift fails (is "adeemed") because the person who made the will no longer owns the property when he or she dies. Often this happens because the property has been sold, destroyed, or given away to someone other than the beneficiary named in the will. A bequest may also be adeemed when the will maker, while still living, gives the property to the intended beneficiary (called "ademption by satisfaction"). When a bequest is adeemed, the beneficiary named in the will is out of luck; he or she doesn't get cash or a different item of property to replace the one that was described in the will. For example, Mark writes in his will, "I leave to Rob the family vehicle," but then trades in his car for a jet ski. When Mark dies, Rob will receive nothing. Frustrated beneficiaries may challenge an ademption in court, especially if the property was not clearly identified in the first place.

admissible evidence

The evidence that a trial judge or jury may consider because the rules of evidence deem it reliable. See *evidence, inadmissible evidence.*

admission

1. An out-of-court statement by your adversary that you offer into evidence as an exception to the hearsay rule.
2. One side's statement that certain facts are true in response to a request from the other side during discovery.

adverse possession

A means by which one can legally take another's property without paying for it. The requirements for adversely possessing property vary among states, but usually include continuous and open use for a period of five or more years and payment of taxes on the property in question.

age of majority

Adulthood in the eyes of the law. After reaching the age of majority, a person is permitted to vote, make a valid will, enter into binding contracts, enlist in the armed forces, and purchase alcohol. Also, parents may stop making child support payments when a child reaches the age of majority. In most states the age of majority is 18, but this varies depending on the activity. For example, people are allowed to vote when they reach the age of 18, but can't purchase alcohol until they're 21.

agent

A person authorized to act for and under the direction of another person when dealing with third parties. The person who appoints an agent is called the principal. An agent can enter into binding agreements on the principal's behalf and may even create liability for the principal if the agent causes harm while carrying out his or her duties. See also *attorney-in-fact*.

aggravate

To make more serious or severe.

aggravating circumstances

Circumstances that increase the seriousness or outrageousness of a given crime and that, in turn, increase the wrongdoer's penalty or punishment. For example, the crime of aggravated assault is a physical attack made worse because it is committed with a dangerous weapon, results in severe bodily injury, or is made in conjunction with another serious crime. Aggravated assault is usually considered a felony, punishable by a prison sentence.

alternate beneficiary

A person, an organization, or an institution that receives property through a will, trust, or insurance policy when the first-named beneficiary is unable or refuses to take the property. For example, in his will, Jake leaves his collection of sheet music to his daughter, Mia, and names the local symphony as alternate beneficiary. When Jake dies, Mia decides that the symphony can make better use of the sheet music than she can, so she refuses (disclaims) the gift, and the manuscripts pass directly to the symphony. In insurance law, the alternate beneficiary, usually the person who receives the insurance proceeds because the initial or primary beneficiary has died, is called the secondary or contingent beneficiary.

alternative dispute resolution (ADR)

A catchall term that describes a number of methods used to resolve disputes out of court, including negotiation, conciliation, mediation, and the many types of arbitration. The common denominator of all ADR methods is that they are faster, less formal, cheaper, and often less adversarial than a court trial. In recent years the term "alternative dispute resolution" has begun to lose favor in some circles and ADR has come to mean "appropriate dispute resolution." The point of this semantic change is to emphasize that ADR methods stand on their own as effective ways to resolve disputes and should not be seen simply as alternatives to a court action.

amicus curiae

Latin for "friend of the court." This term describes a person or an organization that is not a party to a lawsuit as a plaintiff or a defendant but that has a strong interest in the case and wants to file its opinion with the court, usually in the form of a written brief. For example, the ACLU often submits materials to support a person who claims a violation of civil rights even though that person is represented by a lawyer.

ancillary probate

A probate proceeding conducted in a different state from the one in which the deceased person resided at the time of death. Ancillary probate proceedings are usually necessary if the deceased person owned real estate in another state.

annuity

A purchased policy that pays a fixed amount of benefits each year—although most annuities actually pay monthly—for the life of the person who is entitled to those benefits. In a simple life annuity, when the person receiving the annuity dies, the benefits stop; there is no final lump sum payment and no provision to pay benefits to a spouse or another survivor. A continuous annuity pays monthly installments for the life of the retired worker, and provides a smaller continuing annuity for the worker's spouse or another survivor after the worker's death. A joint and survivor annuity pays monthly benefits as long as the retired worker is alive, and then continues to pay the worker's spouse for life.

annulment

A court procedure that dissolves a marriage and treats it as if it never happened. Annulments are rare since the advent of no-fault divorce, but may be obtained in most states for one of the following reasons: misrepresentation, concealment (for example, of an addiction or criminal record), misunderstanding, and refusal to consummate the marriage.

answer

A defendant's written response to a plaintiff's initial court filing (called a complaint or petition). An answer normally denies some or all facts asserted by the complaint, and sometimes seeks to turn the tables on the plaintiff by making allegations or charges against the plaintiff (called counterclaims). Normally, a defendant has 30 days in which to file an answer after being served with the plaintiff's complaint. In some courts, an answer is simply called a "response."

appeal

A written request to a higher court to modify or reverse the judgment of a trial court or intermediate-level appellate court. Normally, an appellate court accepts as true all the facts that the trial judge or jury found to be true, and decides only whether the judge made mistakes in understanding and applying the law. If the appellate court decides that a mistake was made that changed the outcome, it will direct the lower court to conduct a new trial, but often the mistakes are deemed "harmless" and the judgment is left alone. Some mistakes—such as a miscalculation of money damages—are corrected by the appellate court without sending the case back to the trial court. An appeal begins when the loser at trial—or in an intermediate-level appellate court—files a notice of appeal, which must be done within strict time limits (often 30 days from the date of judgment). The loser (called the appellant) and the winner (called the appellee) submit written arguments (called briefs) and often make oral arguments explaining why the lower court's decision should be upheld or overturned.

appellant

A party to a lawsuit who appeals a losing decision to a higher court in an effort to have it modified or reversed.

appellate court

A higher court that reviews the decision of a lower court when a losing party files for an appeal.

appellee

A party to a lawsuit who wins in the trial court—or sometimes on a first appeal—only to have the other party (called the appellant) file for an appeal. An appellee files a written brief and often makes an oral argument before the appellate court, asking that the lower court's judgment be upheld. In some courts, an appellee is called a respondent.

arbitration

A noncourt procedure for resolving disputes using one or more
neutral third parties—called the arbitrator or arbitration panel.
Arbitration uses rules of evidence and procedure that are less formal
than those followed in trial courts, which usually leads to a faster
and less expensive resolution. There are many types of arbitration in
common use. Binding arbitration is similar to a court proceeding
in that the arbitrator has the power to impose a decision, although
this is sometimes limited by agreement—for example, in "hi-lo
arbitration," the parties may agree in advance to a maximum and
minimum award. In nonbinding arbitration, the arbitrator can
recommend but not impose a decision. Many contracts—including
those imposed on customers by many financial and health care
organizations—require mandatory arbitration in the event of a
dispute. This may be reasonable when the arbitrator really is neutral,
but is justifiably criticized when the large company that writes the
contract is able to influence the choice of arbitrator.

arraignment

A court appearance in which the defendant is formally charged with
a crime and asked to respond by pleading guilty, not guilty, or *nolo
contendere*. Other matters often handled at an arraignment are setting
the bail and arranging for the appointment of an attorney at public
expense if the defendant is unable to afford one.

arrearages

Overdue alimony or child support payments. In recent years, state
laws have made it almost impossible to get rid of arrearages; they
can't be discharged in bankruptcy, and courts usually will not cancel
them retroactively. A spouse or parent who falls on tough times and is
unable to make payments should request a temporary modification of
the payments before the arrearages build up.

arrest

A situation in which the police detain a person in a manner that, to
any reasonable person, makes it clear he or she is not free to leave.

A person can be "under arrest" even though the police have not announced it; handcuffs or physical restraint are not necessary to constitute an arrest. Questioning an arrested person about his or her involvement in or knowledge of a crime must be preceded by the *Miranda* warnings if the police intend to use the answers against the person in a criminal case. If the arrested person chooses to remain silent, the questioning must stop.

arrest warrant

A document issued by a judge or magistrate that authorizes the police to arrest someone. Warrants are issued when law enforcement personnel present evidence to a judge or magistrate that convinces him or her that it is reasonably likely that a crime has taken place and that the person to be named in the warrant is criminally responsible for that crime.

articles of incorporation

A document filed with state authorities (usually the secretary of state or corporations commissioner, depending on the state) to form a corporation. As required by the general incorporation law of the state, the articles normally include the purpose of the corporation, its principal place of business, the names of its initial controlling directors, and the amounts and types of stock it is authorized to issue.

assault

A crime that occurs when one person tries to physically harm another in a way that makes the person under attack feel immediately threatened. Actual physical contact is not necessary; threatening gestures that would alarm any reasonable person can constitute an assault. Compare *battery*.

assignee

A person to whom a property right is transferred. For example, an assignee may take over a lease from a tenant who wants to permanently move out before the lease expires. The assignee takes control of the property and assumes all the legal rights and responsibilities of the tenant, including payment of rent. However, the original tenant remains legally responsible if the assignee fails to pay the rent.

assignment

A transfer of property rights from one person to another, called the assignee.

attestation

The act of watching someone sign a legal document, such as a will or power of attorney, and then signing your own name as a witness. When you witness a document in this way, you are attesting—that is, stating and confirming—that the person you watched sign the document in fact did so. Attesting to a document does not mean that you are vouching for its accuracy or truthfulness. You are only acknowledging that you watched it being signed by the person whose name is on the signature line.

attorneys' fees

The payment made to a lawyer for legal services. These fees may take several forms:
- hourly
- per job or service—for example, $350 to draft a will
- contingency (the lawyer collects a percentage of any money won for the client and nothing if there is no recovery), or
- retainer (usually a down payment as part of an hourly or per-job fee agreement).

Attorneys' fees must usually be paid by the client who hires a lawyer, though occasionally a law or contract will require the losing party of a lawsuit to pay the winner's court costs and attorneys' fees. For example, a contract might contain a provision that says the loser of any lawsuit between the parties to the contract will pay the winner's attorneys' fees. Many laws designed to protect consumers also provide for attorneys' fees—for example, most state laws that require landlords to provide habitable housing also specify that a tenant who sues and wins using that law may collect attorneys' fees. And in family law cases—divorce, custody, and child support—judges often have the power to order the more affluent spouse to pay the other spouse's attorneys' fees, even when there is no clear victor.

attorney general

Head of the United States Department of Justice and chief law officer of the federal government. The attorney general represents the United States in legal matters, oversees federal prosecutors, and provides legal advice to the president and to heads of executive governmental departments. Each state also has an attorney general, responsible for advising the governor and state agencies and departments about legal issues, and for overseeing state prosecuting attorneys.

attorney work product privilege

A rule that protects materials prepared by a lawyer in preparation for trial from being seen and used by the adversary during discovery or trial.

attorney-client privilege

A rule that keeps any communication between an attorney and his or her client confidential and bars it from being used as evidence in a trial, or even being seen by the opposing party during discovery.

attorney-in-fact

A person named in a written power of attorney document to act on behalf of the person who signs the document, called the principal. The attorney-in-fact has only the powers and responsibilities that are granted in the specific power of attorney document. An attorney-in-fact is an agent of the principal.

attractive nuisance

Something on a piece of property that attracts children but also endangers their safety. For example, unfenced swimming pools, open pits, farm equipment, and abandoned refrigerators, have all qualified as attractive nuisances.

authenticate

To offer testimony that tells the judge what an item of evidence is and establishes its connection to the case.

avowal

A direct statement or declaration. Also, a statement made by a witness after the judge has ruled that his or her testimony is not admissible at trial. This statement "preserves" the testimony so that it may be considered by the court if the trial's outcome is an appeal.

bail

The money paid to the court, usually at arraignment or shortly thereafter, to ensure that an arrested person who is released from jail will show up at all required court appearances. The amount of bail is determined by the local bail schedule, which is based on the seriousness of the offense. The judge can increase the bail if the prosecutor convinces him or her that the defendant is likely to flee (for example, if he has failed to show up for court in the past), or he or she can decrease it if the defense attorney shows that the defendant is unlikely to run (for example, he has strong ties to the community by way of a steady job and a family).

bailiff

A court official usually classified as a peace officer (sometimes as a deputy sheriff, or marshal) and usually wearing a uniform. A bailiff's main job is to maintain order in the courtroom. In addition, bailiffs often help court proceedings go smoothly by shepherding witnesses in and out of the courtroom and handing evidence to witnesses as they testify. In criminal cases, the bailiff may have temporary charge of any defendant who is in custody during court proceedings.

bailor

Someone who delivers an item of personal property to another person for a specific purpose. For example, a person who leaves a broken DVD player with a repairperson in order to get it fixed would be a bailor.

bankruptcy

A legal proceeding that relieves you of the responsibility of paying your debts or provides you with protection while attempting to repay your debts. There are two types of bankruptcy: liquidation, in which your debts are wiped out (discharged), and reorganization, in which you provide the court with a plan for how you intend to repay your debts. For both consumers and businesses, liquidation bankruptcy is called Chapter 7. For consumers, reorganization bankruptcy is called Chapter 13. Reorganization bankruptcy for consumers with an extraordinary amount of debt and for businesses is called Chapter 11. Reorganization bankruptcy for family farmers is called Chapter 12.

bankruptcy trustee

A person appointed by the court to oversee the case of a person or business that has filed for bankruptcy. In a consumer Chapter 7 case, the trustee's role is to gather, liquidate, and distribute proportionally the debtor's nonexempt property to his or her creditors. In a Chapter 13 case, the trustee's role is to receive the debtor's monthly payments and distribute them proportionally to his or her creditors.

battery

A crime consisting of physical contact that is intended to harm someone. Unintentional harmful contact is not battery, no matter how careless the behavior or how severe the injury. A fistfight is a common battery; being hit by a wild pitch during a baseball game is not.

bench

The seat (usually a chair rather than a bench) where a judge sits in the courtroom. Sometimes the word "bench" is used in place of the word "judge"—for example, someone might say she wants a bench trial, meaning a trial by a judge without a jury.

bench trial

A trial before a judge with no jury. The term derives from the fact that the stand on which the judge sits is called the bench.

beneficiary

A person or an organization legally entitled to receive benefits through a legal device, such as a will, trust, or life insurance policy.

bequeath

A legal term sometimes used in wills that means "leave"—for example, "I bequeath my garden tools to my brother-in-law, Buster Jenkins."

bequest

The legal term for personal property (anything but real estate) left in a will.

best evidence rule

A rule of evidence that demands that the original of any document, photograph, or recording be used as evidence at trial, rather than a copy. A copy will be allowed into evidence only if the original is unavailable.

beyond a reasonable doubt

The burden of proof that the prosecution must carry in a criminal trial to obtain a guilty verdict. Reasonable doubt is sometimes explained as being convinced "to a moral certainty." The jury must be convinced that the defendant committed each element of the crime before returning a guilty verdict.

bifurcate

To separate the issues in a case so that one issue or set of issues can be tried and resolved before the others. For example, death penalty cases are always bifurcated: The court first hears the evidence of guilt and reaches a verdict, and then hears evidence about and decides which punishment to impose (death or life in prison without parole). Bifurcated trials are also common in product liability class action lawsuits in which many people claim that they were injured by the same defective product: The issue of liability is tried first, followed by the question of damages. Bifurcation is authorized by Rule 42(b) of the Federal Rules of Civil Procedure.

binding precedent

The decisions of higher courts that set the legal standards for similar cases in lower courts within the same jurisdiction.

blue law

A statute that forbids or regulates an activity, such as the sale of liquor on Sundays.

blue-sky laws

The laws that aim to protect people from investing in sham companies that consist of nothing but "blue sky." Blue-sky laws require that companies seeking to sell stock to the public submit information to and obtain the approval of a state or federal official who oversees corporate activity.

bond

1. A written agreement purchased from a bonding company that guarantees a person will properly carry out a specific act, such as managing funds, showing up in court, providing good title to a piece of real estate, or completing a construction project. If the person who purchased the bond fails at his or her task, the bonding company will pay the aggrieved party an amount up to the value of the bond.

2. An interest-bearing document issued by a government or company as evidence of a debt. A bond provides predetermined payments at a set date to the bondholder. Bonds may be "registered" bonds, which provide payment to the bondholder whose name is recorded with the issuer and appears on the bond certificate, or "bearer" bonds, which provide payments to whomever holds the bond in hand.

breach

A failure or violation of a legal obligation.

breach of contract

A legal claim that one party failed to perform as required under a valid agreement with the other party. For example you might say,

"The roofer breached our contract by using substandard supplies when he repaired my roof."

brief

A document used to submit a legal contention or argument to a court. A brief typically sets out the facts of the case and a party's argument as to why he or she should prevail. These arguments must be supported by legal authority and precedent, such as statutes, regulations, and previous court decisions. Although it is usually possible to submit a brief to a trial court (called a trial brief), briefs are most commonly used as a central part of the appeal process (an appellate brief). But don't be fooled by the name—briefs are usually anything but brief, as pointed out by writer Franz Kafka, who defined a lawyer as "a person who writes a 10,000-word decision and calls it a brief."

burden of proof

A party's job of convincing the decision maker in a trial that the party's version of the facts is true. In a civil trial, it means that the plaintiff must convince the judge or jury "by a preponderance of the evidence" that the plaintiff's version is true—that is, over 50% of the believable evidence is in the plaintiff's favor. In a criminal case, because a person's liberty is at stake, the government has a harder job, and must convince the judge or jury beyond a reasonable doubt that the defendant is guilty.

burglary

The crime of breaking into and entering a building with the intention to commit a felony. Modern burglary statutes often dispense with the "breaking and entering" requirement and operate whenever a person enters a building with the intent to commit any type of felony. For instance, someone would be guilty of burglary if he entered a house through an unlocked door in order to commit a murder.

business records exception

An exception to the hearsay rule that allows a business document to be admitted into evidence if a proper foundation is laid to show it is reliable.

bylaws

The rules that govern the internal affairs or actions of a corporation. Normally bylaws are adopted by the shareholders of a profit-making business or the board of directors of a nonprofit corporation. Bylaws generally include procedures for holding meetings and electing the board of directors and officers. The bylaws also set out the duties and powers of a corporation's officers.

capital case

A prosecution for murder in which the jury is asked to decide if the defendant is guilty and, if he or she is, whether he or she should be put to death. A prosecutor who brings a capital case (also called a death penalty case), must charge one or more "special circumstances" that the jury must find to be true in order to sentence the defendant to death. Each state (and the federal government) has its own list of special circumstances, but common ones include multiple murders, use of a bomb, or a finding that the murder was especially heinous, atrocious, or cruel.

capital punishment

The decision by a jury, in the second phase of a capital case, that the convicted defendant should be put to death.

caption

A heading on all pleadings submitted to the court. It states basic information such as the parties' names, court, and case number.

case

A term that most often refers to a lawsuit—for example, "I filed my small claims case." "Case" also refers to a written decision by a judge—or for an appellate case, a panel of judges. For example, the U.S. Supreme Court's decision legalizing abortion is commonly referred to as the *Roe v. Wade* case. Finally, the term also describes the evidence a party submits in support of his or her position—for example, "I have made my case," or, "My case-in-chief has been completed."

cause of action

A specific legal claim—such as for negligence, breach of contract, or medical malpractice—for which a plaintiff seeks compensation. Each cause of action is divided into discrete elements, all of which must be proved to present a winning case.

certified copy

A copy of a document issued by a court or government agency that is guaranteed to be a true and exact copy of the original. Many agencies and institutions require certified copies of legal documents before permitting certain transactions. For example, a certified copy of a death certificate is required before a bank will release the funds in a deceased person's payable-on-death account to the person who has inherited them.

challenge for cause

A party's request that the judge dismiss a potential juror from serving on a trial jury by providing a valid legal reason why he or she shouldn't serve. Potential bias is a common reason potential jurors are challenged for cause—for example, the potential juror is a relative of a party or one of the lawyers, or admits to a prejudice against one party's race or religion. Judges can also dismiss a potential juror for cause. There is no limit on the number of successful challenges for cause. Compare *peremptory challenge*.

chambers

A fancy word for a judge's office. Trial court judges often schedule pretrial settlement conferences and other informal meetings in chambers.

Chapter 7 bankruptcy

The most familiar type of bankruptcy, in which many or all of your debts are wiped out completely in exchange for giving up your nonexempt property.

Chapter 13 bankruptcy

The reorganization bankruptcy for consumers, in which you partially or fully repay your debts. In Chapter 13 bankruptcy, you keep your property and use your income to pay all or a portion of the debts over a period of years. The minimum amount you must pay is roughly equal to the value of your nonexempt property. In addition, you must pledge your disposable net income—after subtracting reasonable expenses—for the period during which you are making payments. At the end of the payment period, the balance of what you owe on most debts is erased.

charge

A formal accusation of criminal activity. The prosecuting attorney decides on the charges, after reviewing police reports, witness statements, and any other evidence of wrongdoing. Formal charges are announced at an arrested person's arraignment.

circuit court

The name used for the principal trial court in many states. In the federal system, appellate courts are organized into 13 circuits. Eleven of these cover different geographical areas of the country—for example, the United States Court of Appeal for the Ninth Circuit covers Alaska, Arizona, California, Hawaii, Idaho, Montana, Nevada, Oregon, and Washington. The remaining circuits are the District of Columbia Circuit and the Federal Circuit, (which hears patent, customs, and other specialized cases, based on subject matter). The term derives from an age before mechanized transit, when judges and lawyers rode "the circuit" of their territory to hold court in various places.

circumstantial evidence

Evidence that proves a fact by means of an inference. For example, from the evidence that a person was seen running away from the scene of a crime, a judge or jury may infer that the person committed the crime.

civil case

A noncriminal lawsuit, usually involving private property rights. For example, lawsuits involving breach of contract, probate, divorce, negligence, and copyright violations are just a few of the many hundreds of varieties of civil lawsuits.

civil procedure

The rules used to handle a civil case from the time the initial complaint is filed through pretrial discovery, the trial itself, and any subsequent appeal. Each state adopts its own rules of civil procedure (often set out in a separate Code of Civil Procedure), but many are influenced by or modeled on the Federal Rules of Civil Procedure.

class action

A lawsuit in which the interests of a large number of unnamed people with similar legal claims join together in a group (the class) and are represented by named plaintiffs who have been similarly affected by the wrongdoing alleged in the lawsuit. Common class actions involve cases in which a product has injured many people, or in which a group of people has suffered discrimination at the hands of an organization.

clear and present danger

Speech that poses a "clear and present danger" to the public or government will not be protected under the First Amendment's guarantee of free speech. The classic example is that falsely shouting "Fire!" in a crowded theatre is not protected speech.

close corporation

A corporation owned and operated by a few individuals, often members of the same family, rather than by public shareholders. State laws permit close corporations to function more informally than regular corporations. For example, shareholders can make decisions without holding meetings of the board of directors, and can fill vacancies on the board without a vote of the shareholders.

closing argument

At trial, a speech made by each party after all the evidence has been presented. The purpose is to review the testimony and evidence presented during the trial as part of a forceful explanation of why your side should win. Especially in trials before a judge without a jury, it is common for both parties to waive their closing argument on the theory that the judge has almost surely already arrived at his or her decision.

codicil

A supplement or addition to a will. Codicils must be signed and witnessed in the same manner as the underlying will. A codicil may explain, modify, add to, subtract from, qualify, alter, or revoke existing provisions in a will. Because a codicil changes a will, it must be signed in front of witnesses, just like a will.

collateral

Property that guarantees payment of a secured debt.

collateral estoppel

See *estoppel*.

common law marriage

In some states, a type of marriage in which couples can become legally married by living together for a long period of time, representing themselves as a married couple, and intending to be married. Contrary to popular belief, the couple must intend to be married and act as though they are in order for a common law marriage to take effect—merely living together for a long time won't do it.

community property

A method for defining the ownership of property acquired and the responsibility for debts incurred during marriage. Generally, in states that follow community property principles, all earnings during marriage and all property acquired with those earnings are considered community property. Likewise, all debts incurred during marriage are community property debts. Upon divorce, community property and community debts are generally divided equally between the spouses. At the death of one spouse, his or her half of the community property will go to the surviving spouse unless he or she leaves a will that directs otherwise. Community property laws exist in Alaska, Arizona, California, Idaho, Louisiana, Nevada, New Mexico, Texas, Washington, and Wisconsin. Compare *equitable distribution* and *separate property*.

community property with right of survivorship

A way for married couples to hold title to property, available in Alaska, Arizona, California, Idaho, Nevada, and Wisconsin. It allows one spouse's half-interest in community property to pass to the surviving spouse without probate.

comparable rectitude

A doctrine that grants the spouse least at fault a divorce when both spouses have shown grounds for divorce. It is a response to an old common law rule that prevented a divorce when both spouses were at fault.

competent evidence

Legally admissible evidence. Competent evidence tends to prove the matter in dispute. In a murder trial, for example, competent evidence might include the murder weapon with the defendant's fingerprints on it.

complaint

Papers filed with a court clerk by the plaintiff to initiate a lawsuit by setting out facts and legal claims (usually called causes of action). In some states and in some types of legal actions, such as divorce, complaints are called petitions and the person filing is called the petitioner. To complete the initial stage of a lawsuit, the plaintiff's complaint must be served on the defendant, who then has the opportunity to respond by filing an answer. In practice, few lawyers prepare complaints from scratch. Instead they use—and sometimes modify—predrafted complaints widely available in form books.

confidential communication

Information exchanged between two people who:
- have a relationship in which private communications are protected by law, and
- intend that the information be kept in confidence. The law recognizes certain parties whose communications will be considered confidential and protected, including spouses, doctor and patient, attorney and client, and priest and confessor. Communications between these individuals cannot be disclosed in court unless the protected party waives that protection. The intention that the communication be confidential is critical. For example, if an attorney and his client are discussing a matter in the presence of an unnecessary third party—for example, in an elevator with other people present—the discussion will not be considered confidential and may be admitted at trial. Also known as privileged communication.

conformed copy

An exact copy of a document filed with a court. To conform a copy, the court clerk will stamp the document with the filing date and add any handwritten notations to the document that exist on the original, including dates and the judge's signature. A conformed copy may or may not be certified.

consanguinity

An old-fashioned term referring to the relationship of "blood relatives"—people who have a common ancestor. Consanguinity exists, for example, between brothers and sisters but not between husbands and wives.

conservator

Someone appointed by a judge to oversee the affairs of an incapacitated person. A conservator who manages financial affairs is often called a "conservator of the estate." One who takes care of personal matters, such as health care and living arrangements, is known as a "conservator of the person." Sometimes, one conservator is appointed to handle all these tasks. Depending on where you live, a conservator may also be called a guardian, committee, or curator.

consideration

The basis of a contract. Consideration is a benefit or right for which the parties to a contract must bargain; the contract is founded on an exchange of one form of consideration for another. Consideration may be a promise to perform a certain act—for example, a promise to fix a leaky roof—or a promise not to do something, such as build a second story on a house that will block the neighbor's view. Whatever its particulars, consideration must be something of value to the people who are making the contract.

constructive eviction

A provision for housing that is so substandard that, for all intents and purposes, a landlord has evicted the tenant. For example, the landlord may refuse to provide light, heat, water, or other essential services, destroy part of the premises, or refuse to clean up an environmental health hazard, such as lead paint dust. Because the premises are unlivable, the tenant has the right to move out and stop paying rent without incurring legal liability for breaking the lease. Usually, the tenant must first bring the problem to the landlord's attention and allow a reasonable amount of time for the landlord to make repairs.

contempt of court

Behavior in or out of court that violates a court order, or otherwise disrupts or shows disregard for the court. Refusing to answer a proper question, to file court papers on time, or to follow local court rules can expose witnesses, lawyers, and litigants to contempt findings. Contempt of court is punishable by fine or imprisonment.

contest [as in to contest a will]

To oppose, dispute, or challenge through formal or legal procedures. For example, the defendant in a lawsuit almost always contests the case made by the plaintiff. Or, a disgruntled relative may formally contest the provisions of a will.

contingency

A provision in a contract stating that some or all of the terms of the contract will be altered or voided by the occurrence of a specific event. For example, a contingency in a contract for the purchase of a house might state that if the buyer does not approve the inspection report of the physical condition of the property, the buyer does not have to complete the purchase.

contingency fee

A method of paying a lawyer for legal representation by which, instead of an hourly or per-job fee, the lawyer receives a percentage of the money his or her client obtains after settling or winning the case. Often, contingency fee agreements—which are most commonly used in personal injury cases—award the successful lawyer between 20% and 50% of the amount recovered. Lawyers representing defendants charged with crimes may not charge contingency fees. In most states, contingency fee agreements must be in writing.

contingent beneficiary

1. An alternate beneficiary named in a will, trust, or other document.
2. Any person entitled to property under a will if one or more prior conditions are satisfied. For example, if Fred is entitled to take property under a will only if he's married at the time of the will

maker's death, Fred is a contingent beneficiary. Similarly, if Ellen is named to receive a house only in the event her mother, who has been named to live in the house, moves out of it, Ellen is a contingent beneficiary.

continuance

The postponement of a hearing, a trial, or another scheduled court proceeding, at the request of one or both parties, or by the judge without consulting the parties. Unhappiness with long trial court delays has resulted in the adoption by most states of "fast track" rules that sharply limit the ability of judges to grant continuances.

contract

A legally binding agreement involving two or more people or businesses (called parties) that sets forth what the parties will or will not do. Most contracts that can be carried out within one year can be either oral or written. Major exceptions include contracts involving the ownership of real estate and commercial contracts for goods worth $500 or more, which must be in writing to be enforceable. A contract is formed when competent parties—usually adults of sound mind, or business entities—mutually agree to provide each other some benefit (called consideration), such as a promise to pay money, in exchange for a promise to deliver specified goods or services or the actual delivery of those goods and services. A contract normally requires one party to make a reasonably detailed offer to do something—including, typically, the price, time for performance, and other essential terms and conditions—and the other to accept without significant change. For example, if I offer to sell you ten roses for $5 to be delivered next Thursday and you say "It's a deal," we've made a valid contract. On the other hand, if one party fails to offer something of benefit to the other, there is no contract. For example, if Maria promises to fix Josh's car, there is no contract unless Josh promises something in return for Maria's services.

conviction

A finding by a judge or jury that the defendant is guilty of a crime.

copyright

A legal device that provides the owner the right to control how a creative work is used. A copyright comprises a number of exclusive rights, including the right to make copies, authorize others to make copies, make derivative works, sell and market the work, and perform the work. Any one of these rights can be sold separately through transfers of copyright ownership.

corporation

A legal structure authorized by state law that allows a business to organize as a separate legal entity from its owners. A corporation is often referred to as an "artificial legal person," meaning that, like an individual, it can enter into contracts, sue and be sued, and do the many other things necessary to carry on a business. One advantage of incorporating is that a corporation's owners (shareholders) are legally shielded from personal liability for the corporation's liabilities and debts (unpaid taxes are often an exception). In theory, a corporation can be organized either for profit-making or nonprofit purposes. Most profit-making corporations are known as C corporations and are taxed separately from their owners, but those organized under Subchapter S of the Internal Revenue Code are pass-through tax entities, meaning that all profits are federally taxed on the personal income tax returns of their owners.

corpus delicti

Latin for the "body of the crime." Used to describe physical evidence, such as the corpse of a murder victim or the charred frame of a torched building.

cosigner

A person who signs his or her name to a loan agreement, lease, or credit application. If the primary debtor does not pay, the cosigner is fully responsible for the loan or debt. Many people use cosigners to qualify for a loan or credit card. A landlord may require a cosigner when renting to a student or someone with a poor credit history.

counterclaim

A defendant's court papers that seek to reverse the thrust of the lawsuit by claiming that it was the plaintiff—not the defendant—who committed legal wrongs, and that as a result it is the defendant who is entitled to money damages or other relief. Usually filed as part of the defendant's answer—which also denies plaintiff's claims—a counterclaim is commonly, but not always, based on the same events that form the basis of the plaintiff's complaint. For example, a defendant in an auto accident lawsuit might file a counterclaim alleging that it was really the plaintiff who caused the accident. In some states, the counterclaim has been replaced by a similar legal pleading called a cross-complaint. In other states and in federal court, where counterclaims are still used, a defendant must file any counterclaim that stems from the same events covered by the plaintiff's complaint or forever lose the right to do so. In still other states where counterclaims are used, they are not mandatory, meaning a defendant is free to raise a claim that it was really the plaintiff who was at fault either in a counterclaim or later as part of a separate lawsuit.

counteroffer

The rejection of an offer to buy or sell that simultaneously makes a different offer, changing the terms in some way. For example, if a buyer offers $5,000 for a used car, and the seller replies that he wants $5,500, the seller has rejected the buyer's offer of $5,000 and made a counteroffer to sell at $5,500. The legal significance of a counteroffer is that it completely voids the original offer, so that if the seller decided to sell for $5,000 the next day, the buyer would be under no legal obligation to buy the car.

court calendar

A list of the cases and hearings that will be held by a court on a particular day, week, or month. Because the length of time it will take to conduct a particular hearing or trial is at best a guess and many courts have a number of judges, accurately scheduling cases is difficult, with the result that court calendars are often revised and cases are often heard later than initially planned. A court calendar is sometimes called a docket, trial schedule, or trial list.

court costs

The fees charged for the use of a court, including the initial filing fee, fees for serving the summons, complaint, and other court papers, fees to pay a court reporter to transcribe deposition and in-court testimony, and, if a jury is involved, to pay the daily stipend of jurors. Often costs to photocopy court papers and exhibits are also included. Court costs must be paid by both parties as the case progresses, but ultimately, the losing party will be responsible for both parties' costs.

covenant

A restriction on the use of real estate that governs its use, such as a requirement that the property will be used only for residential purposes. Covenants are found in deeds or in documents that bind everyone who owns land in a particular development. See *covenants, conditions, and restrictions.*

covenants, conditions, and restrictions (CC&Rs)

The restrictions governing the use of real estate, usually enforced by a homeowners' association and passed on to the new owners of property. For example, CC&Rs may tell you how big your house can be, how you must landscape your yard, or whether you can have pets. If property is subject to CC&Rs, buyers must be notified before the sale takes place.

creditor

A person or an entity (such as a bank) to whom a debt is owed.

crime

A type of behavior that has been defined by the state as deserving of punishment, which usually includes imprisonment. Crimes and their punishments are defined by Congress and state legislatures.

criminal case

A lawsuit brought by a prosecutor employed by the federal, state, or local government that charges a person with the commission of a crime.

criminal insanity

A mental defect or disease that makes it impossible for a person to understand the wrongfulness of his or her acts or, even if he or she understands them, to distinguish right from wrong. Defendants who are criminally insane cannot be convicted of a crime, since criminal conduct involves the conscious intent to do wrong—a choice that the criminally insane cannot meaningfully make.

criminal law

Laws written by Congress and state legislators that make certain behavior illegal and punishable by fines and/or imprisonment. By contrast, civil laws are not punishable by imprisonment. In order for a defendant to be found guilty of a criminal law, the prosecution must show that the defendant intended to act as he or she did; in civil law, you may sometimes be responsible for your actions even though you did not intend the consequences. For example, civil law makes you financially responsible for a car accident you unintentionally caused.

cross-complaint

Sometimes called a cross-claim, legal paperwork that a defendant files to initiate his or her own lawsuit against the original plaintiff, a co-defendant, or someone who is not yet a party to the lawsuit. A cross-complaint must concern the same events that gave rise to the original lawsuit. For example, a defendant accused of causing an injury when she failed to stop at a red light might cross-complain against the mechanic who recently repaired her car, claiming that his negligence resulted in the brakes failing and, hence, that the accident was his fault. In some states where the defendant wishes to make a legal claim against the original plaintiff and no third party is claimed to be involved, a counterclaim, and not a cross-complaint, should be used.

cross-examination

At trial, the opportunity to question any witness, including your opponent, who testifies against you on direct examination. The opportunity to cross-examine usually occurs as soon as a witness completes his or her direct testimony—often the opposing lawyer or party, or sometimes the judge, signals that it is time to begin cross-examination by saying, "Your witness." Typically, there are two important reasons to engage in cross-examination: to attempt to get the witness to say something helpful to your side, or to cast doubt on (impeach) the witness by getting him or her to admit something that reduces his or her credibility—for example, that her eyesight is so poor that she may not have seen an event clearly.

custodial interference

The taking of a child from his or her parent with the intent to interfere with that parent's physical custody of the child. This is a crime in most states, even if the taker also has custody rights.

custodian

A term used by the Uniform Transfers to Minors Act for the person named to manage property left to a child under the terms of that Act. The custodian will manage the property if the gift-giver dies before the child has reached the age specified by state law—usually 21. When the child reaches the specified age, he or she will receive the property and the custodian will have no further role in its management.

custody (of a child)

The legal authority to make decisions affecting a child's interests (legal custody) and the responsibility of taking care of the child (physical custody). When parents separate or divorce, one of the hardest decisions they have to make is which parent will have custody. The most common arrangement is for one parent to have custody (both physical and legal) while the other parent has a right of visitation. But it is not uncommon for the parents to share legal custody, even though one parent has physical custody. The most uncommon arrangement is for the parents to share both legal and physical custody.

damages

In a lawsuit, money awarded to one party based on injury or loss caused by the other. There are many different types or categories of damages that occasionally overlap, including:

compensatory damages

Damages that cover actual injury or economic loss. Compensatory damages are intended to put the injured party in the position he or she was in prior to the injury. Compensatory damages typically include medical expenses, lost wages, and the repair or replacement of property (also called "actual damages").

general damages

Damages intended to cover injuries for which an exact dollar amount cannot be calculated. General damages are usually composed of pain and suffering, but can also include compensation for a shortened life expectancy, loss of the companionship of a loved one, and, in defamation cases (libel and slander), loss of reputation.

nominal damages

A term used when a judge or jury finds in favor of one party to a lawsuit—often because a law requires them to do so—but concludes that no real harm was done and therefore awards a very small amount of money. For example, if one neighbor sues another for libel based on untrue things the second neighbor said about the first, a jury might conclude that although libel technically occurred, no serious damage was done to the first neighbor's reputation and consequentially award nominal damages of $1.

punitive damages

Sometimes called exemplary damages, awarded over and above special and general damages to punish a losing party's willful or malicious misconduct.

special damages

Damages that cover the winning party's out-of-pocket costs. For example, in a vehicle accident, special damages typically include medical expenses, car repair costs, rental car fees, and lost wages. Often called "specials."

statutory damages

Damages required by statutory law. For example, in many states if a landlord doesn't return a tenant's security deposit in a timely fashion or give a reason why it is being withheld, the state statutes give the judge authority to order the landlord to pay damages of double or triple the amount of the deposit.

treble damages

(Lawyerspeak for triple damages.) To penalize lawbreakers, some statutes occasionally give judges the power to award the winning party in a civil lawsuit the amount it lost as a result of the other party's illegal conduct, plus damages of three times that amount.

debenture

A type of bond (an interest-bearing document that serves as evidence of a debt) that does not require security in the form of a mortgage or lien on a specific piece of property. Repayment of a debenture is guaranteed only by the general credit of the issuer. For example, a corporation may issue a secured bond that gives the bondholder a lien on the corporation's factory. But if it issues a debenture, the loan is not secured by any property at all. When a corporation issues debentures, the holders are considered creditors of the corporation and are entitled to payment before shareholders if the business folds.

debtor

A person or an entity (such as a bank) who owes money.

decedent

A person who has died, also called "deceased."

decision

The outcome of a proceeding before a judge, an arbitrator, a government agency, or another legal tribunal. "Decision" is a general term often used interchangeably with the terms "judgment" or "opinion." To be precise, however, a judgment is the written form of the court's decision in the clerk's minutes or notes, and an opinion is a written document setting out the reasons for reaching the decision.

declaration under penalty of perjury

A signed statement, sworn to be true by the signer, that will make the signer guilty of the crime of perjury if the statement is shown to be materially false—that is, the lie is relevant and significant to the case.

declaratory judgment

A court decision in a civil case that tells the parties what their rights and responsibilities are, without awarding damages or ordering them to do anything. Unlike most court cases, where the plaintiff asks for damages or other court orders, the plaintiff in a declaratory judgment case simply wants the court to resolve an uncertainty so that it can avoid serious legal trouble in the future. Courts are usually reluctant to hear declaratory judgment cases, preferring to wait until there has been a measurable loss. But especially in cases involving important constitutional rights, courts will step in to clarify the legal landscape. For example, many cities regulate the right to assemble by requiring permits to hold a parade. A disappointed applicant who thinks the decision-making process is unconstitutional might hold his parade anyway and challenge the ordinance after he's cited; or he might ask a court beforehand to rule on the constitutionality of the law. By going to court, the applicant may avoid a messy confrontation with the city—and perhaps a citation, as well.

dedimus potestatum

An outdated legal procedure that permitted a party to take and record the testimony of a witness before trial, but only when that testimony might otherwise be lost. For example, a party to a lawsuit might use the procedure to obtain the testimony of a witness who was terminally ill and might not be able to testify at the trial. Nowadays, the Federal Rules of Civil Procedure routinely permit the taking of testimony before trial if that testimony might otherwise be lost.

deed

A document that transfers ownership of real estate.

defamation

A false statement that injures someone's reputation and exposes him or her to public contempt, hatred, ridicule, or condemnation. If the false statement is published in print or through broadcast media, such as radio or TV, it is called libel. If it is only spoken, it is called slander. Libel is considered more serious than slander because the communication is permanently recorded in print or because it was broadcast to a large number of people. Defamation is a tort (a civil wrong) that entitles the injured party to compensation if he or she can prove that the statement damaged his or her reputation.

For example, if a worker can show that she lost her job because a coworker started a false rumor that she came to work drunk, she might be able to recover monetary damages. In certain extreme cases, such as a false accusation that a person committed a crime or has a feared disease, the plaintiff need not prove that she was damaged because the law presumes that damage was done. These cases are called "libel per se" or "slander per se." Public officials or figures who want to prove defamation must meet a higher standard than the standard for private citizens; they must prove that the person who issued the false statements knew they were false or recklessly disregarded a substantial likelihood that they were false.

default

A failure to perform a legal duty. For example, a default on a mortgage or car loan happens when you fail to make the loan payments on time, fail to maintain adequate insurance, or violate some other provision of the agreement. Default on a student loan occurs when you fail to repay a loan according to the terms you agreed to when you signed the promissory note, and the holder of your loan concludes that you do not intend to repay.

default judgment

At trial, a decision awarded to the plaintiff when a defendant fails to contest the case. To appeal a default judgment, a defendant must first file a motion in the court that issued it to have the default vacated (set aside).

defeasance

A clause in a deed, lease, or will or another legal document that completely or partially negates the document if a certain condition occurs or fails to occur. Defeasance also means the act of rendering something null and void. For example, a will may provide that a gift of property is defeasable—that is, it will be void—if the beneficiary fails to marry before the will maker's death.

defendant

The person against whom a lawsuit is filed. In certain states, and in certain types of lawsuits, the defendant is called the respondent. Compare *plaintiff*.

demurrer

A request made to a court, asking it to dismiss a lawsuit on the grounds that no legal claim is asserted. For example, you might file a demurrer if your neighbor sued you for parking on the street in front of her house. Your parking habits may annoy your neighbor, but the curb is public property and parking there doesn't cause any harm recognized by the law. After a demurrer is filed, the judge holds a hearing at which both sides can make their arguments about the matter. The judge may dismiss all or part of the lawsuit, or may allow the party who filed the lawsuit to amend its complaint. In some states and in federal court, the term demurrer has been replaced by "motion to dismiss for failure to state a claim" (called a "12(b)(6) motion" in federal court) or similar term.

deponent

Someone whose deposition is being taken.

deposition

An important tool used in pretrial discovery where one party questions the other party or a witness who is in the case. Often conducted in an attorney's office, a deposition requires that all questions be answered under oath and be recorded by a court reporter, who creates a deposition transcript. Increasingly, depositions are being videotaped. Any deponent may be represented by an attorney. At trial, deposition testimony can be used to cast doubt on (impeach) a witness's contradictory testimony or to refresh the memory of a suddenly forgetful witness. If a deposed witness is unavailable when the trial takes place—for example, if he or she has died—the deposition may be read to the jury in place of live testimony.

devise

An old legal term that is generally used to refer to real estate left to someone under the terms of a will, or to the act of leaving such real estate. In some states, "devise" now applies to any kind of property left by will, making it identical to the term bequest. Compare *legacy*.

dictum

A remark, a statement, or an observation of a judge that is not a necessary part of the legal reasoning needed to reach the decision in a case. Although dictum may be cited in a legal argument, it is not binding as legal precedent, meaning that other courts are not required to accept it. For example, if a defendant ran a stop sign and caused a collision, the judge's comments about the mechanical reliability of the particular make of the defendant's car would not be necessary to reach a decision in the case, and would be considered dictum. In future cases, lower court judges are free to ignore the comments when reaching their decisions. Dictum is an abbreviation of the Latin phrase "obiter dictum," which means a remark by the way, or an aside.

direct examination

At trial, the initial questioning of a party or witness by the side that called him or her to testify. The major purpose of direct examination is to explain your version of events to the judge or jury and to undercut your adversary's version. Good direct examination seeks to prove all facts necessary to satisfy the plaintiff's legal claims or causes of action—for example, that the defendant breached a valid contract and, as a result, the plaintiff suffered a loss.

directed verdict

A ruling by a judge, typically made after the plaintiff has presented all of his or her evidence but before the defendant puts on his or her case, that awards judgment to the defendant. A directed verdict is usually made because the judge concludes the plaintiff has failed to offer the minimum amount of evidence to prove his or her case even if there were no opposition. In other words, the judge is saying that, as a matter of law, no reasonable jury could decide in the plaintiff's favor. In a criminal case, a directed verdict is a judgment of acquittal for the defendant.

discharge (of debts)

A bankruptcy court's erasure of the debts of a person or business that has filed for bankruptcy.

discharge (of probate administrator)

A court order releasing the administrator or executor from any further duties connected with the probate of an estate. This typically occurs when the duties have been completed but may happen sooner if the executor or administrator wishes to withdraw or is dismissed.

dischargeable debts

Debts that can be erased by going through bankruptcy. Most debts incurred prior to declaring bankruptcy are dischargeable, including back rent, credit card bills, and medical bills. Compare *nondischargeable debts*.

disclaim

1. To refuse or give away a claim or a right to something. For example, if your aunt leaves you a white elephant in her will and you don't want it, you can refuse the gift by disclaiming your ownership rights.
2. To deny responsibility for a claim or act. For example, a merchant that sells goods secondhand may disclaim responsibility for a product's defects by selling it "as is."

disclaimer

1. A refusal or renunciation of a claim or right.
2. A refusal or denial of responsibility for a claim or an act.
3. The written clause or document that sets out the disclaimer. See also *disclaim*.

disclosure

The making known of a fact that had previously been hidden; a revelation. For example, in many states you must disclose major physical defects in a house you are selling, such as a leaky roof or potential flooding problem.

discovery

A formal investigation—governed by court rules—that is conducted before trial. Discovery allows one party to question other parties, and sometimes witnesses. It also allows one party to force the others to produce requested documents or other physical evidence. The most common types of discovery are interrogatories, consisting of written questions the other party must answer under penalty of perjury, and depositions, which involve an in-person session at which one party to a lawsuit has the opportunity to ask oral questions of the other party or his or her witnesses under oath while a written transcript is made by a court reporter. Other types of pretrial discovery consist of written requests to produce documents and requests for admissions, by which one party asks the other to admit or deny key facts in the case. One major purpose of discovery is to assess the strength or weakness of an opponent's case, with the idea of opening settlement talks. Another is to gather information to use at trial. Discovery is also present in criminal cases, in which by law the prosecutor must turn over to the defense any witness statements and any evidence that might tend to exonerate the defendant. Depending on the rules of the court, the defendant may also be obliged to share evidence with the prosecutor.

disinherit

To deliberately prevent someone from inheriting something. This is usually done by a provision in a will stating that someone who would ordinarily inherit property—a close family member, for example—should not receive it. In most states, you cannot completely disinherit your spouse; a surviving spouse has the right to claim a portion (usually one-third to one-half) of the deceased spouse's estate. With a few exceptions, however, you can expressly disinherit children.

dissolution

A term used instead of divorce in some states.

distributee

Anyone who receives something. Usually, the term refers to someone who inherits a deceased person's property. If the deceased person dies without a will (called intestate), state law determines what each distributee will receive. Also called a beneficiary.

district attorney (D.A.)

A lawyer who is elected to represent a state government in criminal cases in a designated county or judicial district. A D.A.'s duties typically include reviewing police arrest reports, deciding whether to bring criminal charges against arrested people, and prosecuting criminal cases in court. The D.A. may also supervise other attorneys, called deputy district attorneys or assistant district attorneys. In some states, a district attorney may be called a prosecuting attorney, county attorney, or state's attorney. In the federal system, the equivalent to the D.A. is a United States attorney. The country has many U.S.

attorneys, each appointed by the president, who supervise regional offices staffed with prosecutors called assistant United States attorneys.

district court

In federal court and in some states, the name of the main trial court. Thus, if you file suit in federal court, your case will normally be heard in federal district court. States may also group their appellate courts into districts—for example, the First District Court of Appeal.

diversity jurisdiction

The power of the federal courts to decide cases between two citizens of different states, provided the amount the plaintiff seeks in damages exceeds $75,000.

docket

See *court calendar.*

doing business as (DBA)

A situation in which a business owner operates a company under a name different from his or her real name. When starting a new business that is named in this way, the owner must file a "fictitious name statement" or similar document with the appropriate county or state agency—for example, the county clerk or secretary of state's office. Putting this document on file enables consumers to discover the names of the business owners, which will be important if a consumer needs to sue the business. It also allows the business owner to conduct transactions in the business's name, such as opening bank accounts and obtaining a taxpayer identification number; and to bring lawsuits under the business's name for business-related debts. Filing a fictitious name statement does not in itself confer trademark protection for the name.

dominant tenement

Property that carries a right to use a portion of a neighboring property. For example, property that benefits from a beach access trail across another property is the dominant tenement.

dower and curtesy

A surviving spouse's right to receive a set portion of the deceased spouse's estate—usually one-third to one-half. Dower (not to be confused with a "dowry") refers to the portion to which a surviving wife is entitled, while curtesy refers to what a man may claim. Until recently, these amounts differed in a number of states. However, because discrimination on the basis of sex is now illegal in most cases, most states have abolished dower and curtesy and generally provide the same benefits regardless of sex—and this amount is often known simply as the statutory share. Under certain circumstances, a living spouse may not be able to sell or convey property that is subject to the other spouse's dower and curtesy or statutory share rights.

durable power of attorney

A power of attorney that remains in effect if the principal becomes incapacitated. If a power of attorney is not specifically made durable, it automatically expires if the principal becomes incapacitated. See *durable power of attorney for finances, durable power of attorney for health care.*

durable power of attorney for finances

A legal document that gives someone authority to manage your financial affairs if you become incapacitated. The person you name to represent you is called an attorney-in-fact.

durable power of attorney for health care

A legal document that you can use to give someone permission to make medical decisions for you if you are unable to make those decisions yourself. The person you name to represent you may be called an attorney-in-fact, health care proxy, agent, or patient advocate, depending on where you live.

dynamite charge

A judge's admonition to a deadlocked jury to go back to the jury room and try harder to reach a verdict. The judge might remind the jurors to respectfully consider the opinions of others and will often assure them that if the case has to be tried again, another jury won't necessarily do a better job than they're doing. Because of its coercive nature, some states prohibit the use of a dynamite charge as a violation of their state constitution, but the practice passed Federal constitutional muster in the case of *Allen v. Gainer*. The instruction is also known as a dynamite instruction, shotgun instruction, *Allen* charge, or third-degree instruction.

easement

A right to use another person's real estate for a specific purpose. The most common type of easement is the right to travel over another person's land, known as a right of way. In addition, property owners commonly grant easements for the placement of utility poles, utility trenches, water lines, or sewer lines. The owner of property that is subject to an easement is said to be "burdened" with the easement, because he or she is not allowed to interfere with its use. For example, if the deed to John's property permits Sue to travel across John's main road to reach her own home, John cannot do anything to block the road. On the other hand, Sue cannot do anything that exceeds the scope of her easement, such as widening the roadway.

easement by prescription

A right to use property, acquired by a long tradition of open and obvious use. For example, if hikers have been using a trail through your backyard for ten years and you've never complained, they probably have an easement by prescription through your yard to the trail.

effluxion of time

The normal expiration of a lease due to the passage of time, rather than due to a specific event that might cause the lease to end, such as destruction of the building.

emancipation

The act of freeing someone from restraint or bondage. For example, on January 1, 1863, slaves in the Confederate states were declared free by an executive order of President Lincoln, known as the "Emancipation Proclamation." After the Civil War, this emancipation was extended to the entire country and made law by the ratification of the Thirteenth Amendment to the Constitution. Nowadays, emancipation refers to the point at which a child is free from parental control. It occurs when the child's parents no longer perform their parental duties and surrender their rights to the care, custody, and earnings of their minor child. Emancipation may be the result of a voluntary agreement between the parents and child, or it may be implied from their acts and ongoing conduct. For example, a child who leaves her parents' home and becomes entirely self-supporting without their objection is considered emancipated, while a child who goes to stay with a friend or relative and gets a part-time job is not. Emancipation may also occur when a minor child marries or enters the military.

emergency protective order

Any court-issued order meant to protect a person from harm or harassment. An emergency protective order is issued by the police, when court is out of session, to prevent domestic violence. An emergency protective order is a stopgap measure, usually lasting only for a weekend or holiday, after which the abused person is expected to seek a temporary restraining order (TRO) from a court.

eminent domain

The power of the federal or state government to take private property for a public purpose, even if the property owner objects, provided that the property owner is compensated for the loss. The Fifth Amendment to the United States Constitution allows the government to take private property if the taking is for a public use and the owner is "justly compensated" (usually, paid fair market value) for his or her loss. A public use is virtually anything that is sanctioned by a federal or state legislative body, but such uses may include roads, parks, reservoirs, schools, hospitals, or other public buildings. Sometimes called condemnation, taking, or expropriation.

encroachment

The building of a structure entirely or partly on a neighbor's property. Encroachment may occur due to faulty surveying or sheer obstreperousness on the part of the builder. Solutions range from paying the rightful property owner for the use of the property to the court-ordered removal of the structure.

equitable distribution

A legal principle, followed by most states, under which assets and earnings acquired during marriage are divided equitably (fairly) at divorce. Typically this means a 50-50 split, but not always. In theory, equitable means equal, but in practice it often means that the higher wage earner gets two-thirds to the lower wage earner's one-third. If a spouse obtains a fault divorce, the "guilty" spouse may receive less than his or her equitable share upon divorce.

escheat

The forfeit of all property to the state when a person dies without heirs.

estate

Generally, all the property you own when you die. The term is also used when referring to a person's probate estate (the property actually passing through the probate process) and bankruptcy estate (the property subject to the bankruptcy court's jurisdiction).

estoppel

A legal principle that prevents a person from asserting or denying something in court that contradicts what has already been established as the truth. Types of estoppel include:

equitable estoppel

A type of estoppel that bars a person from adopting a position in court that contradicts his or her past statements or actions when that contradictory stance would be unfair to another person who relied on the original position. For example, if a landlord agrees to allow a tenant to pay the rent ten days late for the next six months, it would be unfair to allow the landlord to bring a court action in the fourth month to evict the tenant for being a week late with the rent. The landlord would be estopped from asserting his right to evict the tenant for late payment of rent. Also known as estoppel in pais.

estoppel by deed

A type of estoppel that prevents a person from denying the truth of anything that he or she stated in a deed, especially regarding who has valid ownership of the property. For example, someone who grants a deed to real estate before he actually owns the property can't later go back and undo the sale for that reason if, say, the new owner strikes oil in the backyard.

estoppel by silence

A type of estoppel that prevents a person from asserting something when he or she had both the duty and the opportunity to speak up earlier, and his or her silence put another person at a disadvantage. For example, Edwards' Roofing Company has the wrong address and begins ripping the roof from Betty's house by mistake. If Betty sees this but remains silent, she cannot wait until the new roof is installed and then refuse to pay, asserting that the work was done without her agreement.

promissory estoppel

1. A type of estoppel that prevents a person who made a promise from reneging when someone else has reasonably relied on the promise and will suffer a loss if the promise is broken. For example, Forrest tells Antonio to go ahead and buy a boat without a motor, because he will sell Antonio an old boat motor at a very reasonable price. If Antonio relies on Forrest's promise and buys the motorless boat, Forrest cannot then deny his promise to sell Antonio the motor at the agreed-upon price.

2. A legal doctrine that prevents the relitigation of facts or issues that were previously resolved in court. For example, Alvin loses control of his car and accidentally sideswipes

several parked cars. When the first car owner sues Alvin for damages, the court determines that Alvin was legally drunk at the time of the accident. Alvin will not be able to deny this fact in subsequent lawsuits against him. This type of estoppel is most commonly called collateral estoppel.

evidence

The many types of information presented to a judge or jury designed to convince them of the truth or falsity of key facts. Evidence typically includes testimony of witnesses, documents, photographs, items of damaged property, government records, videos, and laboratory reports. Rules that are as strict as they are quirky and technical govern what types of evidence can be properly admitted as part of a trial. For example, the hearsay rule purports to prevent secondhand testimony of the "he said, she said" variety, but the existence of dozens of exceptions often means that hairsplitting lawyers can find a way to introduce such testimony into evidence. See also *admissible evidence, inadmissible evidence.*

exclusionary rule

A rule of evidence that disallows the use of illegally obtained evidence in criminal trials. For example, the exclusionary rule would prevent a prosecutor from introducing at trial evidence seized during an illegal search.

executive privilege

The privilege that allows the president and other high officials of the executive branch to keep certain communications private if disclosing those communications would disrupt the functions or decision-making processes of the executive branch. As demonstrated by the Watergate hearings, this privilege does not extend to information germane to a criminal investigation.

executor

The person named in a will to handle the property of someone who has died. The executor must collect and manage the property, pay debts and taxes, and then distribute what's left as specified in the will. In addition, the executor handles any probate court proceedings (with the help of a lawyer, if necessary) and takes care of day-to-day tasks—for example, terminating leases and credit cards, and notifying people and organizations of the death. Executors are also called personal representatives.

express warranty

A guarantee about the quality of goods or services made by a seller, such as, "This item is guaranteed against defects in construction for one year." Most express warranties come directly from the manufacturer or are included in the sales contract. If you want to hold the seller to an oral guarantee, it's best to get it in writing or have witnesses to the guarantee so that it doesn't come down to your word against the seller's if a problem arises.

expunge

To intentionally destroy, obliterate, or strike out records or information in files, computers, and other depositories. For example, state law may allow the criminal records of a juvenile offender to be expunged when he reaches the age of majority to allow him to begin his adult life with a clean record. Or, a company or government agency may routinely expunge out-of-date records to save storage space.

failure of consideration

The refusal or inability of a contracting party to perform its side of a bargain.

failure of issue

A situation in which a person dies without children who could have inherited his or her property.

fair use rule

A law that authorizes the use of copyrighted materials for certain purposes without the copyright owner's permission. Generally, uses intended to further scholarship, education, or an informed public are considered fair use, but recent years have seen severe limits placed on the amount of a work that can be reproduced under the fair use rule.

false imprisonment

Intentionally restraining another person's freedom of movement without having the legal right to do so. It's not necessary that physical force be used; threats or a show of apparent authority are sufficient. False imprisonment is a misdemeanor and a tort (a civil wrong). If the perpetrator confines the victim for a substantial period of time (or moves him or her a significant distance) in order to commit a felony, the false imprisonment may become a kidnapping. People who are arrested and get the charges dropped, or are later acquitted, often think that they can sue the arresting officer for false imprisonment (also known as false arrest). These lawsuits rarely succeed: As long as the officer had probable cause to arrest the person, the officer will not be liable for a false arrest, even if it turns out later that the information the officer relied upon was incorrect.

family court

A separate court, or more likely a separate division of the regular state trial court, that considers only cases involving divorce (dissolution of marriage), child custody and support, guardianship, adoption, and other cases having to do with family-related issues, including the issuance of restraining orders in domestic violence cases.

fault divorce

A tradition that required one spouse to prove that the other spouse was legally at fault, to obtain a divorce. The "innocent" spouse was then granted the divorce from the "guilty" spouse. Today, 35 states still allow a spouse to allege fault in obtaining a divorce. The traditional fault grounds for divorce are adultery, cruelty, desertion, confinement in prison, physical incapacity, and incurable insanity. These grounds are also generally referred to as marital misconduct.

federal court

A branch of the United States government with power derived directly from the U.S. Constitution. Federal courts decide cases involving the U.S. Constitution, federal law—for example, patents, federal taxes, labor law, and federal crimes, such as robbing a federally chartered bank—and cases where the parties are from different states and are involved in a dispute for $75,000 or more.

felony

A serious crime (contrasted with misdemeanors and infractions, less serious crimes), usually punishable by a prison term of more than one year or, in some cases, by death. For example, murder, extortion, and kidnapping are felonies; a minor fistfight is usually charged as a misdemeanor, and a speeding ticket is generally an infraction.

Feres doctrine

A legal doctrine that prevents people who are injured as a result of military service from successfully suing the federal government under the Federal Tort Claims Act. The doctrine comes from the U.S. Supreme Court case *Feres v. United States*, in which servicemen who picked up highly radioactive weapons fragments from a crashed airplane were not permitted to recover damages from the government. Also known as the *Feres-Stencel* doctrine or the *Feres* rule.

fictitious name

Any name a person uses that is not his or her real name. Fictitious names are often used in conducting a business. (See *doing business as.*) They may also be used when filing a lawsuit against a party whose real name is unknown or when, with the consent of the court, it is appropriate to conceal the true name of the party. John Doe is often used for an unknown male and Jane Roe is used for an unknown female. For example, the most well-known use of a fictitious name in a court case is *Roe v. Wade*, the case that established a woman's right to have an abortion without undue interference from the government. Jane Roe was a fictitious name for the plaintiff in that case.

fieri facias

Latin for "that you cause to be done." This is a court document that instructs a sheriff to seize and sell a defendant's property in order to satisfy a monetary judgment against the defendant.

final beneficiary

The person or institution designated to receive trust property upon the death of a life beneficiary. For example, Jim creates a trust through which his wife, Jane, receives income for the duration of her life. Their daughter, the final beneficiary, receives the trust principal after Jane's death.

forbearance

Voluntarily refraining from doing something, such as asserting a legal right. For example, a creditor may forbear on its right to collect a debt by temporarily postponing or reducing the borrower's payments.

foreclosure

The forced sale of real estate to pay off a loan on which the owner of the property has defaulted.

forfeiture

The loss of property or a privilege due to breaking a law. For example, a landlord may forfeit his or her property to the federal or state government if the landlord knows it is a drug-dealing site but fails to stop the illegal activity. Or, you may have to forfeit your driver's license if you commit too many moving violations or are convicted of driving under the influence of alcohol or drugs.

form interrogatories

Preprinted or "canned" sets of questions that one party in a lawsuit asks an opposing party. Form interrogatories cover the issues commonly encountered in the kind of lawsuit at hand. For example, lawyers' form books have sets of interrogatories designed for contract disputes, landlord-tenant cases, and many others. Form interrogatories are often supplemented by questions written by the lawyers and designed for the particular issues in the case.

forum

Refers to the court in which a lawsuit is filed or in which a hearing or trial is conducted.

forum nonconveniens

Latin for "inconvenient court." Because these days strict written rules of jurisdiction and venue are used to decide where a case can and cannot be properly filed, this term has largely lost any real meaning, except as yet another example of a confusing Latin term that lawyers take pleasure in using.

forum shopping

The process by which a plaintiff chooses among two or more courts that have the power—technically, the correct jurisdiction and venue—to consider his or her case. This decision is based on which court is likely to consider the case most favorably. In some instances, a case can properly be filed in two or more federal district courts as well as in the trial courts of several states—and this makes forum shopping a complicated business. It often involves weighing a number of factors, including proximity to the court, the reputation of the judge in the particular legal area, the likely type of available jurors, and subtle differences in governing law and procedure.

fraud

Intentionally deceiving another person and causing him or her to suffer a loss. Fraud includes lies and half-truths, such as selling a lemon and claiming "she runs like a dream."

future interest

A right to property that cannot be enforced in the present, but only at some time in the future. For example, John's will leaves his house to his sister Marian, but only after the death of his wife, Hillary. Marian has a future interest in the house.

garnishment

A court-ordered process that takes property from a person to satisfy a debt. For example, a person who owes money to a creditor may have her wages garnished if she loses a lawsuit filed by the creditor. Up to 25% of her wages can be deducted from her check to pay the debt before she ever sees her check on payday.

general partner

A person who joins together with at least one other to own and operate a business for profit—and who, unlike the owners of a corporation, is personally liable for all the business's debts. In addition to being responsible for all partnership debts and obligations, a general partner can take actions that legally bind the entire business. That means, for example, that if one partner signs a contract on behalf of the partnership, it will be fully enforceable against the partnership and each individual partner, even if the other partners weren't consulted in advance and didn't approve the contract. In contrast, a limited partner is liable only to the extent of the capital he or she has invested in the business. The term general partner may also refer to the managing partner of a limited partnership who is responsible for partnership debts over and above his or her individual investment in the partnership. See also *partnership, limited partnership*.

general power of attorney

See *power of attorney*.

grand jury

In criminal cases, a group (usually between 17 and 23 persons) that decides whether there is enough evidence to justify an indictment (formal felony charges) and a trial. A grand jury indictment is the first step, after arrest, in any formal prosecution of a felony.

grandfather clause

A provision in a new law that limits its application to people who are new to the system; people already in the system are exempt from the new regulation. For example, when Washington, DC, raised its drinking age from 18 to 21, people between those ages, who could drink under the old law, were allowed to retain the right to legally consume alcohol under a grandfather clause.

grant deed

A deed containing an implied promise that the person transferring the property actually owns the title and that it is not encumbered in any way, except as described in the deed. This is the most commonly used type of deed. Compare *quitclaim deed.*

gravamen

The essential element of a lawsuit. For example, the gravamen of a lawsuit involving a car accident might be the careless driving of the defendant.

gross lease

A commercial real estate lease in which the tenant pays a fixed amount of rent per month or year, regardless of the landlord's operating costs, such as maintenance, taxes, and insurance. A gross lease closely resembles the typical residential lease. The tenant may agree to a "gross lease with stops," meaning that the tenant will pitch in if the landlord's operating costs rise above a certain level. In real estate lingo, the point when the tenant starts to contribute is called the "stop level," because that's where the landlord's share of the costs stops.

guarantor

A person who makes a legally binding promise to either pay another person's debt or perform another person's duty if that person defaults or fails to perform. The guarantor gives a "guaranty," which is an assurance that the debt or other obligation will be fulfilled.

guaranty

When used as a verb, to agree to pay another person's debt or perform another person's duty, if that person fails to come through. As a noun, the written document in which this assurance is made. For example, if you cosign a loan, you have made a guaranty and will be legally responsible for the debt if the borrower fails to repay the money as promised. The person who makes a guaranty is called the guarantor. Also known as a guarantee or warranty.

guardian

An adult who has been given the legal right by a court to control and care for a minor or (in some states) an incapacitated adult, and his or her property. Someone who looks after a child's property is called a "guardian of the estate." An adult who has legal authority to make personal decisions for the child, including responsibility for his or her physical, medical, and educational needs, is called a "guardian of the person." Sometimes just one person will be named to take care of all these tasks. An individual appointed by a court to look after an incapacitated adult may also be known as a guardian, but is more frequently called a conservator.

guardian *ad litem*

A person, not necessarily a lawyer, who is appointed by a court to represent and protect the interests of a child or an incapacitated adult during a lawsuit. For example, a guardian *ad litem* (GAL) may be appointed to represent the interests of a child whose parents are locked in a contentious battle for custody, or to protect a child's interests in a lawsuit where there are allegations of child abuse. The GAL may conduct interviews and investigations, make reports to the court, and participate in court hearings or mediation sessions. Sometimes called court-appointed special advocates (CASAs).

guardianship

A legal relationship created by a court between a guardian and his or her ward—either a minor child or an incapacitated adult. The guardian has a legal right and duty to care for the ward. This may involve making personal decisions on his or her behalf, managing property, or both. Guardianships of incapacitated adults are more typically called conservatorships.

habeas corpus

Latin for "You have the body." For example, a prisoner files a petition for writ of *habeas corpus* in order to challenge the authority of the prison or jail warden to continue to hold him. If the judge orders a hearing after reading the writ, the prisoner gets to argue that his confinement is illegal. These writs are frequently filed by convicted prisoners who challenge their conviction on the grounds that the trial attorney failed to prepare the defense and was incompetent. Prisoners sentenced to death also file *habeas* petitions challenging the constitutionality of the state death penalty law. *Habeas* writs are different from and do not replace appeals, which are arguments for reversal of a conviction based on claims that the judge conducted the trial improperly. Often, convicted prisoners file both.

hearing

In the trial court context, a legal proceeding (other than a full-scale trial) held before a judge. During a hearing, evidence and arguments are presented in an effort to resolve a disputed factual or legal issue. Hearings typically, but by no means always, occur prior to trial when a party asks the judge to decide a specific issue—often on an interim basis—such as whether a temporary restraining order or preliminary injunction should be issued, or temporary child custody or child support awarded. In the administrative or agency law context, a hearing is usually a proceeding before an administrative hearing officer or judge representing an agency that has the power to regulate a particular field or oversee a governmental benefit program. For example, the Federal Aviation Board has the authority to hold hearings on airline safety, and a state Workers' Compensation Appeals Board has the power to rule on the appeals of people whose applications for benefits have been denied.

hearsay rule

A rule of evidence that prohibits the consideration of secondhand testimony at a trial. For example, if an eyewitness to an accident later tells another person what she saw, the second person's testimony would normally be excluded from a trial by the hearsay rule. The major reason for this rule is that secondhand testimony is thought to be inherently unreliable in large part because the opposing party has no ability to confront and cross-examine the person who has firsthand knowledge of the event. However, there are a great many exceptions to the hearsay rule in situations where courts have concluded that a particular type of hearsay is likely to be reliable. These exceptions include statements by an opposing party that contradict what he or she has said in court (called "admissions against interest"), government records, the statements of dying people, spontaneous statements (something a person blurts out when excited or startled), and statements about a person's state of mind or future intentions, to name just a few. One important feature of alternative dispute resolution proceedings, such as arbitration and mediation, is that statements that would be barred from being introduced in court as hearsay are allowed.

heir

One who receives property from someone who has died. While the traditional meaning includes only those who had a legal right to the deceased person's property, modern usage includes anyone who receives property from the estate of a deceased person.

heir apparent

One who expects to receive property from the estate of a family member, as long as he or she outlives that person.

heir at law

A person entitled to inherit property under intestate succession laws.

hold harmless

In a contract, a promise by one party not to hold the other party responsible if the other party carries out the contract in a way that causes damage to the first party. For example, many leases include a hold harmless clause in which the tenant agrees not to sue the landlord if the tenant is injured due to the landlord's failure to maintain the premises. In most states, these clauses are illegal in residential tenancies, but may be upheld in commercial settings.

holographic will

A will that is completely handwritten, dated, and signed by the person making it. Holographic wills are generally not witnessed. Although it's legal in many states, making a holographic will is never advised except as a last resort.

homestead

1. The house in which a family lives, plus any adjoining land and other buildings on that land.
2. Real estate that is not subject to the claims of creditors as long as it is occupied as a home by the head of the household. After the head of the family dies, homestead laws often allow the surviving spouse or minor children to live on the property for as long as they choose.
3. Land acquired out of the public lands of the United States. The term "homesteaders" refers to people who got their land by settling it and making it productive, rather than purchasing it outright.

homestead declaration

A form filed with the county recorder's office to put on record your right to a homestead exemption. In most states, the homestead exemption is automatic—that is, you are not required to record a homestead declaration in order to claim the homestead exemption. A few states do require such a recording, however.

homicide

The killing of one human being by the act or omission of another. The term applies to all such killings, whether criminal or not. Homicide is considered noncriminal in a number of situations, including deaths as the result of war and putting someone to death by the valid sentence of a court. Killing may also be legally justified or excused, as it is in cases of self-defense or when someone is killed by another person who is attempting to prevent a violent felony.

Criminal homicide occurs when a person purposely, knowingly, recklessly, or negligently causes the death of another. Murder and manslaughter are both examples of criminal homicide.

hung jury

A jury unable to come to a final decision, resulting in a mistrial. Judges do their best to avoid hung juries, typically sending juries back into deliberations with an assurance (sometimes known as a "dynamite charge") that they will be able to reach a decision if they try harder. If a mistrial is declared, the case is tried again unless the parties settle the case (in a civil case) or the prosecution dismisses the charges or offers a plea bargain (in a criminal case).

illusory promise

A promise that pledges nothing, because it is vague or because the promisor can choose whether or not to honor it. Such promises are not legally binding. For example, if you get a new job and promise to work for three years, unless you resign sooner, you haven't made a valid contract and can resign or be fired at any time.

impeach

1. To discredit. To impeach a witness's credibility, for example, is to show that the witness is not believable. A witness may be impeached by showing that he has made statements that are inconsistent with his present testimony, or that he has a reputation for not being a truthful person.
2. The process of charging a public official, such as the president or a federal judge, with a crime or misconduct and removing the official from office.

implied warranty

A guarantee about the quality of goods or services purchased that is not written down or explicitly spoken. Virtually everything you buy comes with two implied warranties, one for "merchantability" and one for "fitness." The implied warranty of merchantability is an assurance that a new item will work for its specified purpose.

The item doesn't have to work wonderfully, and if you use it for something it wasn't designed for, say trimming shrubs with an electric carving knife, the warranty doesn't apply. The implied warranty of fitness applies when you buy an item for a specific purpose. If you notified the seller of your specific needs, the item is guaranteed to meet them. For example, if you buy new tires for your bicycle after telling the store clerk that you plan to use them for mountain cycling and the tires puncture when you pass over a small rock, the tires don't conform to the warranty of fitness.

implied warranty of habitability

A legal doctrine that requires landlords to offer and maintain livable premises for their tenants. If a landlord fails to provide habitable housing, tenants in most states may legally withhold rent or take other measures, including hiring someone to fix the problem or moving out. See *constructive eviction*.

in camera

Latin for "in chambers." A legal proceeding is *in camera* when a hearing is held before the judge in his or her private chambers or when the public is excluded from the courtroom. Proceedings are often held *in camera* to protect victims and witnesses from public exposure, especially if the victim or witness is a child. There is still, however, a record made of the proceeding, typically by a court stenographer. The judge may decide to seal this record if the material is extremely sensitive or likely to prejudice one side or the other.

in terrorem

Latin meaning "in fear." This phrase is used to describe provisions in contracts or wills meant to scare a person into complying with the terms of the agreement. For example, a will might state that an heir will forfeit her inheritance if she challenges the validity of the will. Of course, if the will is challenged and found to be invalid, then the clause itself is also invalid and the heir takes whatever she would have inherited if there were no will.

in toto

Latin for "in its entirety" or "completely." For example, if a judge accepts a lawyer's argument *in toto*, it means that he's bought the whole thing, hook, line, and sinker.

inadmissible evidence

Testimony or other evidence that fails to meet state or federal court rules governing the types of evidence that can be presented to a judge or jury. The main reason that evidence is ruled inadmissible is because it falls into a category deemed so unreliable that a court should not consider it as part of deciding a case—for example, hearsay evidence, or an expert's opinion that is not based on facts generally accepted in the field. Evidence will also be declared inadmissible if it suffers from some other defect—for example, as compared to its value, it will take too long to present or risks inflaming the jury, as might be the case with graphic pictures of a homicide victim. In addition, in criminal cases, evidence that is gathered using illegal methods is commonly ruled inadmissible. Because the rules of evidence are so complicated (and because contesting lawyers waste so much time arguing over them), there is a strong trend toward using mediation or arbitration to resolve civil disputes. In mediation and arbitration, virtually all evidence can be considered. See *evidence, admissible evidence.*

incapacity

1. A lack of physical or mental abilities that results in a person's inability to manage his or her own personal care, property, or finances.
2. A lack of ability to understand one's actions when making a will or other legal document.
3. The inability of an injured worker to perform his or her job. This may qualify the worker for disability benefits or workers' compensation.

indispensable party

A person or an entity (such as a corporation) that must be included in a lawsuit in order for the court to render a final judgment that will be just to everyone concerned. For example, if a person sues his neighbors to force them to prune a tree that poses a danger to his house, he must name all owners of the neighboring property in the suit.

information

The name of the document, sometimes called a criminal complaint or petition, in which a prosecutor charges a criminal defendant with a crime, either a felony or a misdemeanor. The information tells the defendant what crime he or she is charged with, against whom and when the offense allegedly occurred, but the prosecutor is not obliged to go into great detail. A defendant who wants more specifics must ask for it by way of a discovery request. Compare *indictment*.

informed consent

An agreement to do something or to allow something to happen, made with complete knowledge of all relevant facts, such as the risks involved or any available alternatives. For example, a patient may give informed consent to medical treatment only after the health care professional has disclosed all possible risks involved in accepting or rejecting the treatment. A health care provider or facility may be held responsible for an injury caused by an undisclosed risk. In another context, a person accused of committing a crime cannot give up his or her constitutional rights—for example, to remain silent or to talk with an attorney—unless and until he or she has been informed of those rights, usually via the well-known *Miranda* warnings.

infraction

A minor violation of the law that is punishable only by a fine—for example, a traffic or parking ticket. Not all vehicle-related violations are infractions, however; refusing to identify oneself when involved in an accident is a misdemeanor in some states.

injunction

A court decision that is intended to prevent harm—often irreparable harm—as distinguished from most court decisions, which are designed to provide a remedy for harm that has already occurred. Injunctions are orders that one side refrain from or stop certain actions, such as an order that an abusive spouse stay away from the other spouse or that a logging company not cut down first-growth trees. Injunctions can be temporary, pending a consideration of the issue later at trial (these are called interlocutory decrees or preliminary injunctions). Judges can also issue permanent injunctions at the end of trials, in which a party may be permanently prohibited from engaging in some conduct—for example, infringing a copyright or trademark or making use of illegally obtained trade secrets. Although most injunctions order a party not to do something, occasionally a court will issue a "mandatory injunction" to order a party to carry out a positive act—for example, return stolen computer code.

injunctive relief

A situation in which a court grants an order, called an injunction, telling a party to refrain from doing something—or in the case of a mandatory injunction, to carry out a particular action. Usually injunctive relief is granted only after a hearing at which both sides have an opportunity to present testimony and legal arguments.

intangible property

Personal property that has no physical existence, such as stocks, bonds, bank notes, trade secrets, patents, copyrights, and trademarks. Such "untouchable" items may be represented by a certificate or license that fixes or approximates the value, but others (such as the goodwill or reputation of a business) are not easily valued or embodied in any instrument. Compare *tangible personal property*.

intellectual property (IP) law

The area of law that regulates the ownership and use of creative works, including patent, copyright, and trademark law.

intentional tort

A deliberate act that causes harm to another, for which the victim may sue the wrongdoer for damages. Examples of intentional torts include assault, battery, libel, and intentional infliction of emotional distress. Acts of domestic violence, such as assault and battery, are intentional torts (as well as crimes).

inter vivos trust

The Latin name, favored by some lawyers, for a living trust. *Inter vivos* is Latin for "between the living."

interlocutory decree

A court judgment that is not final until the judge decides other matters in the case or until enough time has passed to see if the interim decision is working. In the past, interlocutory decrees were most often used in divorces. The terms of the divorce were set out in an interlocutory decree, which would become final only after a waiting period. The purpose of the waiting period was to allow the couple time to reconcile. They rarely did, however, so most states no longer use interlocutory decrees of divorce.

interrogatory

Written questions designed to discover key facts about an opposing party's case that a party to a lawsuit asks an opposing party (but not a nonparty witness, who can only be questioned in person at a deposition). Interrogatories are part of the pretrial discovery stage of a lawsuit, and must be answered under penalty of perjury. Court rules tightly regulate how, when, and how many interrogatories can be asked. Lawyers can write their own sets of questions, or can use form interrogatories, designed to cover typical issues in common lawsuits.

intestate

The condition of dying without a valid will. The probate court appoints an administrator to distribute the deceased person's property according to state law.

intestate succession

The method by which property is distributed when a person dies without a valid will. Each state's law provides that the property be distributed to the closest surviving relatives. In most states, the surviving spouse, children, parents, siblings, nieces and nephews, and next of kin inherit, in that order.

inure

To take effect, or to benefit someone. In property law, the term means "to vest." For example, Jim buys a beach house that includes the right to travel across the neighbor's property to get to the water. That right of way is said, cryptically, "to inure to the benefit of Jim."

invitee

A business guest, or someone who enters property held open to members of the public, such as a visitor to a museum. Property owners must protect invitees from dangers on the property. In an example of the perversion of legalese, social guests that you invite into your home are called "licensees."

ipse dixit

Latin for "he himself said it." The term labels something that is asserted but unproved.

ipso facto

Latin for "by the fact itself." This term is used by Latin-addicted lawyers when something is so obvious that it needs no elaboration or further explanation. For example, it might be said that a blind person, *ipso facto*, is not qualified to obtain to a driver's license.

irrevocable trust

A permanent trust. Once you create it, it cannot be revoked, amended, or changed in any way unless a court finds that a change is necessary for the trust to serve the purpose for which it was created.

issue

A term generally meaning all your children and their children down through the generations, including grandchildren, great-grandchildren, and so on. Also called "lineal descendants."

JNOV

See *judgment notwithstanding the verdict.*

joint tenancy

A way for two or more people to share ownership of real estate or other property. When two or more people own property as joint tenants and one owner dies, the other owners automatically own the deceased owner's share. For example, if a parent and child own a house as joint tenants and the parent dies, the child automatically becomes full owner. Because of this right of survivorship, no will is required to transfer the property; it goes directly to the surviving joint tenants without the delay and costs of probate.

judgment

A final court ruling resolving the key questions in a lawsuit and determining the rights and obligations of the opposing parties. For example, after a trial involving a vehicle accident, a court will issue a judgment determining which party was at fault—or most at fault—and how much money that party must pay the other. Most judgments can be appealed by the losing party, except judgments issued by default (the defendant doesn't show up), which normally require that the defendant first promptly move to vacate (set aside) the default and reopen the case.

judgment notwithstanding the verdict (JNOV)

Reversal of a jury's verdict by a judge when the judge believes that there were insufficient facts on which to base the jury's verdict, or that the verdict did not correctly apply the law. This procedure is similar to a situation in which a judge orders a jury to arrive at a particular verdict, called a directed verdict. In fact, a judgment notwithstanding the verdict is occasionally made when a jury refuses to follow a judge's instruction to arrive at a certain verdict. Incidentally, for those of a scholarly bent, this term has its roots in the Latin *non obstante verdicto*, meaning notwithstanding the verdict.

jurisdiction

The authority of a court to hear and decide a case. To make a legally valid decision in a case, a court must have both "subject matter jurisdiction" (power to hear the type of case in question, which is granted by the state legislatures and Congress) and "personal jurisdiction" (power to make a decision affecting the parties involved in the lawsuit, which a court gets as a result of the parties' actions). For example, state courts' subject matter jurisdiction includes the civil and criminal laws that the state legislature has passed, but does not include the right to hear patent disputes or immigration violations, which Congress has decided may only be heard in federal courts. And no court can entertain a case unless the parties agree to be there or live in the state (or federal district) where the court sits, or have enough contacts with the state or district that it's fair to make them answer to that court. (Doing business in a state, owning property there, or driving on its highways will usually be enough to allow the court to hear the case.) The term jurisdiction is also commonly used to define the amount of money a court has the power to award. For example, small claims courts have jurisdiction only to hear cases up to a relatively low monetary amount—depending on the state, typically in the range of $2,000 to $10,000. If a court doesn't have personal jurisdiction over all the parties and the subject matter involved, it "lacks jurisdiction," which means it doesn't have the power to render a decision.

jury nullification

A decision by the jury to acquit a defendant who has violated a law that the jury believes is unjust or wrong. Jury nullification has always been an option for juries in England and the United States, although judges will prevent a defense lawyer from urging the jury to acquit on this basis. Nullification was evident during the Vietnam war (when selective service protesters were acquitted by juries opposed to the war) and currently appears in criminal cases when the jury disagrees with the punishment—for example, in "three strikes" cases when the jury realizes that conviction of a relatively minor offense will result in lifetime imprisonment.

jus naturale

Latin for "natural law." This is a system of legal principles ostensibly derived from universal divine truths.

kindred

Under some state's probate codes, all relatives of a deceased person.

larceny

Another term for theft. Although the definition of this term differs from state to state, it typically means taking property belonging to another with the intent to permanently deprive the owner of the property. If the taking is nonforceful, it is larceny; if it is accompanied by force or fear directed against a person, it is robbery, a much more serious offense.

lawful issue

Formerly, statutes governing wills used this phrase to specify children born to married parents, and to exclude those born out of wedlock. Now, the phrase means the same as issue and "lineal descendant."

lease

An oral or written agreement (a contract) between two people concerning the use by one of the property of the other. A person can lease real estate (such as an apartment or business property) or personal property (such as a car or a boat). A lease should cover basic issues such as when the lease will begin and end, the rent or other costs, how payments should be made, and any restrictions on the use of the property. The property owner is often called the "lessor," and the person using the property is called the "lessee."

legacy

An outdated legal word meaning personal property left by a will. The more common term for this type of property is bequest. Compare *devise*.

legislative immunity

A legal doctrine that prevents legislators from being sued for actions performed and decisions made in the course of serving in government. This doctrine does not protect legislators from criminal prosecution, nor does it relieve them from responsibility for actions outside the scope of their office, such as the nefarious activities of former Senator Bob Packwood back in the 1990s.

letters testamentary

The document given to an executor by the probate court authorizing the executor to settle the estate according to either a will or the state's intestate succession laws.

lex loci

Latin for the "law of the place." It means local law.

liability

1. The state of being liable—that is, legally responsible for an act or omission.

   EXAMPLE: Peri hires Paul to fix a broken pipe in her bathroom, but the new pipe bursts the day after Paul installs it, ruining the bathroom floor. This raises the issue of liability: Who is responsible for the damage? Peri claims that Paul is responsible, and sues him for the cost of hiring another plumber to fix the pipe and replacing the floor. Paul, in turn, claims that the pipe manufacturer is responsible, because they supplied him with faulty materials. Both Peri and Paul must prove their claims in court; if Paul and/or the manufacturer is found liable, one or both will have to pay damages to Peri.

2. Something for which a person is liable. For example, a debt is often called a liability.

libel

An untruthful statement about a person, published in writing or through broadcast media, that injures the person's reputation or standing in the community. Because libel is a tort (a civil wrong), the injured person can bring a lawsuit against the person who made the false statement. Libel is a form of defamation, as is slander (an untruthful statement that is spoken, but not published in writing or broadcast through the media).

lien

The right of a secured creditor to grab a specific item of property if you don't pay a debt. Liens can also be created by court judgments (judgment liens) and by claims asserted by those who work to improve a person's real estate (mechanic's liens). Liens to which you agree are called security interests, and include mortgages, home equity loans, car loans, and personal loans for which you pledge property to guarantee repayment. Liens created without your consent are called nonconsensual liens, and include judgment liens (liens filed by a creditor who has sued you and obtained a judgment), tax liens, and mechanic's liens (liens filed by a contractor who worked on your house but wasn't paid).

life beneficiary

A person who receives benefits, under a trust or by will, for his or her lifetime.

limited liability

The maximum amount a business owner can lose if the business is subject to debts, claims, or other liabilities. An owner of a limited liability company or a person who invests in a corporation (a share-holder) generally stands to lose only the amount of money invested in the business. This means that if the limited liability company or corporation folds, creditors cannot seize or sell an owner's home, car, or other personal assets. (This is known as "limited personal liability.") By contrast, owners of a sole proprietorship or general partnership have unlimited liability for business debts, as do the general partners in a limited partnership and limited partners who take part in managing the business.

limited liability company (LLC)

A relatively new and flexible business ownership structure. Particularly popular with small businesses, the LLC offers its owners the advantage of limited personal liability (like a corporation) and a choice of how the business will be taxed. Partners can choose for the LLC to be taxed as a separate entity (again, like a corporation) or as a partnership-like entity in which profits are passed through to partners and taxed on their personal income tax returns. Although state laws governing creation of LLCs and IRS regulations controlling their federal tax status are still evolving, because of their flexibility LLCs are increasingly regarded as the small business legal entity of choice.

limited liability partnership (LLP)

A type of partnership recognized in a majority of states that protects a partner from personal liability for negligent acts committed by other partners or by employees not under his or her direct control. Many states restrict this type partnership to professionals, such as lawyers, accountants, architects, and health care providers.

limited partnership

A business structure that allows one or more partners (called limited partners) to enjoy limited personal liability for partnership debts while another partner or partners (called general partners) have unlimited personal liability. The key difference between a general and limited partner concerns management decision making: General partners run the business, and limited partners, who are usually passive investors, are not allowed to make day-to-day business decisions. If they do, they risk being treated as general partners with unlimited personal liability.

lis pendens

Latin for "a suit pending." The term may refer to:

1. any pending lawsuit.
2. a written notice that a lawsuit has been filed concerning real estate, involving either the title to the property or a claimed ownership interest in it. The notice is usually filed in the county land records office. Recording a *lis pendens* against a piece of property alerts a potential purchaser or lender that the property's title is in question, which makes the property less attractive to a buyer or lender. After the notice is filed, anyone who nevertheless purchases the land or property described in the notice is subject to the ultimate decision of the lawsuit.

living trust

A trust you can set up during your life. Living trusts are an excellent way to avoid the cost and hassle of probate because, after death of the founder of the trust, the property you transfer into the trust during your life passes directly to the trust beneficiaries after you die, without court involvement. The successor trustee—the person you appoint to handle the trust after your death—simply transfers ownership to the beneficiaries you named in the trust. Living trusts are also called "*inter vivos* trusts."

living will

A legal document in which you state your wishes about certain kinds of medical treatments and life-prolonging procedures. The document takes effect if you can't communicate your own health care decisions at the time they have to be made. A living will may also be called a health care directive, advance directive, or directive to physicians.

malfeasance

Doing something that is illegal. This term is often used when a professional or public official commits an illegal act that interferes with the performance of his or her duties. For example, an elected official who accepts a bribe in exchange for political favors has committed malfeasance. Compare *misfeasance*.

malpractice

The delivery of substandard care or services by a lawyer, doctor, dentist, accountant, or other professional. Generally, malpractice occurs when a professional fails to provide the quality of care that should reasonably be expected in the circumstances, with the result that his or her patient or client is harmed. In the area of legal malpractice, you need to prove two things to show that you were harmed: first, that your lawyer screwed up; and second, that if the lawyer had handled the work properly, you would have won your original case.

mandamus

Latin for "we command." A writ of *mandamus* is a court order that requires another court, government official, public body, corporation, or individual to perform a certain act. For example, after a hearing, a court might issue a writ of *mandamus* forcing a public school to admit certain students on the grounds that the school illegally discriminated against them when it denied them admission. A writ of *mandamus* is the opposite of an order to cease and desist, or stop doing something. Also called a "writ of mandate."

marital property

Most of the property accumulated by spouses during a marriage, called community property in some states. States differ as to exactly what is included in marital property; some states include all property and earnings during the marriage, while others exclude gifts and inheritances.

mechanic's lien

A legal claim placed on real estate by someone who is owed money for labor, services, or supplies contributed to the property for the purpose of improving it. Typical lien claimants are general contractors, subcontractors, and suppliers of building materials. A mechanic's lien claimant can sue to have the real estate sold at auction and recover the debt from the proceeds. Because property with a lien on it cannot be easily sold until the lien is satisfied (paid off), owners have a great incentive to pay their bills.

mediation

A dispute resolution method designed to help warring parties resolve their own dispute without going to court. In mediation, a neutral third party (the mediator) meets with the opposing sides to help them find a mutually satisfactory solution. Unlike a judge in a courtroom or an arbitrator conducting a binding arbitration, the mediator has no power to impose a solution. No formal rules of evidence or procedure control mediation; the mediator and the parties usually agree on their own informal ways to proceed.

mens rea

The mental component of criminal liability. To be guilty of most crimes, a defendant must have committed the criminal act (the *actus reus*) in a certain mental state (the *mens rea*). The *mens rea* of robbery, for example, is the intent to permanently deprive the owner of his or her property.

minimum contacts

A requirement that must be satisfied before a defendant can be sued in a particular state. In order for the suit to go forward in the chosen state, the defendant must have some connections with that state. For example, advertising or having business offices within a state may provide minimum contacts between a company and the state.

minor

In most states, any person under 18 years of age. All minors must be under the care of a competent adult (parent or guardian) unless they are "emancipated"—in the military, married, or living independently with court permission. Property left to a minor must be handled by an adult until the minor becomes an adult under the laws of the state where he or she lives.

Miranda warning

A warning that the police must give to a suspect before conducting an interrogation; otherwise, the suspect's answers may not be used as evidence in a trial. The *Miranda* warning requires that the suspect be told that he or she has the right to remain silent, the right to have an attorney present when being questioned, the right to a court appointed attorney if a private attorney is unaffordable, and the fact that any statements made by the suspect can be used against him or her in court. Giving the *Miranda* warning is also known as "reading a suspect his or her rights."

misdemeanor

A crime, less serious than a felony, punishable by no more than one year in jail. Petty theft (of articles worth less than a certain amount), first-time drunk driving, and leaving the scene of an accident are all common misdemeanors.

misfeasance

Performing a legal action in an improper way. This term is frequently used when a professional or public official does his job in a way that is not technically illegal, but is nevertheless mistaken or wrong. Here are some examples of misfeasance in a professional context: a lawyer who is mistaken about a deadline and files an important legal document too late, an accountant who makes unintentional errors on a client's tax return, or a doctor who writes a prescription and accidentally includes the wrong dosage. Compare *malfeasance*.

mistrial

A trial that ends prematurely and without a judgment, due either to a mistake that jeopardizes a party's right to a fair trial or to a jury that can't agree on a verdict (a hung jury). If a judge declares a mistrial in a civil case, he or she will direct that the case be set for a new trial at a future date. Mistrials in criminal cases can result in a retrial, a plea bargain, or a dismissal of the charges.

motion

During a lawsuit, a request to the judge for a decision—called an order or ruling—to resolve procedural or other issues that come up during litigation. For example, after receiving hundreds of irrelevant interrogatories, a party might file a motion asking that the other side be ordered to stop engaging in unduly burdensome discovery. A motion can be made before, during, or after trial. Typically, one party submits a written motion to the court, at which point the other party has the opportunity to file a written response. The court then often schedules a hearing at which each side delivers a short oral argument. The court then approves or denies the motion. Most motions cannot be appealed until the case is over.

motion *in limine*

A request submitted to the court before trial in an attempt to exclude evidence from the proceedings. A motion *in limine* is usually made by a party when simply the mention of the evidence would prejudice the jury against that party, even if the judge later instructed the jury to disregard the evidence. For example, if a defendant in a criminal trial were questioned and confessed to the crime without having been read his *Miranda* rights, his lawyer would file a motion *in limine* to keep evidence of the confession out of the trial.

natural person

A living, breathing human being, as opposed to a legal entity such as a corporation. Different rules and protections apply to natural persons and corporations, such as the Fifth Amendment right against self-incrimination, which applies only to natural persons.

naturalization

The process by which a foreign person becomes a U.S. citizen. Almost everyone who goes through naturalization must first have held a green card for several years. A naturalized U.S. citizen has virtually the same rights as a native-born American citizen.

negotiable instrument

A written document that represents an unconditional promise to pay a specified amount of money upon the demand of its owner. Examples include checks and promissory notes. Negotiable instruments can be transferred from one person to another, as when you write "pay to the order of" on the back of a check and turn it over to someone else.

net lease

A commercial real estate lease in which the tenant regularly pays not only for the space (as in a gross lease) but for a portion of the landlord's operating costs as well. When all three of the usual costs—taxes, maintenance, and insurance—are passed on, the arrangement is known as a "triple net lease." Because these costs are variable and almost never decrease, a net lease favors the landlord. Accordingly, it may be possible for a tenant to bargain for a net lease with caps or ceilings, which limits the amount of rent the tenant must pay. For example, a net lease with caps may specify that an increase in taxes beyond a certain point (or any new taxes) will be paid by the landlord. The same kind of protection can be designed to cover increased insurance premiums and maintenance expenses.

no-fault divorce

Any divorce in which the spouse who wants to split up does not have to accuse the other of wrongdoing, but can simply state that the couple no longer gets along sufficiently. Until no-fault divorce arrived in the 1970s, the only way a person could get a divorce was to prove that the other spouse was at fault for the marriage not working. No-fault divorces are usually granted for reasons such as incompatibility, irreconcilable differences, or irretrievable or irremediable breakdown of the marriage. Also, some states allow incurable insanity as a basis for a no-fault divorce. Compare *fault divorce.*

nolle prosequi

Latin for "we shall no longer prosecute." At trial, this is an entry made on the record by a prosecutor in a criminal case stating that he or she will no longer pursue the matter. An entry of *nolle prosequi* may be made at any time after charges are brought and before a verdict is returned or a plea entered. Essentially, it is an admission on the part of the prosecution that some aspect of its case against the defendant has fallen apart. Abbreviated "nol. pros." or "nol-pros." Most of the time, prosecutors need a judge's permission to "nol-pros" a case.

nolo contendere

Latin for "I will not defend it." A plea entered by the defendant in response to being charged with a crime. When defendants plead *nolo contendere*, they neither admit nor deny that they committed the crime, but agree to a punishment (usually a fine or jail time) as if guilty. Usually, this type of plea is entered because it can't be used as an admission of guilt in a civil suit against the defendant. By not admitting guilt during the criminal trial, the defendant can defend the civil case without having to explain such an admission.

nondischargeable debts

Debts that cannot be erased by filing for bankruptcy. If you file for Chapter 7 bankruptcy, these debts will remain when your case is over. If you file for Chapter 13 bankruptcy, the nondischargeable debts will have to be paid in full during your plan or you will have a balance at the end of your case. Examples of nondischargeable debts include alimony and child support, most income tax debts, many student loans, and debts for personal injury or death caused by drunk driving. Compare *dischargeable debts*.

nondisclosure agreement

A legally binding contract in which a person or business promises to treat specific information as a trade secret and not disclose it to others without proper authorization. Nondisclosure agreements are often used when a business discloses a trade secret to another person or business for such purposes as development, marketing, evaluation, or securing financial backing. Although nondisclosure agreements are usually in the form of written contracts, they may also be implied if the context of a business relationship suggests that the parties intended to make an agreement. For example, a business that conducts patent searches for inventors is expected to keep information about the invention secret, even if no written agreement is signed, because the nature of the business is to deal in confidential information.

nonprofit corporation

A legal structure authorized by state law allowing people to come together to either benefit members of an organization (a club, or mutual benefit society) or for some public purpose (such as a hospital, an environmental organization, or a literary society). Nonprofit corporations, despite the name, can make a profit, but the business cannot be designed primarily for profit-making purposes, and the profits must be used for the benefit of the organization or purpose the corporation was created to help. When a nonprofit corporation dissolves, any remaining assets must be distributed to another non-profit, not to board members. As with for-profit corporations, directors of nonprofit corporations are normally shielded from personal liability for the organization's debts. Some nonprofit corporations qualify for a federal tax exemption under Section 501(c)(3) of the Internal Revenue Code, with the result that contributions to the nonprofit are tax deductible by their donors.

novation

The substitution of a new contract for an old one. A novation may change one of the parties to the contract or the duties that must be performed by the original parties.

nuisance

Something that interferes with the use of property by being irritating, offensive, obstructive, or dangerous. Nuisances include a wide range of conditions, everything from a chemical plant's noxious odors to a neighbor's dog barking. The former would be a "public nuisance," one affecting many people, while the other would be a "private nuisance," limited to making your life difficult, unless the dog was bothering others. Lawsuits may be brought to abate (remove or reduce) a nuisance. See *quiet enjoyment, attractive nuisance.*

nulla bona

Latin for "no goods." This is what the sheriff writes when he or she can find no property to seize in order to pay off a court judgment.

oath

An attestation that one will tell the truth, or a promise to fulfill a pledge, often calling upon God as a witness. The best-known oath is probably the witness's pledge "to tell the truth, the whole truth, and nothing but the truth" during a legal proceeding. In another context, a public official, for example, usually takes an "oath of office" before assuming his or her position, in which he or she declares that he or she will faithfully perform his or her duties.

offer of proof

At trial, a party's explanation to a judge as to how a proposed line of questioning, or a certain item of physical evidence, would be relevant to its case and admissible under the rules of evidence. Offers of proof arise when a party begins a line of questioning that the other side objects to as calling for irrelevant or inadmissible information. If the judge thinks that the questions might lead to proper evidence, the judge will stop the trial, ask the parties to "approach the bench," and give the questioner a chance to show how, if allowed, the expected answers will be both relevant and admissible. This explanation is usually presented out of the jury's hearing, but it does become part of the trial record. If the matter is later heard on appeal, the appellate court will use the record to decide whether the judge's ruling was correct.

opening statement

A statement made by an attorney or self-represented party at the beginning of a trial before evidence is introduced. The opening statement outlines the party's legal position and previews the evidence that will be introduced later. The purpose of an opening statement is to familiarize the jury with what it will hear—and why it will hear it—not to present an argument as to why the speaker's side should win (that comes after all evidence is presented as part of the closing argument).

order

A decision issued by a court. It can be a simple command—for example, ordering a recalcitrant witness to answer a proper question—or it can be a complicated and reasoned decision made after a hearing, directing that a party either do or refrain from some act. For example, following a hearing, the court may order that evidence gathered by the police not be introduced at trial; or a judge may issue a temporary restraining order. This term usually does not describe the final decision in a case, which most often is called a judgment.

order to show cause

An order from a judge that directs a party to come to court and convince the judge why he or she shouldn't grant an action proposed by the other side or by the judge on his or her own (*sua sponte*). For example, in a divorce, at the request of one parent a judge might issue an order directing the other parent to appear in court on a particular date and time to show cause why the first parent should not be given sole physical custody of the children. Although it would seem that the person receiving an order to show cause is at a procedural disadvantage—being, after all, the one who is told to come up with a convincing reason why the judge shouldn't order something—both sides normally have an equal chance to convince the judge to rule in their favor.

ordinance

A law adopted by a town or city council, a county board of supervisors, or another municipal governing board. Typically, local governments issue ordinances establishing zoning and parking rules and regulating noise, garbage removal, and the operation of parks and other areas that affect people who live or do business within the locality's borders.

own recognizance (OR)

A way the defendant can get out of jail, without paying bail, by promising to appear in court when next required to be there. Sometimes called "personal recognizance." Only those with strong ties to the community, such as a steady job, local family, and no history of failing to appear in court, are good candidates for "OR" release. If the charge is very serious, however, OR may not be an option.

palimony

A nonlegal term coined by journalists to describe the division of property or alimony-like support given by one member of an unmarried couple to the other after they break up.

par value

The face value of a stock, assigned by a corporation at the time the stock is issued. The par value is often printed on the stock certificate, but the market value of the stock may be much more or much less than par.

partnership

When used without a qualifier such as "limited" or "limited liability," usually refers to a legal structure called a general partnership. This is a business owned by two or more people (called partners or general partners) who are personally liable for all business debts. To form a partnership, each partner normally contributes money, valuable property, or labor in exchange for a partnership share, which reflects the amount contributed. Partnerships are easy to form since no registration is required with any governmental agency (although tax registration and other requirements to conduct business may still apply). Although not required, it is an excellent idea to prepare a written partnership agreement between the partners to define items such as ownership percentages, how profits and losses will be divided, and what happens if a partner dies or becomes disabled. Partnerships themselves do not pay federal or state income taxes; rather, profits are passed through to partners who report and pay income taxes on their personal returns. See also *limited partnership*, *limited liability partnership*.

party

A person, a corporation, or another legal entity that files a lawsuit (the plaintiff or petitioner) or defends against one (the defendant or respondent).

pendente lite

Latin for "while the action is pending." This phrase is used to describe matters that are contingent upon the outcome of a lawsuit. For example, money may be deposited by the defendant with the court *pendente lite* in order to compensate the plaintiff if the defendant loses the case. If the defendant wins, he or she gets her money back.

per stirpes

Latin for "by right of representation." Under a will, a method of determining who inherits property when a joint beneficiary has died before the will maker, leaving living children of his or her own. For example, Fred leaves his house jointly to his son Alan and his daughter Julie. But Alan dies before Fred, leaving two young children. If Fred's will states that heirs of a deceased beneficiary are to receive the property "per stirpes," Julie will receive one-half of the property, and Alan's two children will share his half in equal shares (through Alan by right of representation). If, on the other hand, Fred's will states that the property is to be divided per capita, Julie and the two grandchildren will each take a third.

peremptory challenge

During jury selection, an opportunity for a party to a lawsuit to dismiss or excuse a potential juror without having to give a valid reason, as would be the case when a juror is challenged for cause. Depending on court rules, each party typically gets to make from five to 15 peremptory challenges. Although parties may generally use their peremptory challenges as they see fit, the U.S. Constitution has been interpreted to prohibit their use to eliminate all jurors of a particular race or gender from a jury.

personal injury

An injury not to property, but to your body, mind, or emotions. For example, if you slip and fall on a banana peel in the grocery store, personal injury covers any actual physical harm (broken leg and bruises) you suffered in the fall as well as the humiliation of falling in public, but not the harm of shattering your watch.

petition

A formal written request made to a court, asking for an order or ruling on a particular matter. For example, if you want to be appointed conservator for an elderly relative, you must file a petition with a court. See also *complaint*.

piercing the veil

A judicial doctrine that allows a plaintiff to hold otherwise immune corporate officers and directors personally liable for damages caused by a corporation under their control. The veil is pierced when officers have acted intentionally and illegally, or when their actions exceeded the power given them by the company's articles of incorporation.

plaintiff

The person, corporation, or other legal entity that initiates a lawsuit. In certain states and for some types of lawsuits, the term petitioner is used instead of plaintiff. Compare *defendant, respondent.*

plea

The defendant's formal answer to criminal charges. Typically, defendants enter one of the following pleas: guilty, not guilty, or *nolo contendere.* A plea is usually entered when charges are formally brought (at arraignment).

plea bargain

A negotiation between the defense and prosecution (and sometimes the judge) that settles a criminal case. The defendant typically pleads guilty to a lesser crime (or fewer charges) than originally charged, in exchange for a guaranteed sentence that is shorter than what the defendant could face if convicted at trial. The prosecution gets the certainty of a conviction and a known sentence; the defendant avoids the risk of a higher sentence; and the judge gets to move on to other cases.

pleading

A statement of the plaintiff's case or the defendant's defense, set out in generally accepted legal language and format. Today, in many states, the need to plead a case by drafting legal jargon—or borrowing from a legal form book—and printing it on numbered legal paper has been replaced by the use of preprinted forms. In this case, creating a proper pleading consists principally of checking the correct boxes and filling in the requested information.

post hoc

Part of the Latin phrase *post hoc, ergo propter hoc*, which means "after this, therefore because of this." The phrase represents the faulty logic of assuming that one thing was caused by another merely because it followed that event in time.

pot trust

A trust for children in which the trustee decides how to spend money on each child, taking money out of the trust to meet each child's specific needs. One important advantage of a pot trust over separate trusts is that it allows the trustee to provide for one child's unforeseen need, such as a medical emergency. But a pot trust can also make the trustee's life difficult by requiring choices about disbursing funds to the various children. A pot trust ends when the youngest child reaches a certain age, usually 18 or 21.

pour-over will

A will that "pours over" property into a trust when the will maker dies. Property left through the will must go through probate before it goes into the trust.

power of appointment

The legal authority to decide who will receive someone else's property, usually property held in a trust. Most trustees can distribute the income from a trust only according to the terms of the trust, but a trustee with a power of appointment can choose the beneficiaries, sometimes from a list of candidates specified by the grantor. For example, Karin creates a trust with power of appointment to benefit either the local art museum, symphony, library, or park, depending on the trustee's assessment of need.

power of attorney

A document that gives another person legal authority to act on your behalf. If you create such a document, you are called the principal and the person to whom you give this authority is called your attorney-in-fact. A power of attorney may be "general," which gives your attorney-in-fact extensive powers over your affairs. Or it may be "limited" or "special," giving your attorney-in-fact permission to handle a specifically defined task. If you make a durable power of attorney, the document will continue in effect even if you become incapacitated. For examples, see *durable power of attorney for finances, durable power of attorney for health care.*

prayer for relief

What the plaintiff asks of the court—for example, the plaintiff may ask for an award of monetary damages, an injunction to make the defendant stop a certain activity, or both.

precedent

A legal principle or rule created by one or more decisions of a state or federal appellate court. These rules provide a point of reference or authority for judges deciding similar issues in later cases. Lower courts must apply these rules when faced with similar legal issues. For example, if the Montana Supreme Court decides that a certain type of employment contract overly restricts the right of the employee to quit and get another job, all other Montana courts must apply this same rule.

presumption of innocence

One of the most sacred principles in the American criminal justice system, holding that a defendant is innocent until proven guilty. In other words, the prosecution must prove, beyond a reasonable doubt, each element of the crime charged.

pretermitted heir

A child or spouse who is not mentioned in a will and whom the court believes was accidentally overlooked by the person who made the will. For example, a child born or adopted after the will is made may be deemed a pretermitted heir. If the court determines that an heir was accidentally omitted, that heir is entitled to receive the same share of the estate as he or she would have if the deceased had died without a will. A pretermitted heir is sometimes called an "omitted heir."

prima facie

Latin for "on its face." A *prima facie* case is one that at first glance presents sufficient evidence for the plaintiff to win. Such a case must be refuted in some way by the defendant for him or her to have a chance of prevailing at trial. For example, if you can show that someone intentionally touched you in a harmful or offensive way and caused some injury to you, you have established a *prima facie* case of battery. However, this does not mean that you automatically win your case. The defendant would win if he could show that you consented to the harmful or offensive touching.

principal

1. When creating a power of attorney or another legal document, the person who appoints an attorney-in-fact or agent to act on his or her behalf.
2. In criminal law, the main perpetrator of a crime.
3. In commercial law, the total amount of a loan, not including any capitalized fees or interest.
4. In the law of trusts, the property of the trust, as opposed to the income generated by that property. The principal is also known as

the trust *corpus* (Latin for "body"). For example, Arthur establishes a new trust with $100,000, with interest and other income payable to Merlin; the $100,000 is the trust principal or *corpus*.

pro hac vice

Latin meaning "for this one particular occasion." The phrase usually refers to an out-of-state lawyer who has been granted special permission to participate in a particular case, even though the lawyer is not licensed to practice in the state where the case is being tried.

pro per

A term derived from the Latin *in propria persona*, meaning "for one's self," used in some states to describe a person who handles his or her own case without a lawyer. In other states, the term *pro se* is used. A nonlawyer who files his or her own legal papers is expected to write "*in pro per*" at the bottom of the heading on the first page.

pro se

A Latin phrase meaning "for himself" or "in one's own behalf." This term denotes a person who represents him- or herself in court. It is used in some states in place of "*in pro per*" and has the same meaning.

probable cause

The amount and quality of information a judge must have before he or she will sign a search warrant allowing the police to conduct a search or arrest a suspect. If the police have presented reliable information that convinces the judge that it's more likely than not that a crime has occurred and the suspect is involved, the judge will conclude that there is "probable cause" and will issue the warrant. Police also need probable cause to conduct a warrantless search or seizure. When the police do not have time to go to a judge for a warrant (such as when they are in hot pursuit of a suspect), they still must have probable cause before they can arrest or search.

probate

The court process following a person's death that includes:

- proving the authenticity of the deceased person's will
- appointing someone to handle the deceased person's affairs
- identifying and inventorying the deceased person's property
- paying debts and taxes
- identifying heirs, and
- distributing the deceased person's property according to the will or, if there is no will, according to state law.

Formal court-supervised probate is a costly, time-consuming process—a windfall for lawyers—which is best avoided if possible.

probate court

A specialized court or division of a state trial court that considers only cases concerning the distribution of deceased persons' estates. Called "surrogate court" in New York and several other states, this court normally examines the authenticity of a will—or, if a person dies intestate, figures out who receives his or her property under state law. It then oversees a procedure to pay the deceased person's debts and to distribute his or her assets to the proper inheritors. See *probate*.

prosecute

When a local district attorney, state attorney general, or federal United States attorney brings a criminal case against a defendant.

prosecutor

A lawyer who works for the local, state, or federal government to bring and litigate criminal cases.

public defender

A lawyer appointed by the court and paid by the county, state, or federal government to represent clients who are charged with violations of criminal law and are unable to pay for their own defense.

pur autre vie

Legal French meaning "for another's life." It is a phrase used to describe the duration of a property interest. For example, if Bob is given use of the family house for as long as his mother lives, he has possession of the house *pur autre vie*.

quantum meruit

Latin for "as much as is deserved." The reasonable value of services provided, which a winning party may be able to recover from an opponent who broke a contract.

quasi-community property

A form of property owned by a married couple. If a couple moves to a community property state from a non-community-property state, property they acquired together in the non-community-property state may be considered quasi-community property. Quasi-community property is treated just like community property when one spouse dies or if the couple divorces.

quiet enjoyment

The right of a property owner or tenant to enjoy his or her property without interference. Disruption of quiet enjoyment may constitute a nuisance. Leases and rental agreements often contain a "covenant of quiet enjoyment," expressly obligating the landlord to see that tenants have the opportunity to live undisturbed.

quitclaim deed

A deed that transfers whatever ownership interest the transferor has in a particular property. For example, a divorcing husband may quitclaim his interest in certain real estate to his ex-wife, officially giving up any legal interest in the property. The deed does not guarantee anything about what is being transferred, however. Compare *grant deed*.

real property

Another term for real estate. It includes land and things permanently attached to the land, such as trees, buildings, and stationary mobile homes. Anything that is not real property is termed personal property.

recording

The process of filing a copy of a deed or another document concerning real estate with the land records office for the county in which the land is located. Recording creates a public record of changes in ownership of all property in the state.

recusal

A situation in which a judge or prosecutor is removed or steps down from a case. This often happens when the judge or prosecutor has a conflict of interest—for example, a prior relationship with one of the parties.

red herring

A legal or factual issue that is irrelevant to the case at hand.

reformation

The act of changing a written contract when one of the parties can prove that the actual agreement was different than what's written down. The changes are usually made by a court when both parties overlooked a mistake in the document, or when one party has deceived the other.

remainderman

Someone who will inherit property in the future. For instance, if someone dies and leaves his home "to Alma for life, and then to Barry," Barry is a remainderman because he will inherit the home in the future, after Alma dies.

replevin

A type of legal action where the owner of movable goods is given the right to recover them from someone who shouldn't have them. Replevin is often used in disputes between buyers and sellers—for example, a seller might bring a replevin action to reclaim goods from a buyer who failed to pay for them.

request for admission

A discovery procedure, authorized by the Federal Rules of Civil Procedure and the court rules of many states, in which one party asks an opposing party to admit that certain facts are true. If the opponent admits the facts or fails to respond in a timely manner, the facts will be deemed true for purposes of trial. A request for admission is called a "request to admit" in many states.

res ipsa loquitur

A Latin term meaning "the thing speaks for itself." *Res ipsa loquitur* is a legal doctrine or rule of evidence that creates a presumption that a defendant acted negligently simply because a harmful accident occurred. The presumption arises only if:

1. the thing that caused the accident was under the defendant's control, the accident could happen only as a result of a careless act, and
2. the plaintiff's behavior did not contribute to the accident. Lawyers often refer to this doctrine as "*res ips*" or "*res ipsa.*"

res nova

Latin for "a new thing," used by courts to describe an issue of law or case that has not previously been decided.

residuary beneficiary

A person who receives any property by a will or trust that is not specifically left to another designated beneficiary. For example, if Antonio makes a will leaving his home to Edwina and the remainder of his property to Elmo, then Elmo is the residuary beneficiary.

residuary estate

The property that remains in a deceased person's estate after all specific gifts are made, and all debts, taxes, administrative fees, probate costs, and court costs are paid. The residuary estate also includes any gifts under a will that fail or lapse. For example, Connie's will leaves her house and all its furnishings to Andrew, her VW bug to her friend Carl, and the remainder of her property (the residuary estate) to her sister, Sara. She doesn't name any alternate beneficiaries. Carl dies before Connie. The VW bug becomes part of the residuary estate and passes to Sara, along with all of Connie's property other than the house and furnishings. Also called the residual estate or residue.

respondent

A term used instead of defendant or appellee in some states—especially for divorce and other family law cases—to identify the party who is sued and must respond to the petitioner's complaint.

restraining order

An order from a court directing one person not to do something, such as make contact with another person, enter the family home, or remove a child from the state. Restraining orders are typically issued in cases in which spousal abuse or stalking is feared—or has occurred—in an attempt to ensure the victim's safety. Restraining orders are also commonly issued to cool down ugly disputes between neighbors.

restraint on alienation

A provision in a deed or will that attempts to restrict ownership of the property—for example, selling your house to your daughter with the provision that it never be sold to anyone outside the family. These provisions are generally unenforceable.

right of survivorship

The right of a surviving joint tenant to take ownership of a deceased joint tenant's share of the property. See *joint tenancy*.

rule against perpetuities

An exceedingly complex legal doctrine that limits the amount of time that property can be controlled after death by a person's instructions in a will. For example, a person would not be allowed to leave property to her husband for his life, then to her children for their lives, then to her grandchildren. The gift would potentially go to the grandchildren at a point too remote in time.

ruling

Any decision a judge makes during the course of a lawsuit.

running with the land

A phrase used in property law to describe a right or duty that remains with a piece of property no matter who owns it. For example, the duty to allow a public beach access path across waterfront property would most likely pass from one owner of the property to the next.

S corporation

A term that describes a profit-making corporation organized under state law whose shareholders have applied for and received subchapter S corporation status from the Internal Revenue Service. Electing to do business as an S corporation lets shareholders enjoy limited liability status, as would be true of any corporation, but be taxed like a partnership or sole proprietor. That is, instead of being taxed as a separate entity (as would be the case with a regular or C corporation), an S corporation is a pass-through tax entity: Income taxes are reported and paid by the shareholders, not the S corporation. To qualify as an S corporation a number of IRS rules must be met, such as a limit of 75 shareholders and citizenship requirements.

search warrant

An order signed by a judge that directs owners of private property to allow the police to enter and search for items named in the warrant. The judge won't issue the warrant unless he or she has been convinced that there is probable cause for the search—that reliable evidence shows that it's more likely than not that a crime has occurred and that the items sought by the police are connected with it and will be found at the location named in the warrant. In limited situations, the police may search without a warrant, but they cannot use what they find at trial if the defense can show that there was no probable cause for the search.

secured debt

A debt on which a creditor has a lien. The creditor can institute a foreclosure or repossession to take the property identified by the lien, called the collateral, to satisfy the debt if you default. Compare *unsecured debt*.

self-incrimination

The making of statements that might expose you to criminal prosecution, either now or in the future. The Fifth Amendment of the U.S. Constitution prohibits the government from forcing you to provide evidence (as in answering questions) that would or might lead to your prosecution for a crime.

self-proving will

A will that is created in a way that allows a probate court to easily accept it as the true will of the person who has died. In most states, a will is self-proving when two witnesses sign under penalty of perjury that they observed the will maker sign it, he or she told them it was his or her will, and that the will maker appeared to be of sound mind and proper age to make a will. If no one contests the validity of the will, the probate court will accept the will without hearing the testimony of the witnesses or other evidence. To make a self-proving will in other states, the will maker and one or more witnesses must sign an affidavit (sworn statement) before a notary public certifying that the will is genuine and that all will-making formalities have been observed.

sentence

Punishment in a criminal case. A sentence can range from a fine and community service to life imprisonment or death. For most crimes, the sentence is chosen by the trial judge, who is limited by law to a narrow range of options—for example, burglary might be punishable by three, five, or seven years in prison. Some crimes in some states, however, carry an indeterminate sentence—for example, "20 years to life" for first-degree murder. (The state's parole board decides when, if ever, the defendant should be paroled after he or she has served the 20-year minimum.) The jury chooses the sentence only in a capital case, when it must choose between life in prison without parole and death.

separate property

In community property states, property owned and controlled entirely by one spouse in a marriage. In community property states, property acquired by a spouse before the marriage or after separation is typically that spouse's separate property, as is a gift or inheritance received solely by that spouse. In other states, a spouse's separate property is property owned or acquired before the marriage or after separation, and all property to which title is held in that spouse's name. At divorce, separate property is not divided under the state's property division laws, but is kept by the spouse who owns it. Separate property includes all property that a spouse obtained before marriage, through inheritance, or as a gift. It also includes any property that is traceable to separate property—for example, cash from the sale of a vintage car owned by one spouse before marriage and any property that the spouses agree is separate property. Compare *community property* and *equitable distribution*.

servient tenement

Property that is subject to use by another for a specific purpose. For example, a beachfront house that has a public walkway to the beach on its premises would be a servient tenement.

setback

The distance between a property boundary and a building. A minimum setback is usually required by law.

setoff

A claim made by someone who allegedly owes money, that the amount should be reduced because the other person owes him or her money. This is often raised in a counterclaim filed by a defendant in a lawsuit. Banks may try to exercise a setoff by taking money out of a deposit account to satisfy past-due payments on a loan or credit card bill. Such an act is illegal under most circumstances.

severability clause

A provision in a contract that preserves the rest of the contract if a portion of it is invalidated by a court. Without a severability clause, a decision by the court finding one part of the contract unenforceable would invalidate the entire document.

shareholder

An owner of a corporation whose ownership interest is represented by shares of stock in the corporation. A shareholder—also called a stockholder—has rights conferred by state law, by the bylaws of the corporation, and, if one has been adopted, by a shareholder's agreement (often called a buy-sell agreement). These include the right to be notified of annual shareholders' meetings, to elect directors, and to receive an appropriate share of any dividends. In large corporations, shareholders are usually investors whose shares are held in the name of their broker. On the other hand, in incorporated small businesses, owners often wear many hats—shareholder, director, officer, and employee—with the result that distinctions between these legal categories become fuzzy.

slander

A type of defamation. Slander is an untruthful oral (spoken) statement about a person that harms the person's reputation or standing in the community. Because slander is a tort (a civil wrong), the injured person can bring a lawsuit against the person who made the false statement. If the statement is made via broadcast media—for example, over the radio or on TV—or online or via social media, it is considered libel, rather than slander, because the statement has the potential to reach a very wide audience.

small claims court

A state court that resolves disputes involving relatively small amounts of money—usually between $2,000 and $10,000, depending on the state. Adversaries usually appear without lawyers—in fact, some states forbid lawyers in small claims court—and recount their side of the dispute in plain English. Evidence, including the testimony of eyewitnesses and expert witnesses, is relatively easy to present because small claims courts do not follow the formal rules of evidence that govern regular trial cases. A small claims judgment has the same force as does the judgment of any other state court, meaning that if the loser—now called the "judgment debtor"—fails to pay the judgment voluntarily, it can be collected using normal collection techniques, such as property liens and wage garnishments.

sole proprietorship

A business owned and managed by one person (or for tax purposes, a husband and wife). For IRS purposes, a sole proprietor and his or her business are one tax entity, meaning that business profits are reported and taxed on the owner's personal tax return. Setting up a sole proprietorship is cheap and easy since no legal formation documents need be filed with any governmental agency (although tax registration and other permit and license requirements may still apply). Once you file a fictitious name statement (assuming you don't use your own name) and obtain any required basic tax permits and business licenses, you'll be in business. The main downside of a sole proprietorship is that its owner is personally liable for all business debts.

specific bequest

A specific item of property that is left to a named beneficiary under a will. If the person who made the will no longer owns the property when he or she dies, the bequest fails. In other words, the beneficiary cannot substitute a similar item in the estate. Example: If John leaves his 1954 Mercedes to Patti, and when John dies the 1954 Mercedes is long gone, Patti doesn't receive John's current car or the cash equivalent of the Mercedes. See *ademption*.

specific intent

An intent to produce the precise consequences of the crime, including the intent to do the physical act that causes the consequences. For example, the crime of larceny is the taking of the personal property of another with the intent to permanently deprive the other person of the property. A person is not guilty of larceny just because he took someone else's property; it must be proven that he took it with the purpose of keeping it permanently.

specific performance

A remedy provided by a court that orders the losing side to perform its part of a contract rather than, or possibly in addition to, paying money damages to the winner.

spendthrift trust

A trust created for a beneficiary the grantor considers irresponsible about money. The trustee keeps control of the trust income, doling out money to the beneficiary as needed, and sometimes paying third parties (creditors, for example) on the beneficiary's behalf, bypassing the beneficiary completely. Spendthrift trusts typically contain a provision prohibiting creditors from seizing the trust fund to satisfy the beneficiary's debts. These trusts are legal in most states, even though creditors hate them.

stare decisis

Latin for "let the decision stand," a doctrine requiring that judges apply the same reasoning to lawsuits as has been used in prior similar cases.

state court

A court that decides cases involving state law or the state constitution. State courts have jurisdiction to consider disputes involving individual defendants who reside in that state or have minimum contacts with the state, such as using its highways, owning real property in the state, or doing business in the state. State courts have very broad power to hear cases involving all subjects except those involving federal issues and laws, which are in the exclusive jurisdiction of the federal courts. State courts are often divided according to the dollar amount of the claims they can hear. Depending on the state, small claims, justice, municipal, or city courts usually hear smaller cases, while district, circuit, superior, or county courts (or in New York, supreme courts) have jurisdiction over larger cases. Finally, state courts are also commonly divided according to subject matter, such as criminal court, family court, and probate court.

statute of limitations

The legally prescribed time limit in which a lawsuit must be filed. Statutes of limitation differ depending on the type of legal claim, and often the state. For example, many states require that a personal injury lawsuit be filed within one year from the date of injury—or in some instances, from the date when it should reasonably have been discovered—but some allow two years. Similarly, claims based on a written contract must be filed in court within four years from the date the contract was broken in some states and five years in others. Statute of limitations rules apply to cases filed in all courts, including federal court.

sua sponte

Latin for "on its own will or motion." This term is most commonly used to describe a decision or an act that a judge decides upon without having been asked by either party.

subpena

The modern spelling of subpoena. A subpena is a court order issued at the request of a party requiring a witness to appear in court.

subpena duces tecum

A type of subpena, usually issued at the request of a party, by which a court orders a witness to produce certain documents at a deposition or trial. However, when one party wants an opposing party to produce documents, a different discovery device, called a Request for Production of Documents, is often used instead.

subrogation

A taking on of the legal rights of someone whose debts or expenses have been paid. For example, subrogation occurs when an insurance company that has paid off its injured claimant takes the legal rights the claimant has against a third party that caused the injury, and sues that third party.

substituted service

A method for the formal delivery of court papers that takes the place of personal service. Personal service means that the papers are placed directly into the hands of the person to be served. Substituted service, on the other hand, may be accomplished by leaving the documents with a designated agent, with another adult in the recipient's home, with the recipient's manager at work, or by posting a notice in a prominent place and then using certified mail to send copies of the documents to the recipient.

substitution of parties

A replacement of one of the sides in a lawsuit because of events that prevent the party from continuing with the trial. For example, substitution of parties may occur when one party dies or, in the case of a public official, when that public official is removed from office.

sui generis

Latin for "of its own kind," used to describe something that is unique or different.

summary adjudication of issues

A partial summary judgment motion, in which the judge is asked to decide only one or some of the legal issues in the case. For example, in a car accident case, there might be overwhelming and uncontradicted evidence of the defendant's carelessness, but conflicting evidence as to the extent of the plaintiff's injuries. The plaintiff might ask for summary adjudication on the issue of carelessness, but go to trial on the question of injuries.

summary judgment

A final decision by a judge that resolves a lawsuit in favor of one of the parties. A motion for summary judgment is made after discovery is completed but before the case goes to trial. The party making the motion marshals all the evidence in its favor, compares it to the other side's evidence, and argues that a reasonable jury looking at the same evidence could only decide the case one way—for the moving party. If the judge agrees, then a trial would be unnecessary and the judge enters judgment for the moving party.

summons

A paper prepared by the plaintiff and issued by a court that informs the defendant that she has been sued. The summons requires that the defendant file a response with the court—or in many small claims courts, simply appear in person on an appointed day—within a given time period or risk losing the case under the terms of a default judgment.

sunset law

A law that automatically terminates the agency or program it establishes unless it is expressly renewed. For example, a state law establishing and funding a new drug rehabilitation program within state prisons may provide that the program will shut down in two years unless it is reviewed and approved by the state legislature.

sunshine laws

Statutes that provide public access to governmental agency meetings and records.

superior court

The main county trial court in many states, mostly in the West. See *state court*.

Supremacy clause

Provision under Article IV, Section 2, of the U.S. Constitution, providing that federal law is superior to and overrides state law when they conflict.

Supreme Court

America's highest court, which has the final power to decide cases involving the interpretation of the U.S. Constitution, certain legal areas set forth in the Constitution (called federal questions), and federal laws. It can also make final decisions in certain lawsuits between parties in different states. The U.S. Supreme Court has nine justices—one of whom is the chief justice—who are appointed for life by the president and must be confirmed by the U.S. Senate. Most states also have a supreme court, which is the final arbiter of the state's constitution and state laws. However, in several states the highest state court uses a different name—most notably New York and Maryland, where it's called the "Court of Appeals," and Massachusetts, where it's called the "Supreme Judicial Court."

tangible personal property

Personal property that can be felt or touched. Examples include furniture, cars, jewelry, and artwork. However, cash and checking accounts are not tangible personal property. The law is unsettled as to whether computer data is tangible personal property. Compare *intangible property*.

temporary restraining order (TRO)

An order that tells one person to stop harassing or harming another, issued after the aggrieved party appears before a judge. Once the TRO is issued, the court holds a second hearing where the other side can tell his or her story and the court can decide whether to make the TRO permanent by issuing an injunction. Although a TRO will often not stop an enraged spouse from acting violently, the police are more willing to intervene if the abused spouse has a TRO.

tenancy by the entirety

A special kind of property ownership that's only for married couples. Both spouses have the right to enjoy the entire property, and when one spouse dies, the surviving spouse gets title to the property (called a right of survivorship). It is similar to joint tenancy, but it is available in only about half the states.

tenancy in common

A way two or more people can own property together. Each can leave his or her interest upon death to beneficiaries of his or her choosing instead of to the other owners, as is required with joint tenancy. Also, unlike joint tenancy, the ownership shares need not be equal. In most states, each tenant in common may encumber only his or her share of the property, so that the other share is debt-free. In some states, two people are presumed to own property as tenants in common unless they've agreed otherwise in writing.

testate

The circumstance of dying after making a valid will. A person who dies with a will is said to have died "testate." Compare *intestate*.

testify

To provide oral evidence under oath at a trial or at a deposition.

tort

An injury to one person for which the person who caused the injury is legally responsible. A tort can be intentional—for example, an angry punch in the nose—but is far more likely to result from carelessness (called "negligence"), such as riding your bicycle on the sidewalk and colliding with a pedestrian. While the injury that forms the basis of a tort is usually physical, this is not a requirement—libel, slander, and the "intentional infliction of mental distress" are on a good-sized list of torts not based on a physical injury.

tortious interference

The causing of harm by disrupting something that belongs to someone else—for example, interfering with a contractual relationship so that one party fails to deliver goods on time.

trust corpus

Latin for "the body" of the trust. This term refers to all the property transferred to a trust. For example, if a trust is established (funded) with $250,000, that money is the corpus. Sometimes the trust corpus is known as the *res*, a Latin word meaning "thing."

trustee

The person who manages assets owned by a trust under the terms of the trust document. A trustee's purpose is to safeguard the trust and distribute trust income or principal as directed in the trust document. With a simple probate-avoidance living trust, the person who creates the trust is also the trustee.

ultra vires

Latin for "beyond powers." It refers to conduct by a corporation or its officers that exceeds the powers granted by law.

unclean hands

A legal doctrine that prevents a plaintiff who has acted unethically in relation to a lawsuit from winning the suit or from recovering as much money as he or she would have if he or she had behaved honorably. For example, if a contractor is suing a homeowner to recover the price of work he did on the home, his failure to perform the work as specified would leave him with unclean hands.

unconscionability

A seller's taking advantage of a buyer due to their unequal bargaining positions, perhaps because of the buyer's recent trauma, physical infirmity, ignorance, inability to read, or inability to understand the language. The unfairness must be so severe that it is shocking to the average person. It usually includes the absence of any meaningful choice on the part of the buyer and contract terms so one-sided that they unreasonably favor the seller. A contract will be terminated if the buyer can prove unconscionability.

unjust enrichment

A legal doctrine stating that if a person receives money or other property through no effort of his or her own, at the expense of another, the recipient should return the property to the rightful owner, even if the property was not obtained illegally. Most courts will order that the property be returned if the party who has suffered the loss brings a lawsuit.

unsecured debt

A debt that is not tied to any item of property. A creditor doesn't have the right to grab property to satisfy the debt if you default. The creditor's only remedy is to sue you and get a judgment. Compare *secured debt*.

variance

An exception to a zoning ordinance, usually granted by a local government. For example, if you own an oddly shaped lot that could not accommodate a home in accordance with your city's setback requirement, you could apply at the appropriate office for a variance allowing you to build closer to a boundary line.

venue

State laws or court rules that establish the proper court to hear a case, often based on the convenience of the defendant. Because state courts have jurisdiction to hear cases from a wide geographical area (for example, California courts have jurisdiction involving most disputes arising between California residents), additional rules, called rules of venue, have been developed to ensure that the defendant is not needlessly inconvenienced. For example, the correct venue for one Californian to sue another is usually limited to the court in the judicial district where the defendant lives, an accident occurred, or a contract was signed or to be carried out. Practically, venue rules mean that a defendant can't usually be sued far from where he or she lives or does business, if no key events happened at that location. Venue for a criminal case is normally the judicial district where the crime was committed.

vested remainder

An unconditional right to receive real property at some point in the future. A vested interest may be created by a deed or a will. For example, if Julie's will leaves her house to her daughter, but the daughter will gain possession only after Julie's husband dies, the daughter has a vested remainder in the house.

volenti non fit injuria

Latin for "to a willing person, no injury is done." This doctrine holds that a person who knowingly and willingly puts him- or herself in a dangerous situation cannot sue for any resulting injuries.

with prejudice

A final and binding decision by a judge about a legal matter that prevents further pursuit of the same matter in any court. When a judge makes such a decision, he or she dismisses the matter "with prejudice."

witness

A person who testifies under oath at a deposition or trial, providing firsthand or expert evidence. In addition, the term also refers to someone who watches another person sign a document and then adds his or her name to confirm (called "attesting") that the signature is genuine.

wrongful death

A civil claim based upon a death caused by the fault of another. Examples of wrongful conduct that may lead to death include drinking and driving, manufacturing a deficient product, building an unstable structure, or failing to diagnose a fatal disease.

zoning

The laws dividing cities into different areas according to use, from single-family residences to industrial plants. Zoning ordinances control the size, location, and use of buildings within these different areas.

Topic-Specific Research Sites

Bankruptcy. American Bankruptcy Institute Consumer Commons (www.abiworld.org). This is a consumer-friendly site with laws, news, a consumer education center, and links to courts.

Copyright. The U.S. Copyright Office (www.copyright.gov). This site offers regulations, guidelines, forms, and links to other helpful copyright sites.

Stanford University's Copyright and Fair Use site (https://fairuse.stanford.edu).

Intellectual Property Mall at Franklin Pierce Law Center (www.ipmall.info). An excellent general intellectual property site.

Corporate Law. The Securities and Exchange Commission (www.sec.gov). It has all the investment statutes and regulations, current litigation, opinions, and staff legal bulletins.

Business Law Lounge from the 'Lectric Law Library (www.lectlaw.com/bus.html).

Criminal Law and Criminal Justice. Nolo's Criminal Law Center (www.nolo.com/legal-encyclopedia/criminal-law). This is a great place to start for questions about criminal procedure.

At CriminalDefenseLawyer.com (www.criminaldefenselawyer.com) you'll find articles and resources on every aspect of a criminal case.

Divorce. (See also Family Law.) DivorceNet (www.divorcenet.com). A site with excellent legal resources.

DivorceSource (www.divorcesource.com). In addition to background materials on virtually all divorce issues, this site provides a comprehensive series of links to state divorce statutes.

Elder Law. The Senior Law Home Page (www.seniorlaw.com) provides links to articles about guardianships, conservatorships, Medicare and Medicaid, living wills, physician's directives, durable powers of attorney, senior abuse, and other issues that commonly affect seniors.

The National Academy of Elder Law Attorneys (www.naela.org) also provides information and links to elder law resources.

Family Law. American Bar Association's Family Law Section (www.americanbar.org/groups/family_law.html). This site provides numerous links to family law materials available online.

Adoption.com: Where Families Come Together (https://adoption. com). This site provides information about adoption agencies, international adoption, and many other adoption issues.

Domestic Violence: (www.womenslaw.org) provides state-by-state legal information about domestic violence and how to obtain a restraining order, with downloadable forms and links to local resources.

First Amendment/Free Speech. Electronic Frontier Foundation (www.eff.org). This site focuses on free speech law and policy issues in the online environment.

Health Care. American Health Lawyers Association (www.healthlawyers. org/Pages/home.aspx). This site has an extensive set of links to health care and health law sites.

Landlord-Tenant Law. Rentlaw.com (www.rentlaw.com). This site has good summaries of relevant state laws.

TenantNet (www.tenant.net). This site provides information about landlord-tenant law, with a focus on tenants' rights. TenantNet is designed primarily for tenants in New York City, but the site offers links to similar sites in many other states as well as the text of the federal fair housing law.

Lesbian and Gay Issues. GLAD is a legal rights organization dedicated to ending all forms of discrimination against gays and lesbians (www.glad.org).

American Civil Liberties Union's Lesbian and Gay Rights page (www.aclu.org/issues/lgbt-rights?redirect=lgbt-rights).

Patents. The U.S. Patent and Trademark Office (www.uspto.gov). This is the place to go for recent policy and statutory changes and transcripts of hearings on patent law issues.

For current information on what's being patented, check out FreshPatents.com (www.freshpatents.com).

Small Business. Small Business Development Center National Information Clearinghouse (www.sbdcnet.org).

The Small Business Administration (www.sba.gov). This free site provides information about starting, financing, and expanding your small business.

Tax Law. American Bar Association's Tax Section (www.americanbar.org/groups/taxation.html). This site provides numerous links to tax-related materials available online.

The Internal Revenue Service (www.irs.gov). This site has tax information, publications, and forms that you can download.

AccountantsWorld (www.accountantsworld.com).

Federation of Tax Administrators (www.taxadmin.org). This is a complete, reliable site for state tax information.

Tax and Accounting Sites Directory (www.taxsites.com). This is a directory site.

Trademarks. U.S. Patent and Trademark Office (www.uspto.gov). This is the website of choice for trademark searching, trademark registration, papers issued by the USPTO on various trademark and domain name issues, and general information about the trademark laws.

Also available through this site are the rules used by the trademark examiners and descriptions of goods and services deemed acceptable for trademark registration applications.

GGMark (www.ggmark.com). This is a great general-purpose trademark site. It provides background information on virtually every aspect of trademark law and a comprehensive set of links to various trademark-related sites.

ICANN (www.icann.org). This website is the starting place for researching domain name disputes and the rules that apply to them.

Wills and Estate Planning. National Academy of Elder Law Attorneys (www.naela.org).

Workplace Rights. Equal Employment Opportunity Commission (www. eeoc.gov). The EEOC has resources both for employers and employees. Everything you need to know for compliance is here.

National Labor Relations Board (www.nlrb.gov). The NLRB publishes decisions here.

Workplace Fairness (www.workplacefairness.org). This nonprofit provides lots of free information on employment law issues.

Your Money. Get Out of Debt (https://getoutofdebt.org). This is a non-profit online resource dedicated to helping people get out of debt. You'll find free publications, recommended books, a forum for posting your debt questions, and special programs to assist you.

National Consumer Law Center (www.nclc.org). This site offers information and advice on low-income consumer issues.

USA.gov Consumer Protection (www.usa.gov). The government offers consumer money advice at this site.

The Better Business Bureau (www.bbb.org/en/us). This site allows you to file consumer complaints online.

Index